FIND YOUR
UNICORN
SPACE

ALSO BY EVE RODSKY

*Fair Play: A Game-Changing Solution
for When You Have Too Much to Do (and More Life to Live)*

FIND YOUR
UNICORN
SPACE

Reclaim Your Creative Life
in a Too-Busy World

EVE RODSKY

G. P. PUTNAM'S SONS
NEW YORK

PUTNAM
— EST. 1838 —

G. P. Putnam's Sons
Publishers Since 1838
An imprint of Penguin Random House LLC
penguinrandomhouse.com

Library of Congress Cataloging-in-Publication Data
Names: Rodsky, Eve, author.
Title: Find your unicorn space:
reclaim your creative life in a too-busy world / Eve Rodsky.
Description: New York : G. P. Putnam's Sons, [2021] |
Includes bibliographical references and index.
Identifiers: LCCN 2021046693 (print) | LCCN 2021046694 (ebook) |
ISBN 9780593328019 (hardcover) | ISBN 9780593328026 (ebook)
Subjects: LCSH: Goal (Psychology) | Creative ability. |
Self-actualization (Psychology)
Classification: LCC BF505.G6 R63 2021 (print) |
LCC BF505.G6 (ebook) | DDC 158.1—dc23
LC record available at https://lccn.loc.gov/2021046693
LC ebook record available at https://lccn.loc.gov/2021046694

Printed in the United States of America
1st Printing

Book design by Pauline Neuwirth

Book cover lettering and interior artwork by Lindsey Mayer-Beug

Some names and identifying details of people mentioned in this book have been changed to protect their privacy. In some cases, composite characters have been created for the purpose of further disguising the identity of individuals.

Dedicated to the people in these pages—thank you for sharing your stories with the world. To Zach, Ben, and Anna—I hope you always dance in the rain.

Contents

CONTENTS

x

PART III

CULTIVATE THE THREE C'S OF CREATIVITY

✳ Curiosity ✳

✳ Connection ✳

CONTENTS

✳ Completion ✳

Hope your road is a long one.

May there be many summer mornings when,

with what pleasure, what joy,

you enter harbors you're seeing for the first time

—from "Ithaka" by C. P. Cavafy,
translated by Edmund Keeley

Author's Note

Find Your Unicorn Space was written with the intention that all readers feel seen and heard and worthy of the gift to pursue creative expression that brings their lives more joy.

My personal identities include hetero cisgender, white, female identified, born into a Syrian Jewish immigrant family. I am married to a hetero cisgender, white, Jewish man. I grew up in a single-parent, working-class home. However, access to my education and profession have afforded me economic security.

For this book I interviewed individuals who represent an abundant diversity with regard to age, race, ethnicity, socioeconomic status, marital status, educational attainment, employment status, geographical location, religion, and cis, trans, and nonbinary gender identities. Forty-four percent of the people I interviewed identified as people of color, 33 percent identified as members of the LGBTQIA+ community. I recognize my own racial and economic privilege in coming to this topic and have made a concerted effort to talk with people of diverse racial and socioeconomic backgrounds to discover how they live a creative life.

My research for *Find Your Unicorn Space* used a qualitative approach rooted in informal interviews with open-ended questions and observations. You can describe it as my heroine's journey to create my own Unicorn Space, motivated by personal curiosity and fueled by the creative insights of the interesting people I read about and had the privilege to meet. I read through hundreds of articles, original research, and books. When particular themes emerged, I interviewed experts in psychology, sociology, social work, neuroscience, behavioral economics, and law. I reference this as my "book research." I was fortunate to be able to work with one expert (and a fellow Uni) in particular—Professor Darby Saxbe, a clinical psychology professor who is both an expert in the gendered division of labor and actively pursuing her own Unicorn Space as the lead guitarist for an all-women "Mom" band.

In addition to experts, I interviewed approximately 150 individuals for this book and found incredible creativity insights within each story and journey. These particular individuals engage in a variety of creative pursuits, in the sense that they were not scientifically found or selected according to a standardized protocol. I purposefully sought voices from other countries to interview: Argentina, Australia, Canada, El Salvador, the European Continent, Hong Kong, Japan, Mainland China, Mexico, New Zealand, Nigeria, South Africa, the United Kingdom, as well as the United States. These stories are weaved throughout the book as sources of inspiration and are combined with the more than five hundred diverse interviews I completed for my first book, *Fair Play*. Collectively, these two sets of interviews are referenced as my "research interviews." Individuals are referenced by first name only unless they are an expert or self-identified as a public figure. Not every story made it into these pages, but my goal is to tell many more stories through subsequent writing, podcasts, and other mediums.

Many of the people I have had the privilege to meet through my research have become friends, teachers, and integral sources of inspiration for my continued pursuit of creating Unicorn Space and even more motivation for sharing it with the world. I write to honor these women and all women—cisgender women, trans women, femmes, two-spirit people—anyone who identifies with women. I focus on women for two reasons. One, because the *Fair Play* themes address the unfairness of society being built on the backs of the unpaid labor of women and, when paid as care workers, the undervalued labor of women of color. Two, research shows that since women hold two-thirds or more of what it takes to run a home and family, they are less likely to have leisure time for Unicorn Space. As my friend Professor Darby Saxbe puts it, "Men spend a larger proportion of their time at home engaged in leisure . . . Men benefit when they get more leisure time and their wives get less." A couple more things to note: throughout this book I refer to the 3 P's of partner, parent, and professional. I define "professional" as anyone who works for pay or anyone who works unpaid as a caregiver. When discussing communication advice for you and your partner, I am presuming a safe, nonviolent relationship.

Finally, *Find Your Unicorn Space* aims to provide examples of what it means and what it looks like to be a Uni and pursue the unique creative expression that makes you uniquely and vibrantly *you*.

creativity, redefined as Unicorn Space

(yü-nə-ˌkȯrn spās)

The *active* and open pursuit of *self-expression* in any form, and which requires value-based curiosity and purposeful sharing of this pursuit with the world. Like the mythical equine that inspired the name, it doesn't exist until you give yourself permission to reclaim, discover, and nurture the natural gifts and interests that make you ***you***.

TURN THE PAGE TO REDEFINE YOUR OWN
DEFINITION OF CREATIVITY.

PART I

TIME FOR A RESET

What is Unicorn Space,
and why is it so important?

Unleash Your Unicorn

//

Embracing the Power of "the Pause" to Commit to Creativity

CONSIDER:
THE CASE OF THE BAD TINDER DATE

I was visiting my cousin Jessica at Stanz Cafe in Larchmont, New York. As we were digging into a shared plate of avocado toast, the conversation turned toward her new dating life.

"I've started swiping right," she admitted.

"Really?" I said with a near mouthful. "You're ready, then?"

Jessica's life took an unexpected turn when her husband had a catastrophic stroke at the age of thirty-seven. After Jessica served as caretaker to her husband for seven years until he reached a full recovery, while also juggling the needs of their two young kids and working a full-time job, their marriage ultimately dissolved, albeit amicably.

"It's been a year since the divorce," said Jessica, "and I'm proud of myself for all I've been able to do on my own, but truthfully"—she paused—"I don't want to keep doing it all alone. So, yeah, I think I'm ready." She nodded assuredly.

"Okay, then," I encouraged, "show me who's made the cut."

Jessica took out her phone, tapped on the Tinder app, and scrolled until she landed on Andy. "Read his profile," she said, handing me her phone.

Andy had a clean yet intentionally disheveled kind of mountain man look. His smile appeared genuine, and his interests were listed as follows: adventure, travel, and cooking.

"He sounds amazing," I enthused. "He lists 'adventure' as one of his top values. That's totally you." When we were younger, I'd nicknamed my cousin Jessica "Adventure" Cohen, because she didn't have a given middle name and because she saved all of her waitressing tip money to climb Mount Kilimanjaro, explore Machu Picchu, and visit the Choeung Ek memorial in Cambodia.

"*Was* totally me," Jessica corrected.

"And look at this," I continued. "His favorite quote is *your* favorite quote: Vivian Greene's 'Life isn't about waiting for the storm to pass. It's about learning to dance in the rain.' I mean, c'mon, the guy loves adventure *and* inspirational quotes?"

Jessica sighed and leaned in. "I know, but we already went on one date, and it's not going to work out."

"Oh my God. Tell me," I said a little too loudly, attracting the attention of the full table next to ours.

"Well," she confided, "it was a sort of disaster. Ten minutes into our dinner, he asks me, 'What do you do for fun?' Can you imagine?" Jessica rolled her eyes.

I clearly felt her exasperation but didn't similarly share

it. Why was his question so offensive to her? I challenged: "What's wrong with a little fun?"

Her eyes widened. "Who past the age of twenty asks that question? Really, who has time for fun when you're raising kids and juggling a career and taking the dogs to the freaking vet? I had no 'fun' answer for him, so I ended the date early."

I well understood the challenge she was describing, as a working mother with tiny humans underfoot in my own home. Still, fun is not exclusively reserved for Gen Z. Or single people without jobs or pets. Is it?

"Jessica . . ." I straightened and said in my firm but loving voice, "you of all people deserve to rediscover what brings you joy, and you must make time for it."

She gave me the finger and handed me the bill.

♣ ◎ ϟ

On the flight back to Los Angeles, I gave the Case of the Bad Tinder Date some thought. Andy's "what do you do for fun" approach to life seemed like the right antidote for Jessica's malaise. She could definitely use some fun, some time and space for herself. A new adventure. A little less responsibility. A little more joy. How could I help her?

Without a clear answer, I spent the next hour occupying myself by clicking on random YouTube videos. And that's when I discovered Shige-boh. Uncertain as to how I'd navigated there, I landed on a video of elderly Japanese men and women unselfconsciously, super earnestly "busting" hip-hop dance moves in of-the-moment urban streetwear. *What is this?* I couldn't help but break into an ear-to-ear grin at these seniors' jubilant faces, accompanied by CNN anchor Mayu Yoshida's deadpan reporting:

Hip-hop dance lessons for seniors are popping up across Tokyo. This group calls themselves the Senior Monsters. They are part of the latest health craze that proves you are never too old to bust a move.

Never too old, indeed. Yoshida introduced a seventy-two-year-old man named Shige-boh, who demonstrated the complicated footwork of traditional street dance. *He's good!* He explained in English, "I started dancing to hip-hop after I retired. Six months after I started learning hip-hop, I went on a show. It was a bit embarrassing at first, but I invited my family. It was an unforgettable moment. I am very happy when I'm dancing."

I get it. I'm very happy when I'm dancing, too. I rewound my own mental tape twenty-five years to when I practiced my own moves, with great enthusiasm, in front of the television in my mom's cramped New York apartment. At fourteen, my cousin Jessica and I were obsessed with the *In Living Color* Fly Girls. Our *only* future ambition was to become one of them, and we spent hours after school each day choreographing dances in the little space between the television and the sofa. This continued until our hardworking moms and well-meaning school guidance counselors delivered the memo that a sounder plan for our future was required. I kicked off my gold-glitter sneakers and put dance on the back burner in favor of a more traditional professional track—college, law school, mom to three kids. My cousin Jessica, similarly, followed suit.

But to this day, my passion for dance has not waned. Just ask my children, who groan with exaggerated embarrassment when I do the running man while brushing my teeth, flash jazz hands while packing their school lunches, or bust a move as I'm folding the laundry: *Mom, pleassssssse stop!!!*

My husband, Seth, on the other hand, gets a kick out of my clumsy choreography, goading me into a dance routine when we're out with friends (following a couple of glasses of wine, *it happens*). After all, it was our shared love for hip-hop when we met more than fifteen years ago that initially clarified for us both that we were perfectly matched.

Watching the Senior Monsters on the flight home, I had a full-circle moment. Jessica's bad date has an important lesson for us. I pulled out my journal and frantically started writing. "Life is a series of storms. As we get older, they tend to be more frequent. Taking time to have 'fun' is how we weather them. The storms will keep coming, so we must learn to DANCE IN THE RAIN!"

I could hardly wait to share this connection with Jessica. The next morning, with my kids running in circles around me, frantically searching for backpacks and lost shoes, I forwarded the video to Jessica with a note: "MUST WATCH." Ten minutes later, just as I was racing out the door with my two older boys for the school drop-off routine (while balancing their lunches, my laptop, an overstuffed tote, and my car keys in hand), she wrote back: "Is Shige-boh single?"

I responded with an LOL and added: "I think you might be too late and too young for Shige-boh, but there's no expiration date to having a little fun. Pull out your dancing shoes, cuz. It's time to start dancing in the rain."

CREATIVE TIME IS NOT OPTIONAL

I know my cousin and I are not the only people to look up from their busy lives and realize we've left some of our youthful dreaming and passion behind. You might feel it, too. What does *your* heart sing for? What does your body crave? What piques your curiosity? What does your intellect yearn for? What did you give up that you want to get back to?

Do you want to return to school? Pick up an instrument? Learn another language? Go to circus camp? Climb a mountain? Perfect your Cantonese cooking? Or maybe just carve out some quiet time to paint? What's *your* version of hip-hop dance?

To be clear, I'm not talking about identifying or returning to a *hobby*. Let's just retire that word right now. In an article in the *Harvard Business Review, hobby* was defined broadly to be "the intentional, purposeful use of the time you do have for yourself (however short that window may be)." Unfortunately, as many women well know, a hobby is generally regarded as a superfluous nice-to-have that only comes into play *after* all the more important checkboxes in one's already time-constrained life are ticked off.

And while we're at it, let's also throw the term *vanity project* into the wastebasket, too. The vanity project is, typically, a gendered term that refers to unpaid pursuits (usually performed by women) that are often subsidized by a partner and generally devalued by society. There's very little dignity in the term and even less urgency. Both the hobby and vanity project are categorized as enjoyable but inessential.

To be even more clear, I'm not talking about finding a *distraction*, either. Believe me, I'm distracted enough just trying to get through my day. I don't need an idle diversion, and neither do you.

So if it's not a hobby, a vanity project, or a distraction—what are we talking about, exactly? I'm referring to the *active and open* pursuit of *self-expression* in any form, and which requires value-based curiosity and purposeful sharing of this pursuit with the world. Whether it be creating art, expanding your knowledge within your area of expertise, or developing a new skill, I'm talking about an activity that you lose yourself in. That you crave to go back to when you're away from it. That gives you pleasure outside of your work, your family, and your other obligations. It's something you do just for yourself... and because it brings you so much joy, you want to share it with others.

According to a study out of New Zealand, engaging in creative expression like I'm describing contributes to an "upward spiral" of positive emotions, psychological well-being, and feelings of "flourishing" in life, which researchers defined as feeling engaged in daily life, experiencing positive personal growth, and cultivating social connections. This relates to the "broaden and build" theory of positive emotions first developed by Barbara Fredrickson, PhD. Fredrickson explains that when you feel positive, it encourages you to expand your world, thereby eliciting more growth and creativity. Tony Wagner, a senior research fellow at the Learning Policy Institute, takes it a step further with his research showing that creative expression gives us a sense of *purpose*, along with enhancing resilience and contributing to a sense of playfulness and curiosity.

Given the research (and there's so much more that I'll share in the pages ahead), I invite you to begin thinking of the active and open pursuit of your creative self-expression not as optional or as an "add-on" to your current life but as essential and fundamental to your physical, emotional, and mental health as a whole person.

THE POWER OF UNICORN SPACE

So, then, if carving out time for creative pursuits is so essential... why was I still struggling with it? Wasn't I supposed to be the expert in this?

Let me back up. I'm not just a wannabe hip-hop dancer. I'm also a lawyer who runs an organizational management consultancy—I help foundations, companies, and families run more smoothly. A couple of years ago, though, I'd reached a breaking point in my own home organization: fed up with that feeling that I was doing *all* the work to keep my work life humming alongside a busy home life with my husband and three kids, I determined to increase efficiency and save my sanity— and my marriage—in the process.

I started by creating a list of all the invisible, unheralded tasks I was doing—from making dinner to overseeing homework to doing the laundry—to keep our family afloat. I called it the "Sh*t I Do" list, and it detailed every minute yet important but often undervalued task with a time component (signing my kids up for after-school activities, making sure their vaccinations were up to date, getting the boiler inspected) that was often overlooked and yet absolutely essential. The "Sh*t I Do" list became the basis for a system I created called Fair Play. My goal: to divide domestic work and childcare more fairly in my house (and yours), so that *both* partners in a relationship are set up for success. With clearly defined expectations and delineated roles, Fair Play applies the same principles of organizational management in the workplace to the home because I believe that our home is our most important organization.

I shared the Fair Play system with my friends and friends-of-friends, and eventually I turned it into a book. The message resonated: *Fair Play* became an instant *New York Times* bestseller; it was selected as a Reese's Book Club pick; it spun off into a card deck, a podcast, and a documentary; and that little book got me invited to travel to groups and companies all across the United States and the world to talk about the concept of work-life integration and the injustice of building societies on the backs of the unpaid labor of women and the undervalued labor of domestic workers. It was amazing and gratifying to see that a system that introduced a new vocabulary for talking about domestic life resonates with families everywhere.

People embraced the idea of providing a clear organizational strategy to the home, and more than a few couples told me that *Fair Play* had saved their relationships, too. But the true magic was what emerged for everyone—especially women—when domestic responsibilities were divvied up more fairly: more time.

Time is the ultimate reward for increasing efficiency and fairness in our home organizations. Time to relax. Time to focus on ourselves. Time to become curious. Time for sustained attention to the things we love. In *Fair Play*, I called this time Unicorn Space.

WHAT IS UNICORN SPACE?

Creativity redefined as Unicorn Space is the *active* and open pursuit of *self-expression* in any form, built on *value-based curiosity and purposeful sharing* of this pursuit with the world. Whether it be creating art, expanding your knowledge within your area of expertise, or developing a new skill, your Unicorn Space is that thing that makes you uniquely and vibrantly *you*. But like the mythical equine that inspired the name, it doesn't exist until you give yourself permission to reclaim, discover, and nurture it.

POP QUIZ
Which One of These Activities Qualifies as Unicorn Space?

A. Unwinding with your friends over an extended lunch

B. Sinking into a sensory-soothing, aromatic bath

C. Date night: dinner, drinks, and dancing with your partner/spouse

D. An hour of uninterrupted and contented time in the kitchen to roll out homemade pasta and put on to simmer your signature sauce that you will later, and proudly, serve to family and friends for dinner

KEY:

A. This falls under the Fair Play definition of "adult friendships" and is absolutely valuable and essential to happiness but in a category of its own.

B. This falls under the Fair Play definition of "self-care" and is essential to your brain and body functions. (Not to be confused with "commodified wellness", where people try to sell you care you don't need.) True self-care is important, but it does not count as Unicorn Space unless it's connected to a larger goal that can be *shared with the world*.

C. This falls under the Fair Play definition of "partnerships." Making regular time to invest in your relationship will ensure its longevity and overall satisfaction, but you still need pursuits beyond your role as a partner to feel ultimately fulfilled.

D. Bingo! This has all the elements that characterize the active pursuit of self-expression and that includes value-based curiosity and purposeful sharing.

○ ○

Writing *Fair Play* had been my Unicorn Space—I loved writing. Turning a dozen journals filled with my scribbled thoughts and unfinished ideas into a complete and published manuscript was a dream come true, and every time I spoke to couples on the subject, it delivered a Category 5 storm of passion to my life. But as I got busier and *Fair Play* became a full-time (then more than full-time!) job, I realized that calling my work my Unicorn Space was, well, no longer hitting the mark. Even though I loved my new role on the professional front, I was losing time just for me. Would rekindling my childhood dance dreams with my cousin Jessica lead me in the direction of a little more fun? Was this the spark of a creative expression that would reinspire and carry me throughout the inevitable storms of daily life? And could my expanded Unicorn Space inspire others to reclaim or discover their own? I was on the verge of something. I could feel it.

And then the pandemic hit, and all my—and everyone else's—carefully wrought systems, plans, and dreams were upended.

WAIT:
WHY SHOULD *I* MATTER WHEN
THE WORLD IS ON FIRE?

When the fast-spreading coronavirus drove over 20 million people out of the workplace and into the home, one thing became immediately clear: time for more fun was back-burnered as the domestic dirty work of laundry, dishes, and now disinfectant fell directly into the hands of women.

It was not a shocker. As *Fair Play* screamed, women have been doing it all, bearing the brunt of childcare and housework for decades. Despite the fact that, pre-pandemic, women outnumbered men in the paid workforce, women still did almost twice as much unpaid work in the home as their male partners. And at the height of the pandemic, U.S. women's unpaid labor (childcare and housework) increased by 153 percent, contributing to the loss of approximately three million women out of the paid workforce in 2020, according to a study conducted by Katica Roy, CEO of Pipeline Equity. In December 2020 alone, all jobs lost were held by women, and primarily women of color, according to the National Women's Law Center. For those still working, research from Gema Zamarro, PhD, and Maria Prados, PhD, showed that 42 percent of working mothers had to reduce their working hours to provide care for their children, compared to only 30 percent of working fathers. This was found to equate to ten hours more extra childcare per week.

Perhaps it was too optimistic to hope that men, without much of a choice but to stay home during a global pandemic, would retire the tired "I'm not home to help" argument. But no. A substitute claim slid right into its place. It went something like this: "I'd really like to help, but I can't watch the kids / do the dishes / make dinner / bid for cleaning supplies on eBay because I'm 'working' (remotely from the kitchen table while the kids run around and you make dinner for our family while simultaneously disinfecting all the countertops and door handles)." In Jessica Valenti's *Medium* article titled " 'Am I the Asshole?' Reveals America's Sexist Underbelly," she explains

this dynamic: "Part of what's on display . . . is entitled igno-
rance; some men brought up in a sexist world really do believe
that there is a natural gendered order that they just happen to
benefit from."

This "gendered order" that further excused men from family life enraged me, since 44 percent of all US households with
children are comprised of married dual-earner, full-time-
working couples—and so far, I hadn't heard even one woman
use that excuse. Single mothers (many of whom are essential
workers) can't use that excuse. And many working women in
hetero cisgender partnerships were contorting themselves to
juggle job responsibilities, household management, and su-
pervision of their children's remote learning—while also at-
tempting to work remotely alongside their male counterparts
at the kitchen table. Or as one woman told me, "My husband
works at the table, while I work in the bathtub with a kid on
my lap."

"When I'm not on a Zoom call trying to perform—or at least
act as if I'm performing—at maximum efficiency for my job,
off-screen I'm doing *everything for my kids*," my friend Anne
lamented one night over a glass of wine and a FaceTime call,
"including ordering supplies, overseeing weekly art projects,
plus arranging online hangouts so they don't become social-
ly withdrawn, planning for physical activity so they don't
become lumps on the couch, and communicating daily with
teachers so I don't become 'that parent' who doesn't know
when homework's due."

"What's Jeff doing?" I asked the obvious.

"Well," she hedged, "he's home working, too, but I do all the
'extra' stuff because my job is more flexible."

"Is it?" I challenged. Anne works full-time as a financial adviser for a nationally recognized investment company, not a

job typically described as yielding. And given the current global economic crisis, I understood that her professional contribution was more needed than ever. I added, "Or is that *you* are more flexible?"

It turns out, it wasn't just Anne who was more "flexible." Women everywhere were juggling faster and faster. A woman named Meg wrote on *Motherly*: "I am privileged. I have a partner; we can exist on a single income and we have security in a very insecure time. I am also in pain. There is a misconception that stay-at-home moms are living the dream right now—where some moms are pulling their hair out balancing work and kids full-time, we are frolicking happily, with face paint . . . exploring nature and engaging in quality family time. What right do we have to be pained? And yet, the price of the health, safety and happiness of my family was paid for with my goals, dreams, and a large part of my identity and self-worth as I became a stay-at-home mom." Elizabeth Teng, a doctoral student in astrophysics, summarized her experience on Twitter, "Am I working at my regular capacity? No. But am I prioritizing and taking care of the most important tasks? No. But am I at least taking care of myself and my mental health? Also no."

DOUBLING DOWN ON FAIRNESS AT HOME

I, too, was busier than ever. I felt lucky that I was able to work safely from home and still, daily life was a grind. In my household, I hold the "homework card," which in normal times means I help my two elementary-age boys and one preschooler manage and complete their homework assignments. But in pandemic times, that job expanded—soon, I was responsible for logging three kids onto three separate Zoom calls on three separate school iPads (*What's the password?!*), seven times a day, five days a week. And when those gazillion calls were over, I'd ensure that all assignments were completed and submitted through the school portal each day by 3:00 p.m. to be marked by their teachers as "done." This one aspect of domestic life felt like a thankless full-time job with no benefits.

17

Meanwhile, my actual paid job was intense, too. My speaking schedule had also migrated to Zoom, and now that the home had become our whole universe, companies and individuals were hungry for tips on how to set up systems under one roof to infuse more fairness into our relationships. *How*, people asked me every day, *can we create more efficiency in our households—and by extension, the "living where we work" workplace?* A good question, as the three kids at *my* home were pushing me to my breaking point. Emotional eating was becoming my form of self-care, and binge-watching gardening shows now counted as my "outside" time.

This is when I called a time-out in my own home. I suggested to Seth: "We had a solid system in place to keep our household running . . . but we're slipping back into old patterns that are triggering old resentments. Can we agree to check in every night for ten minutes to make sure we're balancing the workload and not hating each other?"

"Yes," he agreed, and joked, "but we can still treat our kids as our common enemy, right?"

I realized that, as difficult as circumstances were, if we could focus on boundaries, systems, and communicating effectively, it would help us in this unprecedented time. Time and system management may sound easy enough, but boundary setting especially was proving difficult if near impossible for many women. So where did that leave us?

I conducted an informal poll of women in my circle and beyond—many of whom I'd originally interviewed for *Fair*

Play and others I'd met in the intervening years. It was a diverse sample from across a range of incomes, geographic backgrounds, race, and ethnicities, whose makeup mirrored that of the US Census as a whole. I asked: "Describe in one word how you feel during this time of juggling work and home life?" Their number one answer:

Drowning.

You sure can't dance in the rain if you're underwater.

This is a recipe for madness!

—POLITICAL SCIENTIST LAUREL ELDER ON THE MENTAL EFFECTS
OF PARENTING IN THE PANDEMIC

Without much solicitation, I began hearing from women all across the country who were seeking some kind of Mayday! relief. Women like Aisa, a friend of mine from high school, who was collapsing under the pressure. She is the general manager for an e-commerce company, and her already demanding job spiked into the red zone with the onset of COVID-19. Literally overnight, she was charged with figuring out a way to deal with the heavy increases in demand and finding ways to deliver essential items to people every day.

"A lot of people's jobs were put on hold during this time. Not mine," she said. "I was grateful to have work, but my particular job became a nonstop, constant. I would get on calls at eight in the morning that would not stop until eight at night. Coupled with trying to juggle childcare for two kids at home while my husband was also working full-time. It was insane."

Aisa, who describes her husband, Matt, as "generous," continued. "We'd both read *Fair Play* a few months before the pandemic hit and we were actively working to share responsibilities at home and to encourage each other to make time and space for our own 'things,'" recounted Aisa on a video call with Matt.

"I could feel that her dial had been turned to eleven," Matt said, jumping in, "and I wanted to support her. One evening after the kids were in bed, I suggested she create some Unicorn Space."

"I gave him a look like, *Yeah, right. When am I going to do that? I* remember thinking to myself, *My job has never been so stressful and there is no end in sight.* I felt strongly that this was not the time to find time for *me.*"

"But I kept nudging her," said Matt, "because I knew she needed more than nonstop work. I could see it on her face. She was drained."

"I finally gave in to his suggestion," Aisa said, "but I was wrestling with *what* I'd do if I made time for me. I couldn't quite wrap my head around the idea of Unicorn Space. I suggested to Matt, 'Maybe I'll get back into my yoga practice.' He corrected, 'No, that's self-care. It's supposed to be something *else.*' I considered joining the PTA given all the uncertainty with remote schooling, and again, Matt said that something extra in service of the kids isn't considered 'unicorn-ing.' I was stumped.

"And then, around this time, I called my uncle who lives in India and who's deep into Hindu astrology. I asked him if he'd read my star chart to help give me a clear direction forward. He told me I was 'transiting out of Saturn and into a different time of life' and a bunch of other things about my 'house and governing planets' that sounds like hocus-pocus to some people but that absolutely captured me. I went down the wormhole with him, and I was *so into it.* I didn't want to come out."

From that moment forward, Aisa created time to foster her new curiosity. She ordered a stack of books on Hindu astrology and stayed up late into the nights reading, researching, and connecting to her Hindu traditions.

"I would pore over those books for hours," she said. "Astrology energized me. It gave me a new drive, the search for something bigger, more existential in a super-stressful time. And, also, it was just fun."

"I could see the benefits for our family, too," interjected Matt. "By reconnecting with her uncle, Aisa was reconnecting with her family history and sharing it with me and our kids."

"I realized that just because I live in the US doesn't mean I should lose this piece of my family history," affirmed Aisa. "My grandmother practiced Hindu astrology for much of her life. She passed it down to my uncle, who is now passing it down to me. It feels really meaningful to carry the tradition forward and share it with my kids . . . and who knows where it goes from here." She smiled.

Finding joy and meaning. Sharing with others. Deepening connections between generations and cosmos. These are just some of the benefits we start to receive when we invest in our creative lives—even (or especially) when the rest of our world feels out of control.

THE POWER OF "THE PAUSE"

Let's pause for a minute. I want to acknowledge the full spectrum of realities caused by the pandemic and nod to the inherent privilege of being able to focus on creative pursuits at all, in a world where so many people are struggling just for food, shelter, and work. Many more are dealing with mental health issues like depression and physical issues like chronic fatigue and insomnia. And too many were, and still are, fighting for their very lives. I want to be sensitive to whatever your personal experience is and also propose, again, that Unicorn Space is essential for *all* people, regardless of your circumstances or financial privilege. (In fact, I discovered that some of the most privileged people had a *harder* time tapping into their creativity, whereas those with fewer resources were *more* likely to have Unicorn Space in their lives. More to come on that.)

Unicorn Space may sound like the stuff of glitter and rainbows, and paradoxically it *is* the magic that will light you up as you inevitably face the hardships of life. But Unicorn Space won't serve to replace or stop the storms from coming. What it will do is help you weather them. The truth is, if we want to avoid burning out, we each *have* to find time to step back; cultivate our curiosities, interests, and passions; and remember who we are apart from our jobs and our family roles. No matter what is affecting your life, creative self-expression like I'm describing is essential to your physical and mental well-being. In fact, it has been found to be a form of "transformative coping" that allows individuals to deal with transitions and stressful events. Additionally, creativity is also essential to the health of your partnerships and your ability to model what a full and meaningful life looks like to your children, your friends and colleagues, and your communities. And as I continued to meet and talk with a variety of people with different backgrounds, I saw strong evidence to support this.

Even amid the struggles we were all facing, more and more I was hearing from women online who were sharing a hopeful message: this "forced pandemic pause" was causing them to slow down, look inward, and reevaluate what in their lives was really making them happy—and what wasn't. This awareness was bolstering their resilience in the face of the current storm.

Abigail, a new friend, direct messaged me: "Check out my celebration cakes that are a party unto themselves! They're interactive and light up because in these times, it's even more important to bring joy into our lives. Particularly when that joy is edible and twirly."

Alexis, a colleague, followed: "I'm launching an improv class online for people who need a creative outlet, a safe space to speak up and act out without fear or judgment."

A message followed on my Instagram, from a woman named Leslie whom I didn't yet know: "We all need inspiration to escape the overwhelm. Women routinely put self-interests at the bottom of their to-do list. Let's change that! Now is the time for a ruthless commitment to caring for yourself and regarding your time as valuable."

Hear! Hear!

And then my mom forwarded me a link titled "Badass Women" with a note: "Read this! It features one of my colleagues from Hunter College who opened a feminist bookstore in Crown Heights. I signed you up for her book club."

I scanned the article, which featured Kalima DeSuze, who self-identifies as an Afro-Latinx feminist, social worker, activist, teacher, army veteran, and new mother. Kalima has a full-time job as a social work educator, and she is also the owner of Cafe con Libros, a bookstore and coffee shop. What resonated most with me about Kalima's story was her emphasis on the radical nature of joy for Black and brown communities. In spite of the inequities in politics, gender, race, education, immigration status, and "otherness" that Kalima has personally experienced or witnessed in other's lives, she says, "We need to think about the things that bring us joy."

I was so intrigued by Kalima's story and mission that I asked Mom to put us in touch. A few days later, Kalima and I spoke by phone. She shared that when the bookstore had to shut its doors due to the global shutdown, "I was fortunate to still have a full-time, paid job, which allowed me to go deeper into what I wanted Cafe con Libros to be because, to me, it's more than just a Black-owned bookstore. It's a community for people to tell their stories, and especially for those who feel marginalized or silenced." Throughout COVID-19 and our country's reckoning with racial injustice, Kalima explained that Cafe con Libros became a safe space for a community of readers and thinkers "to connect and to spread the love of reading as a source of healing and joy."

Wow, I thought, *talk about a Unicorn Space!*

After my call with Kalima, I had to pause and reconsider that not everyone was drowning. Despite the current storm, women like Kalima, Abigail, and Alexis were finding a way to dance in the rain. Could it be that we were on the verge of taking an important step forward for people—partnered and unpartnered, with kids and without, traditionally employed or otherwise—to find ourselves, to express ourselves, and to heal ourselves through creativity?

On further thought, I recognized—*of course!*—the desire for personal expression and human connection would become more pronounced during this period of disruption. Removed from the daily hustle and bustle, those of us who were forced to stay home faced an "involuntary quiet," when our "go-go-go world has slowed to a near halt," as Arthur C. Brooks described in his series "How to Build a Life" in *The Atlantic*. Periods like this, he offered, afford us the "chance to stop and consider the big drivers of our happiness and our sense of purpose." Laura Empson and Jennifer Howard-Grenville echoed in an article in the *Harvard Business Review* that liminal experiences, or "prolonged separation from the normal ways of being and doing . . . are disturbing and disruptive, but they also represent potent opportunities for reflection, discovery, and even reinvention."

And even those of us whose family structure includes medical personnel and all varieties of essential workers were also challenged to get creative in order to carve out important Unicorn Space, even when the world was seemingly on fire.

Case in point—just before the pandemic hit, Roderick was laid off as a pastor. He was fortunate to secure a full-time job at a Walmart in New Jersey as an essential worker. His wife, Imani, who was the primary caretaker of their two children, had just started creative writing classes at the local junior college. "When COVID shut everything down, all the classes went online and my kids needed to be homeschooled," explained Imani. "So, all of a sudden I had to make a choice—give up my classes or find a way to pursue my dream to become a writer. Roderick and I worked around his schedule so that I could write at night."

Roderick added, "I didn't want to cut into her dream. I'd had my season as a pastor, and now it was hers."

"We made it work," said Imani. "And it wasn't easy, but my writing during this time of disruption was really important. Giving up this *one thing for me* would have been a harder choice."

Whether it's a pandemic, a depression, a recession, or during times of war and social unrest, this sort of reflective, creative response to instability and uncertainty is not unusual. As I began researching this further, I found a wealth of smart thinkers in the fields of behavioral science and psychology commenting on this very subject.

In a beautifully written article for *The Riveter*, Kristina Libby, author and educator, offered her historical perspective to this collective creative outgrowth: "There is a long history of creativity in response to trauma. If we look back even in the past century, some of our greatest artists (Frida Kahlo, Georgia O'Keeffe and Virginia Woolf among them) emerged in the wake of our world wars, our forgotten wars and our economic downturns. They, like all of us, used creativity to express the complexity of emotions, perceived and subconscious, that result from the experience of being alive."

Los Angeles–based psychiatrist Will Siu, MD, similarly invited readers to embrace the moment: "Although these times are challenging, they may hold an opportunity to mindfully and actively reassess both our gifts and needs and deepen our relationship to ourselves and others."

I became inspired—okay, *obsessed*—with this creative lens that mirrored my own, and by the psychology of post-traumatic growth that affirms that trauma can be a catalyst for positive change. Marie Forgeard wrote in *Psychology of Aesthetics, Creativity, and the Arts* that difficult times are a bona fide creative force, with the power to redefine ourselves and "expand our capacity for expression."

In a time of destruction, create something: a poem, a parade, a community, a school, a vow, a moral principle; one peaceful moment.

—MAXINE HONG KINGSTON,
NOVELIST AND PROFESSOR

THE RETURN OF GOLD-GLITTER SNEAKERS

Rather than be lulled into the seductive waters of anxiety presented with every news cycle, I determined to take my cue from Kristina Libby's Floral Heart Project, which challenged, "Pick up a pencil. Find clay. Grab for a marker. Locate an empty page.

Arrange some flowers. Take a moment to create." Inspired to create a community, I formed a coalition of sorts—a combination of old friends and new acquaintances from all across the globe and from vastly different circumstances and backgrounds—to join me in the continuation of my quest for Unicorn Space. Included were some of the same women who helped me curate the original "Sh*t I Do" list that became the launching pad of the Fair Play system. Others I'd previously interviewed or met online and at various stops along my speaking tour, and all of whom I considered "spiritual friends" because they each, in one way or another, had been a source of creative inspiration to me. I formed an email thread and sent them the following note—

To: Friends, family, colleagues, fellow working mothers, and partners

From: Eve Rodsky, organizational management specialist currently obsessed with creativity

As many of you have heard me proselytize, making time for *ourselves* and creating space for self-expression is vital to our self-identity, along with our mental and physical well-being. So, beyond being a wonderful partner and parent (if that applies), what activity are you engaging in—if even only for five to ten minutes every day—that makes you feel vibrant, focused, connected, and alive?

Note: I'm not talking about friendships and self-care (also important!), but rather an active pursuit (beyond household responsibilities and childcare) that gives your life a lift. I'm talking about Unicorn Space, a term of which many of you are already familiar: the *active and open* pursuit of *self-expression* in any form that makes you *you,* and which requires value-based curiosity and purposeful sharing by phone, email, social media, or from your front steps!

As I waited for their replies, I reflected on my own Unicorn Space. My dream to become a published author had become a dream fulfilled, and that sense of completion could never be taken away from me. Now, I wanted a *new* dream. What could I pursue next? What could I commit to that would fuel my own creativity while also contributing to my larger community?

I determined: I would commit to a new writing project—forged in that acute pandemic moment but not defined by it—that reimagined and expanded on the idea of Unicorn Space. This idea would show how everyone—*anyone*—can bust through domestic, professional, cultural, and creative barriers if they just commit, day-to-day, to value-based self-expression. And once again, I would play the guinea pig—by fully immersing myself in the process and tracking my successes (and failures) along the way. My new dream was nothing less than jump-starting a creativity revolution!

As part of this experiment, I intended to stay close to my writing and also pull my gold-glitter sneakers out of the back of my closet and freshen up my choreo. And if she was willing, I'd enlist Jessica to once again join me as my dance partner. If it weren't for the travel restrictions in place at that moment, I might have suggested we escape our families and jump on a plane to Tokyo to study hip-hop dance at the feet of Shige-boh—obviously, you know, only because I'm dedicated to my research and not at all because we'd enjoy it. But without that option, my living room would have to double as a dance floor. In the evenings once the kids were asleep and my husband was occupied with the news, I'd pull up the now classic and canonized clips of *In Living Color* and dance it out. Just for fun.

(On second thought, maybe I should make like Shige-boh and update my moves just a bit.)

2

A New Creativity Framework

//

Why Creativity Is Essential— in Difficult Times and Beyond

CREATIVE AVENGERS: ASSEMBLE

Still flush with the excitement of my new plan, I realized I would need some help if I was going to bring the concept of Unicorn Space to the masses and reimagine my 1990s Fly Girl moves. So I turned to my very own ambassador of youth culture for advice on next steps: my twelve-year-old son, Zach.

"Zach!" I called out.

He appeared in the doorway and slumped against the frame. "Yeah?"

"Where can I watch the most current hip-hop dances—you know, how do you and your friends learn to dance?"

"TikTok," he muttered. I did a Macarena-inspired thank-you move as he rolled his eyes and turned on his heels.

So it was settled. I would commemorate my renewed pursuit of Unicorn Space by learning to dance from TikTok, and then by sharing my amateur videos to all who agreed to join me on my quest. I reasoned that watching forty-four-year-old me earnestly attempt to perfect Jalaiah Harmon's Renegade had viable entertainment value, maybe? Plus, I'd just read in *Quartz* that Harvard neuroscientist and bestselling author Dr. John Ratey espouses dance as the best possible exercise in terms of brain health. He did qualify that he meant "vigorous" dance that gets your heart rate up, not just flailing around. (Noted.) And the reason, he says, that this form of dance is so powerful for the brain is because it requires mental focus. "The more demand on the brain . . . the more [brain muscle] you're going to build," encourages Dr. Ratey. So perhaps dancing would not only satisfy my desire to expand my Unicorn Space, but also it might make me smarter. Bonus!

But given my tween's tepid response to my creative endeavor, I knew I was going to need a larger coalition of support to get this project off the ground. Right on cue, as my plan continued to crystalize in my mind, I began to receive encouraging responses to that email invitation I'd sent out to friends, familiars, and colleagues.

Aisa wrote back right away. She was the first to say, "You know I'm in! I'm getting a new astrology book in the mail this week."

Tiffany, a friend from my sons' school, followed: "I would love to make time and space to start and <u>complete</u>"—she underlined the word *complete* for emphasis—"something other than raising my kids and throwing in another load of laundry, both of which I consider to be a labor of love but neither of which are ever really 'done.' "

Blessing, a friend I'd met on the *Fair Play* book tour, was more optimistic, but, she, too, had her own parameters: "We should all be embracing time for ourselves. I'll just have to fit my time in around my boss, who apparently thinks I'm supposed to be working ten to twelve hours a day on top of taking care of three kids." As I read Blessing's response, I quietly reflected on her particular dynamic. She's ambitious, successful, and appears to *have* it all. But this often means *doing* it all, too.

Ashley, another new friend, countered: "I'm the DIY type, so I love spending my free time creating. I'm up for the challenge!"

Darby, a leading clinical psychologist and neuroscientist who'd become a good friend of mine through my research, responded: "I'm always at the lab, so I love spending my free time creating. I'll just have to juggle what's most important right now."

I loved the early enthusiasm, but I was starting to see some threads of doubt and concern layered in their responses. They were already backtracking with some all-too-familiar internalized excuses for why they couldn't prioritize their own time.

PRIORITIZING YOUR CREATIVE LIFE

I hear these lines all the time. I call them Toxic Time messages, and they often enter our minds (and our relationships) without our even realizing it. Some examples of these Toxic Time messages that specifically compromise one's Unicorn Space are:

- I have less time than ever; I cannot make more time.
- Time for what I *need* to do (feed the dog, get to work, and pick up groceries) takes precedence over time for what I *want* to do.

○ At the end of the day, making time for *me* feels like just another thing to put on my list.

○ How can I prioritize creativity when there are so many people hurting in the world?

○ It doesn't pay, so why make the time?

○ There's always something that interrupts or distracts and sidelines my attention. And then, there's no time left.

○ In the grand scheme of things, do I really need creative time for me?

CAUTION AHEAD!
Beware of Toxic Time Messages

The promised land of Unicorn Space will stay forever out of reach until you commit to reframing how you value your time and then intentionally reprioritize time for *you*. One by one, strike down the Toxic Time messages that compromise your time choice and obstruct your path forward to a more fulfilling life.

TIME REFRAME

I jumped in and responded to everyone on the email chain: "Many of us feel as time-compromised as ever—especially now—which is precisely why this is the optimal time to reclaim some for ourselves. There is always more to do—more cleaning, more childcare, more work! Still, I challenge you to engage in an activity (again, beyond household and childcare responsibilities) that feels meaningful and brings you joy. This isn't selfish; it is an imperative. Mia Birdsong, social justice activist who advocates for reclaiming our interdependence, acknowledges, 'Turning away from work can feel like an indulgence, but in the context of capitalism, acts of joy are a form of rebellion and a deep affirmation of life, love, creativity, connectedness, and spirit.'"

I continued, "So be mindful of dismissing time for you as an indulgence or a luxury and make the intentional choice to move Unicorn Space to the top of your to-do list. If you find yourself making the excuse *It doesn't pay* or *I should spend my time in service to my family*, research shows that our individual health can be significantly compromised when our lives become all work and no play. And even if you love your full- or part-time job, you still need time and space to engage in something outside the work you do for money to make you come alive. And especially if you do the heavy-lifting work of a full-time stay-at-home parent, you need your own creative outlet, for sure, and I'm not talking about the grocery outlet or the outlet mall."

Reader: Before we go any further, I must make an important point—none of this works in a vacuum. You cannot find and inhabit your Unicorn Space unless you are committed to prioritizing yourself and your own time. That's rule number one.

I'll dig into the rules of Unicorn Space in part II of this book, but I'll abbreviate the first important one for you here—you have only twenty-four hours in a day. Your time is finite—like diamonds—and thereby valuable. So preserve some of it *for yourself* by making the intentional choice to step away from everything that is demanding it from you. Your space is limited, too, so give yourself permission to be "unavailable" so that you may engage in creative pursuits that fulfill you.

IS PRIORITIZING CREATIVE TIME PARTICULARLY TOUGH FOR WOMEN?

I caught up one afternoon with my friend Darby, the neuroscientist. "Women, in particular, really struggle with this in a way that men often just don't," I lamented to Darby.

She nodded. "Women just have less free time, period. Domestic and childcare time can be all-encompassing and boundaryless, because you're never fully done. Couple that with men statistically taking more leisure time, and not much time is left for women."

She mentioned a study she did at UCLA that focused on dual-income couples with kids. After tracking a typical "week in the life," she found that wives spent the largest share of their time at home on chores and housework, with leisure time coming in at a distant third place. For husbands, this order was flipped: leisure time was their leading activity at home, and chores came in third. In the same study, she found that partners who spent more of their time on housework had weaker evening recovery of their levels of cortisol, a stress hormone—so the extra housework seemed to carry an everyday health toll for women.

The study brought to mind my friend Michelle, who'd told me several months into her stay-at-home COVID-19 life, "My husband is *thriving* in quarantine. He has lost twenty pounds, renovated the front porch, started learning German on Duolingo, and he is actually building a cigar-box ukulele in the basement. It's ridiculous. He's busier than ever at work, too—but he hasn't struggled to carve out his 'me time' and feed the interests and hobbies that make him happy."

I returned to Darby. "It's predictable that men take more leisure time than women, but it's not inevitable. It's 'effing-evitable.'"

Darby laughed. "Yes, you got that point across in *Fair Play*."

Finding your Unicorn Space requires, first and foremost, that you and your partner (if you have one) both reframe how you value space and time . . . and then commit to the goal of rebalancing the hours that domestic work requires between you so that you both can benefit from the true life- and relationship-changing experience of creative living.

Notice that I said so that you can *both* benefit. Unless you're both benefiting, a nasty pot of resentment will begin to brew. I discovered in my research that when there is a lopsided division of labor at home, and especially if there are kids in play, we can quickly become resentful of our partners for engaging in individual pursuits that make them come alive. And it goes both ways.

For example, my neighbor Susan confided to me, "When I hear Jason out in the garage on his electric guitar practicing with his 'band buddies' while I'm stuck inside folding laundry and chasing the kiddos around, I really want to pull the plug— on his guitar, that is."

When I asked Jason separately about the time he spends practicing guitar, he shrugged. "I worked sixty hours this week. This is my downtime and I earned it."

CAUTION AHEAD!
Unicorn Space Is Crucial for a Happy Partnership

This tit for tat is the logic that can signal the downward spiral of an otherwise healthy, functional, even loving relationship. Based on my interviews, when we prevent our partners from engaging in their Unicorn Space, our relationships are likely to suffer and sometimes even fail. Don't despair! Based on every instance I've tracked with this type of imbalance, relationship success significantly improves when you and your partner reframe how you value each other's time. Repeat after me: "My partner and I both deserve and *need* uninterrupted time and attention to focus on the things that we love. It is vital to our relationship longevity and our individual happiness."

Where happiness within your relationship is its own reward, the findings of the Harvard Study of Adult Development, a one-of-its-kind, near-eighty-year longitudinal study on well-being, furthers that good relationships are the *key* to longevity, with study participants who identified as "happiest" in their relationships at fifty were later those identified as the *healthiest* at age eighty.

THE PROMISE OF CREATIVE LIVING

Most of the women I'd enlisted in my social experiment understood the importance of Unicorn Space, but I wanted to give them a chance to reframe some of the Toxic Time messages that may have unconsciously been getting in their way. A week after our initial exchange, I nudged the group again: "How's it going on your journey toward creative living?"

Jakki, another friend from the neighborhood and new to the group, chimed in: "Since we're still confined to our homes, I've been taking my family on 'virtual' vacations. We pick a place on the map and—*go there*. Last week I brought Italy to our outdoor patio with family-style raviolis, a red-checked tablecloth, and the kids wore fedoras and sang to my husband and me as if we were sitting along the street in Florence. It's not a solo pursuit, since we're all enjoying it. But it's Uni-ish, right?"

Ashley, the DIY enthusiast, offered: "I'm a huge Harry Potter fan, so I picked up my crochet needles. I've decided to make a collection of miniature dolls—Harry, Hermione, Ron. Maybe I'll sell them on Etsy or maybe I'll just keep them. Haven't decided."

Darby introduced herself to the group: "I moved my 'Mom' band, the Dahli Mamas, to Zoom. A departure from my virtual lab, but who says scientists can't also be musicians?"

And finally, I happily announced: "I did it—I signed up for advanced-beginner jazz funk dance classes on Zoom! Jessica, will you join me? It'll give you an excuse to be unavailable for an hour."

My cousin Jessica, whom I'd more or less coaxed to join the group, wrote simply, "Let me get back to you when I have a free hour."

I realized that although the *will* was there for so many of us to tap into our more creative selves . . . the framework was lacking. The pathway was unclear. We didn't always know how to get started nor did we know where we were going. Luckily, I had some ideas—and if there's one thing I'm good at, it's digging into a subject and creating solutions. So I got to work.

THE 3 C'S OF UNICORN SPACE

For the past two years, I've amassed a collection of stories of people from all over the world who, whether they put a name to it or not, are figuring out new ways to tap into their own creativity and "unleash their unicorn." In spite of daily challenges to their livelihoods, home life, and relationships, these individuals have each created the time and space to *be* more, *share* more, and *connect* more.

I also kept tabs on my initial focus group I started in the darkest days of the lockdown. As we grew into a creativity coalition of sorts, we started calling ourselves the Unis (short for *Unicorns*). I'll refer to the Unis throughout this book. Along the way, I added more voices to my data set, until we represented a vibrant cross section of real people—women, men, trans people, and nonbinary people, from mixed family configurations, socioeconomic statuses, income, race, ethnicities, and national origins (see my Author's Note to learn more). What began as a short email thread between friends and familiars evolved into hundreds of one-on-one Zoom video calls and in- and out-of-home interviews with some of the most interesting and inspiring people I've ever met, many of whom I'm excited to introduce you to in the pages ahead.

Early on, I took a six-degrees-of-separation approach. If I read an article or heard a TED Talk or a podcast about someone I wanted to meet or interview, I would try to find a way to connect. If that meant dialing up childhood friends, old neighbors, former clients, my favorite college professors, and even my mother's veterinarian, I did it. I also didn't shy away from tracking down people on LinkedIn and Instagram, and I even conducted an informal poll while standing in line at Costco.

I figured, *Why not initiate a conversation?* The worst anyone could say was no.

But to my delight, by allowing my curiosity and tenacity to drive me, I reached people I would've never imagined would agree to sit down and talk to me about creativity and chasing dreams, such as Bob Ballard, the oceanic explorer who discovered the *Titanic*! And Renée Brinkerhoff, who became a formidable race car driver at fifty-six! It turns out that those people who are inhabiting their Unicorn Space love to share their success stories (and even their setbacks) with others.

Out of those conversations, I started to come up with a framework for creative living—what I call the **Three C's: Curiosity, Connection, and Completion**. We'll explore each of these ideas in turn in part III of this book as I discuss them with a myriad of creativity scholars (I tracked many of them down, too!). It was a journey that my Unis and I took together—in real time!—as I was writing this book, following my own interests and digging deeper into these concepts. It took all of us some time to pass through the Three C's of curiosity to connection to completion to arrive at our individual destinations. But we easily discovered that even in small doses—which is all most of us have on any given day—creating uninterrupted space and time for the things that bring us joy and enhance our sense of self, and that we can share with others, infused our lives with greater meaning and purpose.

In many respects, our committed exploration of the Three C's became the antidote to a number of subsequent threats circulating at the outstart of our journey: Burnout. Opting out. Anxiety. Depression. Also, carving out Unicorn Space helped inoculate us from potential resentment intensified by the gender inequities at play in many of our households. Additionally, and maybe most importantly, our exploration addressed a more persistent restlessness—an existential longing to know and honor ourselves more deeply.

TIME FOR A RESET

As the world began to cautiously creep out of dark isolation and step back into the sunlight as the pandemic pause passed, I continued my personal experimentation and research. I gathered the latest studies in the areas of creativity, meaning, and happiness, and I spoke with specialists and researchers in the fields of humanistic psychology, positive psychology, cognitive science, and neuroscience, alongside psychotherapists and life coaches.

As I layered in this data with the organizational management rigors that I espouse, the overarching conclusion was consistently clear: a creative life is not a nice-to-have but a *must*-have. It is essential to our sense of self, our physical and mental well-being, the health of our partnerships, and our ability to model what a full and *meaningful* life looks like to our children, our friends and colleagues, and our communities.

As the people in my growing coalition explored their creative selves more deeply, they described their experience as profound and life-changing. Instead of *I feel like I'm drowning,* they articulated their new reality in a variety of ways that sounded, to me, like the basic essence of being human:

I feel like I'm breathing again.

I'm awake.

I'm falling in love with my life again.

I didn't know I was missing anything until I had it again.

I'm alive.

I'm me.

Alas, when the Unis returned to a new normal as workspaces, offices, and schools reopened and commute hours (along with morning drop-off and afternoon pick-up) resumed with everyday intensity, I noticed a proclivity by many of us to step away from our Unicorn Space. Not all at once, necessarily, but incrementally. Even I found myself lacing up my gold-glitter sneakers less and less, because I was now filling my allotted dance space with time out with friends and running my three kids around. I had to remind the group of us that Unicorn Space is not limited to "the pause." It is a mistake, and it will be to our detriment, if we reframe creative self-expression as a distraction, a privilege, an indulgence, or a simple additive to our lives *during hard times.* No, creativity is essential work. Still. Today. Tomorrow. And during the next hard time.

The words of Sonya Renee Taylor, author, poet, and activist, resonated with me. "We will not go back to normal. Normal never was. Our pre-corona existence was not normal other than we normalized greed, inequity, exhaustion, depletion, extraction, disconnection, confusion, rage, hoarding, hate, and lack. We should not long to return," she poses, because now, "we are being given the opportunity to stitch a new garment, one that fits all of humanity."

And how do we do that? How do we tailor a life cut from new patterns? We start by asking ourselves questions, by being curious:

What's intrinsically valuable and most meaningful in my life? What do I want to keep? Do differently? Let go of entirely? What brings me joy, and how can doing my "thing" foster a deeper connection with myself and by extension . . . the world around me? We can each begin to trim back inequity, exhaustion, depletion, disconnection, confusion, and lack from our lives, leaving them as scraps on the cutting-room floor when we can honestly answer these questions. And only *you* can answer these questions for yourself.

PUSH FORWARD

My research continues, and I invite you to be part of the journey. Welcome, fellow Uni! And back to my earlier question: What would you unleash if you had the uninterrupted time and space to express yourself in your own "being true to you" way, and how would you share it with the world? Whether you are partnered or not, have three children or none, or whether your work is paid or unpaid, in the pages that follow, you will learn how to create time in your already busy life to tap into your unique expression of creativity and find purpose that will allow you to live a more meaningful and fulfilled life.

CAUTION AHEAD!
Let Go of Your "Shoulds"

Don't think you have time for it? Don't think you need it? Not sure what that "thing" is that would provide you with a greater sense of meaning, purpose, and fun? Maybe old guilt is nagging you: I "should" spend my time making a grocery run, balancing the household budget, doing [fill in the blank] in service of my family. Whatever your reason, excuse, or belief that you don't need or deserve more space and time for yourself, read on to understand the costs of sidestepping your inherent right to live a creative life.

3

Identify Yourself

How to Rethink "Success"
and Redefine What Matters to You

CONSIDER:
THE CASE OF THE MISSING IDENTITY

It was my first Target run since the world had gone into lock-down mode. I desperately needed a reason to leave the house, both to replenish a few standard items (diapers and paper towels) and also to stock up on some new essentials (stretchy pants and leg warmers). This had become my new lockdown look. My from-the-waist-down daily Zoom wear. I hardly recognized myself anymore, and as I walked through Target's electric double doors in my LA Clippers beanie pulled down low, dark sunglasses, and face mask, I imagined no one else could recognize me, either, in these times of invisibility. After gathering all my items, I wandered down the notebook and journal aisle. I figured I might as well stock up for all the interviews I was now collecting. As I scanned the shelves, I couldn't help but notice the affirmations adorning a row of journal covers: You Got This! (*Do I?*) Everything Happens for a Reason. (*Does it?*) Only Dead Fish Go with the Flow! (*Huh?*) None quite fit my mood. Just as I was about to leave the aisle, my eye landed on a notebook with the following quote scrolled in bold lettering:

For a Minute There I Lost Myself.

Well, that's fitting. I smiled.

I recognized the quote as a lyric of a popular Radiohead song, and the words now felt especially profound. They spoke directly to me in this moment but also to how so many women feel about themselves—not only during the pandemic, but generally in midlife. In fact, I'd just had a heart-to-heart with an old law firm colleague who'd tearfully admitted, "In my chase to do it all and be it all, I lost myself somewhere. I'm a 'success.' I should be happy, but something's missing."

I responded, "It sounds like what you're missing is *you*."

In nearly every conversation I have with women about finding their Unicorn Space, one way or another, we eventually veer toward themes of overextension, overwhelm, and some version of identity loss—all of which become especially heightened after childbirth and can hit the proverbial roof when a wild card like a job loss, illness, or (God forbid) a death in the family or a pandemic is also thrown into the mix. Erin Erenberg, who runs Totum Women, a community to help support and advance working mothers, said, "I'm hearing women in our community and beyond repeat a refrain of 'I'm disconnected from myself; I don't know what I want anymore. And once I do, is it even available to me?'" It's no wonder that women, specifically, feel disconnected given that 70 percent of US mothers report to working full-time jobs while also carrying the lioness's share of child-rearing and housework. And where, within this chronic, never-seems-to-end "double shift," can a woman possibly find uninterrupted time and space to expand her purpose beyond her roles of what I call the Three P's—partner, parent, and professional (and by professional, I mean any person working for pay or working unpaid in the home)?

Even if we are proud of our achievements, find comfort and belonging in our relationships, and enjoy our standing in our various communities, so many women I speak to voice a longing for a return to the person who once was or who may have been—or who simply hasn't shown up yet. Based on my interviews with hundreds of women, we generally fall into one of two creative types:

1. **The Resigned Dreamer:** You are resigned, albeit a bit resentful, to remain in the longing stage. Becoming More *is a great book title*, you think, *but it's likely an urban legend. I should be grateful for who I am and the life I've built and stop wanting for more.*

2. **The Breakout Star:** You are determined to break free of cultural conditioning and your self-made tethers and seek out more. *I am grateful*, you think, *and still, I know there's another version of me that could give, learn, love, live even more.*

If you're reading this book, it's highly likely, like 99 percent likely, that you're a Breakout Star . . . and I'm here to help you break out so that you're no longer missing out. To put it within the language of pop culture, the Breakout Star often suffers from FOMM (fear of missing me). And yet, you feel like you're on the precipice of a reimagined present and future. You fantasize about jumping on the boat, wherever it went, and before it sets sail again and you miss it. You have the courage, or at least the curiosity, for what comes next, but you're stuck on *What's "next," anyway? What's the "more"? And what's the "happily ever after"? Can someone define that for me?*

POP QUIZ
Did You Sign Up for "Happily Ever After"?

Q: After school, work—and, for those who choose it, partnership and kids—what's next? What's the "after"?

A. Caretaking your parents. Tack on another twenty-one hours a week to your already busy schedule. Welcome to the sandwich generation!

B. Membership to the AARP. Hello, discounts to car insurance and matinee movies!

C. You hit the ceiling at work. Nowhere to go but down!

D. You have an affair and ensuing divorce. Hey, everyone's doing it! Well, more than half—53 percent of married couples do the splits.

E. Death. The milestone that comes with a gravestone.

If your inclination is to choose [none of the above!!], take some comfort that there can be more, and I'm not just talking about a clean mammogram. The shiny bauble beyond the Three P's (partner, parent, and professional) is that you can create new milestones of your own design that connect you to an expression of yourself that you may have buried, forgotten, or haven't discovered yet, and which connects you to a community of like-minded seekers. "We can have multiple identities when we give ourselves permission to think of ourselves outside of our roles," encouraged Dr. Amber Thornton, host of *The Balanced Working Mama* podcast, in our conversation over Zoom. If that's attractive to you, keep reading. . . .

⊙ ⊙ ⊙ ⊙⊙⊙⊙ ⊙ ⊙⊙ ⊙⊙ ⊙⊙⊙⊙⊙ ⊙⊙⊙ ⊙⊙⊙ ⊙ ⊙⊙⊙⊙ ⊙⊙⊙⊙⊙⊙ ⊙⊙ ⊙⊙⊙ ⊙

RETHINKING "SUCCESS"

The inspirational quotes in the Target journal and notebook aisle have yet to define *what* the next step should be—or, just as important, *how* and *when* to make the time and space for that next step in our lives. After all, we've been fed a particular kind of definition of success: leaning in and optimizing performance in our careers, pushing harder and achieving more than the generation before us; earning more money than the previous year; and also being amazing, present partners, parents, and standout citizens. No pressure. How, then, do we reimagine personal success within a culture that applauds milestone markers for women that aren't necessarily fulfilling or sustaining? A friend reflected on Instagram: "Do you ever look into the mirror and think, *Who is this person?* A go-getter? A career woman? And now . . . I don't know what I am or where I'm going next. Was I sold a lie?"

In a rare moment of putting my feet up and sinking back into the couch without a child on either side of me asking for a snack, a show, or a story, I scrolled Instagram and stumbled

upon a *Forbes* article listing the indicators of a midlife crisis. Number ten was: "Willing to walk away from your current 'success' in an effort to pursue passion and live out your
dreams." Come again? The effort to pursue one's passions is
on the top-ten list of midlife *crisis* indicators?! Isn't that a bit
upside down? Shouldn't dreamy living be an indicator of mental health, not mental crisis? I asserted out loud to an empty
room: "And what is 'success,' really, if we *aren't* pursuing the
passions that allow us to live out our dreams?"

I quickly recalled a contrasting opinion made by Arianna
Huffington that made a lot more sense. She posted on Linked-
In: "When we chase a flawed definition of success, the danger
is not only that it takes us to a place that's not truly where we
want to go, it's that on the way we're much more likely to miss
the things that really do bring us happiness and fulfillment,
like connection, meaning, impact."

Don't you like that better? Assuming you do, too, let's go
ahead and turn this formula for success around: rediscovering
your passions beyond partnering, parenting, and your profession is *how* you live out your dreams, and this active pursuit of
self-expression, creativity, and discovery is the antidote, not
only to the storms of life but also to a crisis of identity.

WHAT ARE YOU LOSING?

And the real question is, if you deny yourself permission to live
a creative and more meaningful and fulfilling life, what are you
losing?

Yourself.

Consider the costs of invalidating or revoking your right to
unleash an expanded self:

Y
O
U

Relationship satisfaction, if you are partnered, in the form of pointed resentment, jealousy, and overall dissatisfaction and lack of fulfillment in the relationship. Left unchecked or poorly addressed, I've met people who opt out of their relationships—by having affairs, leaving, or divorcing in an effort to "find themselves again."

Sanity and mental health, in the form of new physical and mental health challenges for your entire family. "This American drive for achievement, optimal productivity and peak human experience is familiar, relentless, exhausting," writes Brigid Schulte, director of Better Life Lab and author of *Overwhelmed.* "Yet, despite these well-intentioned efforts, children—and adults—in America are decidedly unhappier, more anxious and live sicker, shorter lives compared to the children and adults in many other countries."

Emotional longevity. Multiple studies have documented a longitudinal decline in "purpose in life" and emotional well-being and growth in the transition from midlife to older age. In other words, simply living longer doesn't necessarily translate to a good life—reimagining *what* you are engaged with while living that longer life (when you may no longer be partnered or parenting or working) has been identified as that missing link in successful transition beyond the Three P's.

Loss of identity, in the form of a lost sense of your former self (FOMM), and a feeling of disconnection from the passions, skills, and interests that have formerly made you uniquely *you.*

Finances, in the form of your paid or unpaid career due to stagnation, mental fatigue, and burnout. Regarding burnout specifically, studies by occupational psychologists have found that those who rank low in a feeling of personal well-being find their professional work more stressful and are likely to experience burnout more often and sooner in their careers.

YOURSELF. Without Unicorn Space—that space in your life that allows you to express creativity and tap into something deeper and more profound than we usually find in everyday life—you risk losing what makes you uniquely *you.* Yes, the stakes are that high.

But don't despair. There is another way.

CONSIDER:
THE CASE OF THE JOURNEY BACK TO ME

I first "met" Melody on Instagram. She posted about the importance of finding time for her Unicorn Space and tagged me: "I used to be confused by 'alone time,' and I used to feel like I should give it up for family and friends. I now understand the importance of giving myself space to listen to myself, to daydream, to remember those things that make me *me* and make me feel alive. I now plan for 'alone' time. I schedule it, relish it, live for it, and sacrifice other things for it. But I only found that space when I eliminated other things I 'should' be doing in favor of bringing myself to life every day."

I mean, c'mon, pass the collection plate. This woman was speaking the gospel. I had to meet this kindred spirit in real time.

Melody graciously agreed to an interview, and when she appeared on-screen, her bright smile lit up the room. She quickly explained that she hadn't always been so buoyant and light.

"I live in a community where kids are the job, the dream, the passion, the end-all-be-all. And I got lost in that world. Where I felt like every waking minute of the day should be spent in devotion to my kids and my family. And I love my kids dearly, but total devotion just wasn't *me*. I was molding myself into a role that didn't fit . . . and it was painful."

She continued, "I guiltily thought: *But wait, I'm supposed to be happy. I have it all: a wonderful husband, great kids, a house. I have everything I want, right?* Except I had nothing for *me* and that was creating underlying unhappiness. I got pretty low."

Melody began working with a therapist who helped her realize that, as a natural introvert, she needed to create alone time for herself to regenerate and be the best version of herself for her family.

"Once I started giving chunks of time to myself, everything changed," she said. "I was a happier wife, a happier mom, a happier friend and daughter. My life became beautiful to me again."

"What's your Unicorn Space?" I asked her.

"Gardening, photography, and writing. These are the things I do to just be me with *me*."

Just be me with me. That's the opposite of FOMM!—and a great inspirational quote. Now that's what I want to find emblazoned on a blank journal in Target!

She continued, "When I realized how good it was for me to shut everything else out and make time for myself and how happy I was on the other side of it, there was no question that I had to continue giving myself permission to 'shut off' from time to time and do the things that make me feel the most alive. Also, my kids started seeing a more authentic version of me and that brought a breath of new life to our family. For so long I tried to keep the real me from my children, and that was a mistake, such a disservice to myself and to my kids to conform to what I thought a 'good mother' looks and acts like instead of just being who I am. Life is too short and too beautiful to spend it being someone we were not meant to be."

Melody admitted that finding her Unicorn Space didn't happen overnight. Getting "back to me" was just the first step for Melody. From there, it has become a journey of exploring how to move beyond the "me" and share her special gifts with the world. "It was a process of letting things go. I had to eliminate some old habits," she said. "But with every step I took away from the shoulds, I was one step closer to fulfilling bigger dreams."

FIND A NEW HAPPY

Take heart. As Melody beautifully exemplifies, there is much to be gained from cultivating your creativity and living more intentionally. Add to that, there are real, tangible benefits to following your own authentic path: an increase in brain function and efficiency of neural systems. (It'll make you more clearheaded!) Other studies underscore the improved motivation and even life extension that result from creativity. (You'll live longer!) It's also linked with better physiological regulation of stress hormones and inflammatory markers. (Decreased puffiness and far less anxiety!)

Lisa Damour, PhD, psychologist, *New York Times* columnist, and bestselling author wisely posits that the definition of mental health is "having the appropriate emotion at the appropriate time and the capacity to weather it effectively." Unicorn Space gives you that *capacity*, that kick of resilience. It works like an umbrella to help you weather the inevitable storms of life. Look, life is full of rain—giving yourself space and time to focus on the things you love to do is how you weather the hard and the mundane. And those experiences can't be washed away.

Now, before we go any further, I want to underscore that this is not a "how to be happy" book. Even Dr. Laurie Santos, who teaches Psychology and the Good Life—the most popular course in Yale's history—and who many consider to be the reigning happiness expert, advises against pursuing happiness as its own end goal. "Going for happiness for happiness' sake doesn't work," Santos said in our interview. But as you will discover in the pages ahead, it *is* the natural by-product of discovering, inhabiting, and sharing your Unicorn Space with others.

CONSIDER:
THE CASE OF THE CULTURE CLASH

I shared this highlight of my conversation with Laurie Santos with my cousin Jessica. She exhaled for effect. "Are you trying to ruin happiness now? You know, that's not going to make you very popular. People like to be happy."

"Jessica"—I laughed—"I'm not trying to take away anyone's happiness. I'm just suggesting we redefine it. Rather than seek happiness, I'm suggesting we create new milestones, like dusting off our dance moves"—I elbowed her playfully—"that help us to weather unhappy times."

"Dancing is more like a hobby," Jessica dismissed with a wave of her jazz hand.

"Oh, no, you didn't just say 'hobby.' You know I hate that word."

Jessica smiled with the satisfaction of a close family member who likes to get under your skin for their own amusement. "Okay, maybe it's more than a hobby, but 'milestone' is kind of pushing it, don't you think? In our culture, the milestones are marriage, career, kids, making money. If you're lucky, a vacation here and there and a decent retirement party."

"Partnering, parenting, and a profession," I said, rattling them off. "But you're forgetting the fourth P: permission to live a creative life."

"You and the P's . . ." She feigned exasperation.

"What?" I protested. "I love my alliterations."

Jessica turned to me. "Babe, society doesn't value creativity past kindergarten. Expressing yourself is fine when you're under ten, and then life gets real."

Jessica was painting a pretty cloudy picture. I made a mental note to buy her a pair of cheery, gold-glitter sneakers, stat! She did have a point, though: the "real" world does have a way of stifling our creative expression past an, ahem, *certain age*. When our valedictorian at Stuyvesant High School reminded my class that women weren't admitted to my high school until 1969, she encouraged us to fight for our dreams and yet, at the end of the metaphorical day, I retired my gold-glitter sneakers in favor of a more traditional professional track. The unspoken subtext to that inspiring speech and so many others like it was: go ahead and dream but also be practical. In other words, be smart, kid, and lock in a reliable, good-paying job.

What a bunch of bullshit, I thought, now echoing start-up savant Sari Azout's words: "How do we encourage more people to best serve humanity? A good start would be by valuing creativity instead of killing it; to focus instead on realizing our potential, taking chances, creating, imagining, building."

Thankfully, I had the privilege to eventually leave my law career for something more fulfilling, but it took me nearly twenty years of my adult life before I jumped ship. And so many good people I know are still, unhappily, on board, effectively taking an early retirement from their creative life.

We should each ask ourselves: Why did I stop doing what I love? Why did I stop myself from even *identifying* what I love? And more important, why did I start doing something I don't love? Joy Foster, a friend who started TechPixies, an online learning platform helping women return to work, change careers, or start a business, said to me, "So often we encourage our children to follow their dreams, but why do we stop following ours? My son wants to be an artist, architect, actor, footballer, or a cricketer. I *wanted* to be a missionary, an art teacher, a prima ballerina, president of the United States. What did you want to be as a child? Who do you want to be now?"

FIND YOUR COMMUNITY

I thought back to the Senior Monsters. When referring to his dancing, Shige-boh said it was his "reason for being," and that all men and women in the Japanese culture are inspired to find *their* reason because it provides a sense of directed meaning and purpose to one's life. I puzzled: *What's* my *reason?* To Jessica's point, cocktail-hour conversation in our social circles rarely ventured this deep. Outside of my interviews in conjunction with this project, I couldn't remember the last time someone had turned to me and asked: "Hey, Eve, what's your reason for being?"

I wondered: Is this lack of prioritizing our deeper selves a Western shortcoming? Are we a culture that retires our self-expression too early, while people in other countries and at all ages are encouraged to unleash themselves and expand their lives beyond conventional milestones? Is the American drive for achievement what prevents us from actively pursuing and properly crediting what makes us *most* feel alive? Or is it simply a matter of finding your special community, as Shige-boh had done? As I was contemplating this, my friend Mags sent me the following text:

"Hi, dancers! Join me for the first day of Dance for the Revolution!" Mags is the very definition of a person who lives their passion—Mags is an artist and activist who uses dance to protest and inspire transformation—so I knew a dance fest with Mags would be nothing if not a celebration of Unicorn Space with other radical dancers. "The online session starts at seven," they wrote. "Clothing optional because you don't have to leave the privacy of your house!"

Yes! I thought. *This is what Jessica and I need! After sitting in front of screens all day, we need a clothing-optional excuse to stand up and shake it all out.* And that's when I had my lightbulb moment. Finding your community need not be defined by cultural norms or expectations, nor are "your people" necessarily fixed by a physical location. Your community can be found anywhere within a shared space that allows for creative expression, promotes self-discovery, and inspires purposeful connection. Meaning, we can each find and build our own communities, in our own *homes.* Heck, on Zoom. This aha suddenly struck me as supremely obvious. After all, the Unis had started our quest for a more creative life while we were under lockdown. In the beginning we hadn't ventured much farther than pulling garbage bins to the street.

Finding and building your community is the subject of a full chapter later on, so if you're feeling at all lost or without a sense of community right now, hang tight. For now, start right where you are. With identifying where you stand today.

EXERCISE
Start Right Where You Are

Begin your line of self-inquiry with the following questions. Jot your answers down in a separate journal or in the space provided here. Or if you're not in the mood for going "deep" right now, dog-ear the page and return to this exercise later.

- *Who am I now? Describe yourself in the present.* ____
  _____
  _____
  _____

- *What do I like about this version of myself? What do I not like about this version?* ____
  _____
  _____
  _____

- *Who did I used to be? Describe yourself in the past.* __
  _____
  _____
  _____

- *Who had I always imagined myself becoming?* ____
  _____
  _____
  _____

- *In what ways have I stopped myself from becoming "me"?* _____

_____

_____

- *What are the cultural expectations that have prevented me from pursuing what makes me most feel alive?* _____

_____

_____

- *In what communities, groups, or environments do I feel a purposeful connection?* _____

_____

_____

- *In what ways am I willing to modify my current lifestyle, routine, or habits in order to connect or reconnect with aspects of myself and make connections with others?* _____

_____

_____

On our next informal call, I workshopped these questions with some of the Unis. "I need to collect more data," I said, "so indulge me, okay? First question: Who did I used to be?"

Tiffany jumped in first: "Younger."

Darby and Blessing laughed.

I continued, nonplussed: "Who did I always *imagine* myself becoming?"

"Michelle Obama," Jessica cut in.

We were all having fun laughing at ourselves and one another until I asked the last question and the group went quiet.

"Really, is *no one* willing to modify their current lifestyle, routine, or habits to create more Unicorn Space? This is the whole point of our social experiment, and you women are supposed to be my chief ambassadors," I pressed. "C'mon, don't fail me now. I just bought two more pairs of sneakers, on clearance, but still. Jessica, one pair is for you."

"It's not that I'm *unwilling*," returned Tiffany, "but I still struggle to make the time."

Aisa added with apology, "Even though I have a partner who is supportive of my Unicorn Space, I tend to fill my free moments with other things, typically," she said guiltily, "with work."

"Personally, I'm tired of the silent eye roll I get from my partner," interjected Ashley, "when I pull out my craft bins."

"Oh, I know that look," said Blessing, "that clearly says, *You're going to spend your time doing* that?"

Where our group had made significant progress over the past few months, we were now, again, at a crossroads. How could I convince the Unis to keep going, to give them permission to continue on their journey of self-discovery and creative expression?

That's it, isn't it?

I reframed the question: "Is it that you aren't *willing* or that you won't give yourself *permission*?"

They hesitated, and I had my answer. It was a matter of giving *ourselves* permission to pursue our Unicorn Space, to live a creative life.

With these fresh insights, I further understood that before any one of us can set off on the journey from curiosity to connection to completion, we must each first embrace the rules of permission.

○ Permission to be unavailable
○ Permission to burn guilt and shame
○ Permission to use your voice

When we live by these rules, we can write our own "permission slip" to engage in the active and open pursuits that express our uniqueness and, by extension, create purposeful connections that infuse more meaning and joy into our lives. And then, with our permission slip in hand, the road map to "what comes next" suddenly appears before us, and there's no good reason to stand still any longer. Rather, it's time to start dancing in the rain.

PART II

THE RULES OF PERMISSION

Why do each of us deserve the permission to be unavailable, to burn our guilt and shame, and to use our voice to ask for what we need—and how does that allow us to cultivate our creativity and create our own Unicorn Space?

4

RULE #1—
Permission to Be Unavailable

//

How to Find Your Flow and Start Saying No

WHAT'S YOUR LINE?

I would engage in meaningful activities that make me happy beyond my role as partner, parent, and professional, but...

- I don't have enough time to do what I *need* to do to make the time for things I *want* to do.
- It doesn't pay, so why make the time?
- It's on my list. I just haven't gotten to it... *yet.*
- My partner and I take turns making time for our own thing, and it's their turn right now. (*Hmmmm.* When I think about it, it's been their turn for a while now.)
- Every time I start to engage in something outside of work, parenting, or the house, I inevitably get inter-

rupted by work email, paying bills, a clogged toilet, or a child tugging on my sleeve.

○ There's always something that interrupts or distracts and sidelines my attention. After that, there's no time left.

○ I have less time than ever. I don't have any "extra" time for me.

○ Scheduling "me time" feels just like one more thing to do.

Are any of these "I have no time" hurdles preventing you from a more creative life? Do any of these "I'm constantly interrupted" realities rob you of time you may otherwise spend expressing yourself in your own true-to-you way by engaging in an active pursuit that infuses your life with greater meaning and boosts your happiness quotient?

REFRAME TO GAIN

Over the past several years, I've met countless people who respond positively to the *why* of Unicorn Space. They all intuitively understand that taking time for themselves makes good sense. Once introduced to the idea (and especially once I give it a name—Unicorn Space), most people immediately appreciate *why* carving out a place in their lives for creative self-expression is a key component to creating a life of meaning and happiness.

And yet, many women—culturally conditioned to put time for themselves last—especially struggle with the *what* and *how* to make it happen . . . and most definitely the *when*. This is no surprise, really, because there is no "when" when your mental and physical bandwidth is stretched as thin as Saran Wrap.

As my friend LeeAnah describes it, "I'm the human equivalent of a conveyer belt. The work keeps piling up and coming down the line. Meanwhile, my partner is a single plate, and when it's full, he's 'done.'" If you also find yourself single-handedly (or even just predominantly) performing the demanding and intensive work of running a household, being a parent, working a job in or outside the home, and trying to maintain a working relationship with a partner—you likely have nothing left for yourself.

It's time to change that. It's time to give yourself the permission to be unavailable.

> You are complicit in your own oppression when you willingly put yourself and your time second or last.

So many women I meet and speak to still believe, often unconsciously, that in order to "have it all"—the degree, career, partnership, family, home, social standing, etc.—we must *do it all. Make it happen. Get it done.* The net result: Women spend less time on their own health and important self-care and also tend to deny themselves any time for personal pursuits beyond the Three P's (remember, those are partner, parent, and professional). And without enough proper attention to self, women are drowning. They're burning out. (Single mothers, I see you, too.) And I want to hug each one of these women I meet and say, *Honey, you're missing the piece about having something for yourself.*

I know. I've been there myself.

CONSIDER:
THE CASE OF THE "UNAVAILABLE" POST-IT

Repeat after me—time is a limited commodity. It is a finite resource, which means I do not have an *infinite* amount of time. I have twenty-four hours in a day, and I have the right to choose (within reason!) how I spend my hours. If I have a partner, both of us have only twenty-four hours in a day . . . and for each of us, those hours have value. Therefore, we *both* get to make choices about how we use our finite time.

It wasn't until I intentionally reframed the value of my time and asked my partner to also rework the twenty-four hours of the day in his own head that attitudes started to shift within our home. Behaviors, on the other hand, took a bit longer to develop. You see, reframing time is only part of the equation. Boundary setting, in which you intentionally stake and guard your time, makes it whole.

Look back no further than to when our time-space continuum collapsed during the 2020 pandemic, blurring once-distinguishable lines in the workplace and at home. According to a "time diary" study in the *Washington Post*, a couple working at home during the pandemic was interrupted an average of fifteen times per hour by childcare and household demands. The average length of an uninterrupted period of work time was three minutes, twenty-four seconds—and the shortest stretch was mere seconds. According to a study of 3,500 families with two opposite-sex parents by the Institute for Fiscal Studies, the "child-interruption gap" affected women most significantly. Mothers, they found, were dedicating 10.3 hours every day to looking after the kids—2.3 hours more than fathers. Bestselling YA author Nicole C. Kear shared her own version of this "gap" on Facebook: "I'm working in five- to fifteen-minute intervals, punctuated by interruptions from my kids, WHERE'S MY CHARGER? THE ZOOM LINK WON'T WORK! and I'M STARVING AND THERE'S NOTHING TO EAT!"

During that challenging time, boundary setting became a fast necessity in the interest of self-preservation, and I applauded many of my friends who boldly instituted clear lines of their own, in an effort to juggle jobs, partners, kids, pets, and their *sanity* all under one roof. I relished their videos of hiding out in their kitchen pantries and escaping to their bedroom closets. "Double-lock the door," my friend Blessing advised. I laughed at the caution tape, "leave me alone" boxes, and the impossible-to-confuse "DO NOT ENTER" and "Mommy's on a time-out!" signs other friends and Unis posted on bathroom and home office doors.

Caught up in the moment and without totally thinking it through, I followed their lead. When I decided to start writing the first draft of this book, I instituted a similar boundary. I converted a corner of our guest room into a writing nook, where I hoped to work uninterrupted for two hours over each weekend. This seemed feasible. Fair. At breakfast Sunday morning, I announced to my husband and three kids: "After we finish up, I'm going to go work on my book for two hours. I'll be home, but pretend I'm not home." They nodded in vague agreement, and once the table was cleared, I retreated to the guest room and shut the door. Guess what happened? Within five minutes there was a knock on the door.

It was Seth. "Hey, I know you're busy, but I just wanted to let you know that later I need to pick up our curbside groceries. Cool?"

"Cool."

A few minutes later, my nine-year-old barged in. "Mom, when can you read my homework assignment?"

"Later." I waved him away.

Not thirty seconds later, my three-year-old began screaming from the adjacent room: "I WANT MOMMY!"

Good God, the walls are thin. I was quickly gaining a clear understanding of why collaborative workspaces are so popular—it's not really about doing work. For twenty bucks a day, you can escape your family.

The next week, I tried to communicate my boundary a little differently. I explained again that I was taking two hours to write and that I was unavailable to answer questions, make snacks, or change the batteries in the TV remote. "If you need something," I told the kids, "ask Daddy." To hammer home the point, I wrote UNAVAILABLE on a Post-it and stuck it to my T-shirt.

"I'm unavailable," I enunciated slowly and for effect, before calmly excusing myself from the table. Guess what happened this time? Within five minutes there was a knock on the door.

It was Seth. "Hey, I know you're unavailable, but . . ."

"No *buts*—I'm working."

"Sorry." He retreated and shut the door.

A few minutes later, Anna stumbled in, sucking on a lollipop. She sidled up to my chair and pointed at the Post-it. She whispered, "I love you," before running out. Adorable, yes, but still disruptive. But since she was not yet reading, I deduced that her interpretation of *unavailable* meant that interruptions were permissible so long as they were delivered quietly and with love.

After Anna left, I enjoyed ten minutes of solitude, just enough time to settle and focus in on writing, when Ben barged in. I took a deep breath. "What is it?" I asked without exhaling.

"Ummmm . . ." He hedged and looked around the room, as if searching for a viable excuse for his standing there. Not finding one, he tried a distraction technique and pointed at my chest. "Hey, Mom, your Post-it's falling off."

That was it! Before I could stop myself, I stood up and screamed a regretful "GET OUT!" Without missing a beat, I'd reverted to an old communication style of mine—sharp commands, *sir!*

"Sorry," Ben said, teary-eyed and wounded. He slunk out of the room, and I spent the duration of my "unavailable" time equally fuming and feeling guilty. This wasn't working. My Post-it paired with my drill-sergeant delivery was as ineffective as it used to be back when I would place a clean garbage liner on the kitchen counter and glare at Seth, hoping he'd magically figure out that I wanted him to take out the overflowing trash.

When it came to the trash can, I'd learned that a passive-aggressive death stare followed by full-on aggressive stomping around the house and slamming doors was not the most effective way to reach my audience or garner the outcome I desired. Rather, developing shared goals, establishing clear communication of expectations, and setting realistic boundaries was the "magic" solution. These tools were effective in my work as a professional mediator, and they worked in other aspects of my home life, too. It was time for me to practice what I preached and start putting these tools in effect to preserve my Unicorn Space.

At breakfast the following Sunday, I communicated my needs to my family this way. I said, "Hey, I want to try something new today that helps us all get what we need without all the yelling and tears." I paused and locked eyes with each one of them. I registered attention, so I calmly continued . . .

"I love you and I want you to feel seen and heard in this house. *I* want to feel heard and respected, too. I'm asking for two full hours in the morning to write in my office. This time is very important to me. It allows me to use my voice for what I value, which means I have more to give you when I'm done. While I'm writing, Daddy is here to help you with whatever you need." I paused and leveled my eyes at Seth.

"Of course." He nodded.

I resumed. "Then in a couple hours, I'll be one hundred per-cent available to you all. But until then"—I paused again for effect—"please respect my time and space. Okay?"

"Okay," they all mumbled with that glassy-eyed look that in-dicated only partial compliance but a clear desire for me to stop talking. Maybe I hadn't made the situation relatable enough?

I turned to the kids and said, "Think of it this way: if we re-served a private room at the trampoline park for your birthday party and—just as we were cutting the cake—another group of kids burst through the door, demanding cake and proclaiming that it was *their* party room, you'd be upset because it wasn't their turn yet."

Anna flared with indignation at my fictionalized scenario. "That's not fair!" she shouted while pounding her small, clenched fist on the breakfast table.

"No, it's not, baby. And that's my point: don't crash my party."

Effectively setting boundaries is not barking demands, slamming doors, or going on strike. To effectively guard your space and time, you must intentionally set boundaries, not with yellow caution tape or Post-it notes, but by clearly and respectfully communicating what you need and why you need it and by expressing appreciation, ahead of time, for having your boundary honored: *Thank you for respecting my space and time. Now, get outta here.*

I'll go into more detail about *how* to explicitly negotiate these terms with your partner and family when we discuss rule three: *permission to use your voice.* But just knowing that you can (and must) do so is an important first step in the process. Once I set boundaries that felt fair and that my family could understand and appreciate, the behaviors in our house shifted. It was far less contentious and much more collaborative. Understanding what was now possible, Seth took his cue from me and negotiated two uninterrupted hours to himself on Saturdays. Once we set this clear boundary and expectation as a couple, the kids easily settled in. In fact, they started to look forward to their alone time with Mommy on Saturdays (pancakes for lunch) and Daddy on Sundays (extended roughhousing). As long as we continued to regularly check in as a family and clearly set boundaries and define expectations for the weekend, we all got what we needed, at least most of the time.

THE UPSIDE TO BEING UNAVAILABLE: FLOW

When you give yourself permission to be unavailable and recognize you have a right to your own valuable time, a magical thing happens—you're granted mental freedom. Available head room. Space to think! Sustained attention to focus on something you love.

Now, hold on. It will be tempting to flood a quiet mind with another mental to-do list: place Instacart order, return unanswered emails, schedule kids' haircut appointments, and then make the futile attempt to get to the "end" of your Twitter or Instagram feed. Resist! Take this time for *you.* I promise, the rewards are great. You see, an unencumbered mind in the form of more mental space to have singular focus allows you to get into a state of flow.

You know flow, even if you haven't experienced it for a while. Professor Mihaly Csikszentmihalyi, creativity specialist, preeminent researcher, and the author who introduced the concept with his book *Flow: The Psychology of Optimal Experience,* describes it as "the state in which people are so involved in an activity that nothing else seems to matter; the experience itself is so enjoyable that people will do it even at great cost for the sheer sake of doing it." *New York Times* op-ed columnist Jennifer Senior describes it as "that heavenly state of total absorption in a project. Your sense of time vanishes; it's just you and the task at hand, whether it's painting or sinking shots through a basketball hoop."

Bill Burnett and Dave Evans, pop culture authors of *Designing Your Life*, describe flow as "engagement on steroids . . . that state of being in which time stands still, you're totally engaged in an activity." They also describe it as "play for grown-ups."

Natalie Nixon, author of *The Creativity Leap*, asserts that flow "creates the moments that make life worth living."

I resonate with all of these descriptions, while I personally describe flow as *uninterrupted time and sustained attention to something you love.*

When I'm in my writer's flow, I can get pulled into the page and tune out everything around me. Left uninterrupted, I can singularly focus for hours, until my bladder reminds me that it's time to take a pee break. When I'm onstage delivering my message of domestic rebalance and the importance of pursuing our dreams, my space-time continuum collapses, and I rise into an elevated state of heart-pumping adrenaline that extends outward, deepening my connection with my audience. This flow state will typically carry me effortlessly through the last slide of my presentation and the very last line of my talk. Before I know it, I'm taking questions from the audience and thinking, *Wait—what happened? Where did the time go? Wow, what a fun ride!* Flow allows for optimal experiences that can never be taken away from you, even after the moment has passed.

What does flow feel like for you? And when was the last time you experienced it? "I can't remember back that far," recounted Kristine, an elementary school teacher and mom to two teens. "I struggle to find a quiet room, let alone any free time for myself. The other night, I thought I'd stolen a few minutes to write in my journal until I realized that my fourteen-year-old daughter was standing quietly behind the couch and reading over my shoulder! I feel like I'm never alone, which doesn't leave much space for flow."

We love our kids, *but* . . . as artist and culture critic Oubria Tronshaw says, "Your kids will never give you permission to have a moment to be sane. Ever. You have to learn to be an advocate for yourself."

She's right, and I'm just going to say it so you don't have to—our kids are the antithesis of flow.

"When kids are small, their developing brains actually conspire *against* flow," echoes Jennifer Senior, "because they're wired to sweep in as much stimuli as possible, rather than to focus; even when they're older, they're still churning windmills of need."

Our kids are just being kids when they interrupt and ask us questions. They can't help it. Still, understand that raising kids is an inherently nonflow activity and they will continue to be a source of interruption.

A woman named Akanksha posted on a parenting Facebook page, "Yesterday I was sipping freshly brewed coffee . . . [and] I thought to myself, I can finally have some 'me time,' when my toddler swooped in and did some ninja butt move and spilled my entire cup. Just like that my 'moment' vanished. To those who have children, [understand] that your kids' butts will always get in the way of your peace of mind."

BOUNDARIES, NOT BUTTS

I've met many parents who fantasize about sending their kids off to Mars or cryofreezing them to recoup some of their lost uninterrupted space and time. "Or at least sending them off to another room with the iPad," offered my cousin Jessica. "As a single mom, sometimes this feels like my only option when I need time and space." Fair enough, and yet, there is another option beyond bribing the littles with screen time or kicking them out of the house: set boundaries. Your kids will be fine. But if you continue to deny yourself uninterrupted flow time, it's *you* I'd be worried about.

"You need a stretch of continuous, unmolested time to do good work," emphasizes Senior. "Instead, your day is a torrent of interruptions, endlessly divided and subdivided, a Zeno's paradox of infinite tasks . . . There's no flow at all."

And in the absence of flow, cautions Csikszentmihalyi in the first pages of *Flow*, "people often feel like their lives have been wasted. That instead of being [fulfilled] their years were spent with anxiety and boredom."

Yikes, I might not go *that* far, but I can confidently say that at the risk of compromising your creative self-expression, you must say no to achieve your own version of flow.

The opposite of **sustained attention to something you love** is interruption.

NO KIDS, SAME PROBLEM

Have you, too, forgotten the feeling of uninterrupted time in your own home? When was the last time you had literal space apart from your partner, family, or roommates to reclaim your creative space? Even if you're single, without kids, or live alone, you're not immune to interruptions. Boundary crossing is prolific in the workplace, too. We've all had managers and colleagues who call after hours and make requests on weekends because they assume we'll likely say yes.

"There are way too many times when meetings are booked at all times of the day. I'm like, what about lunch? What about dinner? I need to eat at some point," commented a woman who attended one of my work-life integration panels at BlogHer. Another agreed, "I'm tired of letting the interruption of work email rule my life and ruin my productivity."

Long hours and no breaks are closely linked to burnout, exhaustion, and sleep disorders. Additionally, our work-at-all-hours, "answer it now," stay-on-the-online-treadmill society is a chief interrupter of flow and a master Unicorn Space inhibitor. And here's the rub for a significant sector of society, as Kiisha, a woman who attended another one of my panels, pointed out: "If you don't have kids, you don't have an excuse *not* to be interrupted. You can't say, I have to get off the call to go feed my kids." She made an interesting point that time-management consultant and researcher Laura Vanderkam writes about in *Fortune*: "When I was reviewing time logs ... I noticed that people with children or other caregiving responsibilities were far better at creating a stopping point, which makes sense. Someone has to send a sitter home or pick up the kids from day care."

Curious, I determined to explore the "no excuses" idea further, so I DM'd Kiisha and asked her about her ratio of work time to Unicorn Space. She explained that as a single woman in her early thirties, the expectation is that she always be available for work, even during "nonworking" time.

"There are no time and space boundaries," she said.

I countered that she *must* assert a boundary in order to make time and space for life outside of work.

She challenged back: "Ironically, I feel like I need to find my Unicorn Space first and then assert a boundary, otherwise I have no reason to say no to work at all times. Kids and family needs create a sense of urgency in the workplace to attend to other things. It's hard to create that urgency if you don't have kids."

She was probably right that a request to wrap up the day's meetings to, say, scoot home to pop open a bottle of wine and binge-watch Netflix wouldn't be granted. But, as Kiisha suggested, she may get an altogether different response if she asserted a boundary around creative self-expression. Hers was a solid lead and, I thought, worth conducting a new social experiment. I encouraged Kiisha to claim her Unicorn Space and notice how that shifted anything at work.

She accepted the challenge and dusted off a dream that she'd back-burnered: she enrolled in a master mixology course. A few months later, I followed up with her. "My mixology class finally gave me the permission I was looking for to work more regular, less insane hours. I worried that my colleagues might resent me for taking time for me but instead, they became really interested in what I was learning, and over the past several months they've come to respect it, unquestioned. On their request, this past Friday for after-office happy hour, I taught my team how to make the perfect whiskey sour."

GUARD YOUR TIME

The first step to guarding your time is awareness. Do you operate as though your time expands to fit everyone else's needs? Is your unconscious habit to guard the time of your partner/child/colleague/friend while you let your own minutes run out? Do you undervalue time for yourself? Do you regard it as an infinite resource like sand?

Take a moment now and acknowledge that **your time is finite**. It is a limited and valuable resource—like diamonds!—so preserve and protect it by giving yourself permission to step away from the endless cycle of daily to-do's and demands on your precious time. When I speak to women, this singular message is the one that resonates the most because the majority of us do not guard our time. We give it away, day after day, hour by hour, minute by minute. An interruption by your partner, a colleague, the doctor's office, or your child's school may be 100 percent worthy of your attention, but understand that ceaselessly doing for others will continue to consume and compromise *all* your available time until you reframe the value of your time and then reprioritize uninterrupted time for you.

The most important step to protecting your time is to set boundaries. I call this giving yourself permission to be un-available. And again, this suggestion tends to strike a controversial note. A woman who attended another one of my virtual panels wrote in the group chat afterward: *"Do you have permission to be unavailable?"* This is one of the most incredibly powerful questions ever posed to me. Up until relatively recently, my answer to this question would very likely have been 'Urgh, nooope!' It's taken some conscious thinking and retraining myself to allow myself time off. Time to refuel. To fill my cup back up so that I have energy to show up better for everyone else."

"You are the only one who can give yourself permission. Permission to say no to unreasonable requests. Permission to do nothing. Permission to take a break. It's up to you to set boundaries in your life," advocates Pooja Lakshmin, MD, a perinatal psychiatrist and clinical assistant professor of psychiatry at the George Washington University School of Medicine and the founder of Gemma, a digital education platform for women's mental health. Pooja and I met on a panel called "Things No One Tells You About Motherhood" and became fast friends.

"When I've said yes to too many things and too many people, I find myself easily irritated at the smallest request," Dr. Lakshmin freely admits. "Everything ends up feeling like a chore (even things that I usually love to do!)."

Permission Slip

I grant myself permission
to be unavailable.

—signed by: ME

PERMISSION TO BE *EVEN MORE* UNAVAILABLE

My husband, Seth, and I were both enjoying our separate, two uninterrupted hours over the weekends. So much so that I suggested, "What do you think about us each taking a full day off for ourselves?" I'd just interviewed Dr. Stew Friedman, founder in 1991 of the Wharton Work/Life Integration Project and author of several books, including *Parents Who Lead: The*

Leadership Approach You Need to Parent with Purpose, Fuel Your Career, and Create a Richer Life. During our call, Friedman inspired me to think like a leader in my own home. In the context of creating uninterrupted time for creative pursuits, I interpreted this to mean—don't stop at two hours, ask for a whole day!

Before Seth had even a moment to answer, I took another cue from Friedman, who said to effectively lead, "Recognize that a give-and-take attitude holds value for the collective good. In other words, it can't just be about me. It has to be about *us*. In your most intimate relationships," Friedman posed, "how can you align what's most important to you with your partner so that you both benefit?"

With that, I layered in a value proposition I was sure Seth couldn't refuse—"Think about it," I said, tempting him, "a full Saturday for you could include an uninterrupted workout, endless hours of *SportsCenter*, and time with friends...."

"And reading the *Times* cover to cover." His eyes lit up.

"Yes, *all of that*. We haven't had an uninterrupted stretch of time like this since before we had kids," I said.

"That's twelve years," he calculated.

"How cool would it be to get some of that time back?"

"I think it sounds awesome," he said. "And on Sundays...?"

"You'll have the kids all day," I said casually.

I could see his expression shift from optimism to doubt. *How many hours of roughhousing Daddy would that amount to?*

I jumped back in before he jumped ship. "How about we just try it and see? It might be too much. Maybe we dial it down. And maybe it's not every weekend. But," I reiterated, "as long as we continue to regularly check in, we can set reasonable boundaries and expectations. Deal?"

"Deal." He smiled.

Protect your time.

Protect your space. Protect your flow.

The path forward to a more fulfilling life is yours when you commit to reframing how you value your time and then intentionally reprioritize some for *you*. Strike down the Toxic Time messages that compromise your choices and begin to think about creating intentional boundaries to protect your time, space, and flow.

ASK YOURSELF

- *How do I value my own time?*
- *How can I begin to create time and space boundaries?*
- *What would an uninterrupted day or just one free hour to myself look like?*

Repeat once a day: *I have permission to be unavailable.*

5

RULE #2–
Permission to Burn Your Guilt and Shame

How to Carve Out Free Headspace for Creativity

WHAT'S YOUR LINE?

I would engage in meaningful activities that make me happy beyond my role as partner, parent, and professional, but . . .

- ○ I *should* spend my time . . . in service of the family or financially contributing to the household.
- ○ I feel *guilty* taking time away from my kids, especially because I work so much.
- ○ My partner *expects* me to devote my "extra" hours to our marriage and our family.
- ○ I'm better at running the house and raising the kids, so I should focus on where I'm most needed.
- ○ The needs of my family come first.

○ I'd like to engage in something beyond work and home, but I'm embarrassed I don't know what that would be.

○ Whenever I try to take time for *me*, I get pushback from [my partner, kids, friends, colleagues, parents, in-laws . . .], who have their own ideas about how I "should" be spending my time.

○ "Me time" feels so indulgent, almost *selfish*.

Do guilt and the shaming "shoulds" prevent you from pursuing a life beyond your roles as partner, parent, and professional? Do you feel that you've been denied permission by society, your community, your partner, or *yourself* to engage in the interests and talents that you once identified with or wish you had the freedom to explore? Take a minute and consider what beliefs and expectations are holding you back from identifying yourself with more than *your roles*. The messages that negatively critique our behavior (guilt) and undercut our sense of self (shame) in our cultural conversation are strong. As Brené Brown, author, speaker, and preeminent expert in this realm, explains it: "Shame is a focus on self. Guilt is a focus on behavior. Shame is, 'I am bad.' Guilt is, 'I did something bad.' . . . Guilt is, 'I'm sorry. I made a mistake.' Shame is, 'I'm sorry. I am a mistake.'" Both make you feel bad, and in combination, guilt and shame are two of the most powerful and effective tools for denying your personal space and time to rediscover *you*.

CONSIDER:
THE CASE OF THE GUILT AND SHAME SALON

It was a Sunday afternoon, and I was sitting in my local nail salon, waiting for an open chair and reveling in a magical "bonus" hour all to myself. As Seth and I had newly negotiated, I'd already taken advantage of my two hours to write uninterrupted at home in the morning and now, I was about to luxuriate in some well-earned alone time.

85

"I've been looking forward to this," I confided to the woman waiting quietly in a chair next to me. "Away from the house and my family."

She gave me a knowing look and perked up. "Oh, I get it. I have three kids, and it's a small miracle I'm here right now. I'm anticipating a 'When are you coming home?' text any minute."

I leaned over and smiled conspiringly. "I turned my phone off."

"Really?" She looked surprised. "Good for you. I could never do that. I feel like I should always be available for whatever comes up, because there's always something that comes up."

"I left my husband in charge," I returned. "I'm trusting him to handle whatever that something is."

"Ha!" She laughed. "How'd you pull that off?" I took this as my opening to share some of my latest time-management and boundary-setting strategies. "My husband and I created a new weekend schedule where I take the kids all day Saturday, and he has them all day Sunday. This is my first full Sunday 'off.'" I crossed my fingers. "And so far so good." I smiled and sat back, imagining how rewarding it was going to feel to plunge my feet into soapy water.

She raised an eyebrow. "Wait . . . you left him with the kids for the full day?"

I thought, *Here we go again.* Even though all women want more time, they sometimes guilt other women for taking it. After nearly eight years of collecting data on gender inequity in the household, I well understood the expectation that the "good mother" be the parent primarily responsible for maintaining the household and taking care of the children. The research backs this, too. Take, for example, a Pew Research Center study where 50 percent of the married or cohabiting women included in the study reported taking on more child-care responsibilities than their male partners (whereas only 4 percent of men reported doing more childcare work than their female partners). Because this continues to be the discordant reality, no one bats an eye when a mother assumes sole responsibility for her kids for extended hours or, God forbid, extended days because ... *Why would Mom ever need a break?*

Diana Spalding writes about the "good mom" ideology on *Motherly*, the online community where she is the Health and Wellness director: "From the moment we become parents, we begin to experience the gender stereotypes and social norms we have come to accept as, well, norms. ... [My husband] is never asked how he manages to balance a career and a family. We simply do not think to ask these questions of men. He also, admittedly, never goes to sleep at night with an overwhelming sensation of *was I good enough today?* That's my societal baggage to enjoy."

Dr. Amber Thornton summed it up this way: "[Women] mistakenly assume that spending time with our [kids, partner, work] is more important than spending time with ourselves. This leads to neglecting our needs and desires, which then leads to guilt if we dare even to have a moment to ourselves, which then leads to low-quality experiences with our [kids, partner, work] because we are tired from neglecting ourselves and because we think that's what we *should* be doing."

Mom guilt like this used to really trigger me, too. In the not-so-recent past, my salon mate's comments could have poisoned my whole day, causing me to think terrible things about myself: *I'm a horrible mother who abandons her family for a fresh coat of Selfish Shimmer polish.* But today, the unfair disparity between a mother's and father's time and whose is more valuable simply annoys me.

But I didn't say any of that. Instead, I turned back to her and stated simply, without apology, "Yep, he has them for the *full day*."

She regarded me with an air of disbelief. "So, what are you going to do for a full day while he's at home?"

"I'm going to do *me*." I smiled brightly and considered that after the spa I may take an hour to practice my new dance moves.

"Wow, good for you." She turned her gaze to follow another woman leaving the salon. She tilted her head in wonder. "What would I do with a full day to *myself*?"

WHAT WOULD YOU DO WITH ONE FREE DAY?

After my visit to the Guilt and Shame Salon, I put on my research hat and asked my growing community of Unis, both those who are partnered and those who are not: *What would you do for yourself, outside family life, with one free day?*

Their responses landed predominantly in the following three categories:

- ○ Adult friendships ("grab dinner with my best friend"; "book club")
- ○ Self-care ("meditate"; "walk on the beach")
- ○ Unicorn Space ("browse around an art store for new paintbrushes"; "start a vision board for my business idea")

Where the majority of my interviewees became instantly invigorated by how they might fill a "free" day, when I suggested they create their vision in real time, they quickly dismissed it as a "sounds great, *but . . .*" fantasy, and especially from those Unis whose responses fell within the category of creative pursuits and Unicorn Space.

"How am I going to get one full day when I hardly get one free minute?" questioned Jakki.

"A full day off to do my own thing?" Tiffany laughed. "Not without traveling back in time to before marriage and kids."

Jessica half joked: "The one gift I received from my divorce is two full days 'off' every other week without the kids or the guilt. That's one way to get it."

These findings brought to mind a recent business trip from Los Angeles to San Francisco, where I sat next to a man on the plane who was holding a book titled *HBR Guide to Work-Life Balance* from the *Harvard Business Review*. I turned to him with a smile. "I'm curious about what you're reading. If you don't mind, what's the quick synopsis?"

He happily obliged. "It's a work-life balance anthology that focuses on creating boundaries and untouchable time. The authors advocate that at a minimum, you have one full day a week that is yours and yours alone, 'untouched' by any outside factors like work, family responsibilities, et cetera."

"Sounds amazing," I said, thinking that my salon mate—*hell*, make that every woman I know—could use a copy. "Have you been successful? Is it working?"

"To be honest"—he leaned in—"I already have a lot of free time."

"Oh." It was starting to make sense. "Are you single, then?"

"No." He shook his head emphatically. "Wife and two kids."

Hmmm, now it was making less sense. I dug in for answers

without reserve. "Well, then, do you feel at all guilty or shameful about taking 'untouchable' time to pursue your own interests outside of work and family life?"

He laughed. He actually laughed out loud. "My wife may give me shit for it," he said, "but no, I don't feel guilty."

THE GUILT DISCREPANCY

I couldn't get that airplane conversation with Mr. Untouchable out of my head. I realized what was bothering me wasn't just Mr. Untouchable's attitude but the fact that it seemed to be echoed by so many of the women I'd been talking with as well. I looped back with friend and colleague Dr. Pooja Lakshmin, who was working on her own upcoming book on the tyranny of self-care. When she appeared on Zoom, I quickly started in with: "Why do women with kids seem to be perpetuating self-sacrifice? We're still buying into this idea that to be good mothers and partners, we must put ourselves last. Why is untouchable time for men a no-brainer, but for women it's quickly dismissed as a fantasy or an indulgence?"

Dr. Lakshmin responded, "It's the most heartbreaking thing to see—and I see it nearly daily in my clinical practice. Moms who are navigating the endless sea of contradictions that are the reality of leading a professional life while raising a family. The thing is, in our culture, it's impossible to hold these roles simultaneously *and* to feel good about the job you are doing— our system is not set up to support women in that way. So when my patients never feel a sense of rightness or mastery in either role, they understandably beat themselves up."

Dr. Lakshmin continued: "So, to answer your question, guilt holds us back from affording time for ourselves. Research shows us that mothers report higher levels of work-family guilt when compared to fathers. What is really interesting to me is how many women are tied to self-sacrifice as a marker of being the good mother."

"Well, that's because our culture applauds women for their suffering, for giving until the point of empty," I interjected. "And that sense of sacrifice starts early and transcends boundaries of race, class, region, and religion. Even before or if you ever have children, women are conditioned to put their needs second . . . to our parents, our friends and neighbors, our colleagues, even our pets!"

Dr. Lakshmin, nodding along, said, "Exactly. That's the predicament women face. When you identify with the martyr role, your power is paradoxically in your smallness—it's linked to your suffering. Many women don't understand the toxicity of this position and understandably mistake it for real power."

I visibly winced when she said "martyr." I really detest the word. It's so gendered; men never refer to themselves in this way, and women wear it as an identifying name tag at back-to-school night. Why must "martyr" be the female narrative, the female identity? I'd taken to replacing it with the term *Human Giver Syndrome*, which I'd recently read about in the marvelous book *Burnout: The Secret to Unlocking the Stress Cycle* by Emily Nagoski, PhD, and Amelia Nagoski, DMA. The authors describe Human Giver Syndrome, or HGS, as "the contagious false belief that you have a moral obligation to give every drop of your humanity—your time, attention, energy, love, even your body—in support of others, no matter the cost to you." The authors continue, "The implication is that human beings have a moral obligation to be or express their humanity while 'human givers' have a moral obligation to give their humanity. Guess which one women are?"

"Women aren't going to stop overgiving," Dr. Lakshmin cautioned, "until we recognize that the rewards of being a martyr are the opposite of happiness. Shrinking yourself and your needs for the sake of your family nearly always feels like the easier option, but the story ends in the same, sad way: a rageful and existentially exhausted mother. Simply put: losing yourself for the sake of others is not a win."

> It is not honorable for a tree to wilt and shrink
>
> and disappear. It's not honorable
>
> for a woman to, either.
>
> —GLENNON DOYLE, *UNTAMED*

POP QUIZ
Are You a Giving Tree?

Making myself available to accommodate the needs of my partner/family/friends/colleagues at the cost of neglecting myself makes me feel:

A. Noble

B. Righteous

C. Generous

D. Valuable

E. Purposeful

F. Sacrificial

G. Selfless

H. Depleted

I. Resentful

J. Unrecognizable to myself

K. Angry

If your answers fall anywhere within the A to K range, consider that your giving tree may be *over*producing and that your best intentions are creating a few bad apples. To be clear, I'm not dismissing the value of care but I do take issue with giving until you have nothing left. Thankfully, as you'll read next, you, too, can become "a tree who sets healthy boundaries," as Topher Payne advises in his contemporary retelling of the classic children's story, *The Giving Tree*.

○ ○

CONSIDER:
THE CASE OF THE "F*CK MOM
GUILT WORLD TOUR"

As I was writing this chapter, I tuned into one of my favorite podcasts, *The Double Shift*, which challenges the status quo of motherhood. It's co-hosted by the award-winning journalist Katherine Goldstein, whom I'd met through our mutual advocacy work on behalf of caregiving. On this particular episode, Goldstein espoused that "Guilt keeps mothers quiet and small!" and then went on to announce the online relaunch of her F*ck Mom Guilt World Tour. Sign me up!

I reached out to reconnect with her and learn more, and over Zoom, she enthusiastically shared her impetus for creating her "world tour" in the first place. Goldstein, a mother of a six-year-old and twin toddlers, said that the idea came about on a whim, when she was thinking about creating a onetime, fun event to commemorate the launch of the successful first season of her podcast.

"I literally put up an event flyer online and in less than two days, all the tickets were reserved. That's when I realized that there was a significant segment of listeners who just really wanted to go to an event called 'F*ck Mom Guilt,' whatever that meant. I wasn't even sure what the event would become, but it was an invitation to women like me who had felt like a failure. After my first son was born and I lost my job, I felt like everyone else had this working mom thing figured out except me.

"Over time, what I came to realize and now speak openly about at conferences and on my podcast, is that I'm not a failure. Mothers aren't failures. Rather, America has failed us. There are systemic forces and obstacles that make the work of mothers hard, and yet we tend to feel guilty about the space we need away from our children or our partners, the space we need for ourselves to be creative and fulfilled individuals."

Goldstein explained that the F*ck Mom Guilt events (that have now become a series with event stops in New York City; Durham, North Carolina; Oakland; and San Francisco) give women "that space without apology and with full permission. They're a fun night out for women to connect and create community."

Goldstein has made the creation of a Unicorn Space *her Unicorn Space*!

"Women should stop feeling guilty and start getting angry," encourages Goldstein. "This is how we become motivated to challenge the status quo."

BURN GUILT AND SHAME

Three years ago, as I was preparing to leave my three kids at home with their father for two full weeks (insert shock and horror) to travel the country promoting my first book, I had a serious sit-down with guilt and shame. In my absence, I knew I'd be missing many "should be there" moments with my kids.

Countless meals, bedtime stories, and, perhaps the worst of them all—missing a birthday! Cue the guilt. And if I went anyway and missed these "should be there" moments, cue the shame for not feeling guilty enough!

The old me wouldn't have even considered leaving my family behind for an extended amount of time so that I could pursue something solely for myself, but the evolving Eve had begun questioning a lifetime of societally conditioned thinking. *Am I really abandoning my husband and failing my children by going on this book tour? Should I stay home instead so that I don't miss singing the "happy birthday" song and blowing out the cake candles?* Of course I could intentionally choose to stay home, but the real question was: *Should I?*

I thought about so many of the women I'd interviewed who gave in to the "shoulds" and gave up their dreams, allowing a vibrant part of themselves to fade or burn out entirely. Zibby Owens, host of the award-winning podcast *Moms Don't Have Time to Read Books*, described her own flame of discontent this way: "The fire inside me, what made me *me*, had been stamped out after a decade of decline. I'd felt like the inside of an old-fashioned barbecue grill long after dinner, a smoking pit of burnt charcoal briquettes."

If I succumbed to the same societal guilt and denied myself permission to spend time outside the home that wasn't deemed essential or as important as my role as caretaker and moneymaker, I knew I'd regret it. If I listened to the voices that said, "It's not worth it for you to pursue *you*," and withdrew permission to present myself to the world as the engaged and passionate woman I'd worked so hard to become, I'd likely resent my husband. And worse, my kids.

With this fresh insight, my mind automatically rewound to an interview I'd done with a woman named Ellen, who'd felt the pressure to give up her career so that she could better use her time to run the household and raise her children. At the time, this was the societal expectation, and without much protest, she relented. She disengaged from interests beyond motherhood and domestic responsibilities and stepped into the background of her own life. After a near lifetime of selfless contributions, Ellen admitted to me that while her life felt meaningful, she was ultimately unfulfilled. "Honestly, I believe I lost my permission to be interesting," she said, "and I regret that my now-adult children grew up with only a partial me. I was Mom, but I wish I'd shown them the full me earlier.'"

Shit. Will that be Ellen's legacy? To be defined by her sacrifice? Will her friends and loved ones only remember the partial her? The one-dimensional version of a truly multifaceted woman? In a flash, I realized how guilt and shame had not served Ellen and they would not serve me, either. Rather, they were hurdles I had to strike down in order to claim my Unicorn Space. After all, my own mother had taught me the importance of this. As a single mom to two young kids, she'd pursued tenure as a professor. This meant working late at her school and coming home even later. Over the years, she's admitted to feeling guilty for making family sacrifices to pursue her dream. But I realize now that she did the best thing she could for herself and, by extension, for us. And in her absence, I became "schooled" myself by reading some of her favorite feminist authors—like Betty Friedan, who cautioned in her 1963 groundbreaking book, *The Feminine Mystique*, "Faced with the slow death of self, the American woman must begin to take her life seriously ... by fulfilling [her] own unique possibilities as a separate human being."

Snapping back to the present, I combined Betty's wisdom with the insight of new thought pioneer Brené Brown, who writes in *Daring Greatly*, "If we cultivate enough awareness about shame to name it and speak to it, we've basically cut it off at the knees. Shame hates having words wrapped around it." Within hours, I'd created a ritual to mark this notable tick forward in my personal evolution, but rather than "cut it off at the knees," I determined to light it up in flames, baby. The inspiration for my "Burn Guilt and Shame" ritual was inspired by a quote I'd stumbled upon online: "Don't wait for others to light your fire; you have your own matches." And also, this one by author Penny Reid: "You are not required to set yourself on fire to keep other people warm."

I'd written both quotes down in a journal to refer back to and possibly use at a later date. Now was *that* time. I co-opted some beautiful origami paper from my daughter's closet, and with a silver Sharpie, I wrote *Guilt* and *Shame* in my best handwriting. I folded the paper into a tiny square and took it outside, where I lit a match and watched it burn. (If you re-create this ritual for yourself, be mindful to find a safe place to burn your guilt and shame that won't set off your fire alarm or engulf the neighborhood in flames.)

As my origami square went up in flames, I said: "Guilt and shame, you have got me to where I am today, but I don't need you anymore. From this point forward, you will only serve as a distraction, a hurdle in my way. I am willing to let you go. I am setting myself free."

The following morning, I woke up refreshed and newly purposeful. I was ready to embark on my own version of the F*ck Mom Guilt World Tour and promptly ordered a Lyft. I left home for two weeks and didn't look back. Of course I missed my husband and kids, but I didn't feel guilt or shame for choosing to pursue my dream. Rather, I took the treasured time to connect with the best parts of *me*.

Permission Slip

I grant myself permission to
burn guilt and shame.

—signed by: ME

CREATE A FIRE WALL

Have guilt and shame influenced the permission you give your-self? Often, the thing we don't feel permitted to do is the very thing that will reignite our flame within, restoring us to the most alive version of ourselves. Women today have every right to feel angry and victimized by our culture, which makes us second-guess our desire for time for ourselves, but holding on to that suffering, says Martha Beck, PhD, sociologist, life coach, and author of *Breaking Point: Why Women Fall Apart and How They Can Re-Create Their Lives*, is "a recipe for despair."

So, what's a healthier recipe? Dr. Lakshmin suggests, "We need to reframe guilt. It's like a faulty check-engine light. It doesn't give you any productive information about the choices in front of you; it's just a comfortable place for your brain to go. To counteract this, women must learn to build a new muscle, one of permission, that overrides the guilt. It's not about some dramatic life change. It's in the small, daily acts of permission that help you understand that guilt does not need to drive your decisions."

Psychologist Sheryl Gonzalez Ziegler, author of *Mommy Burnout*, also suggests modifying guilt into something more productive. "When you feel guilt, acknowledge it, and then re-frame it," she encouraged when I interviewed her over Zoom. "Instead of saying, 'I feel guilty because I'm [fill in the blank],' say, 'I made this choice because [fill in the blank.]' That's it. Don't apologize. Own your choices. Express conviction in your body language and in the tone of your voice. This makes such a difference. It sends a message to your partner, your kids, your boss that you are certain about your decisions. And more importantly, it makes a difference in how *you* feel about your choices."

Once you reframe guilt and shame as internalized noise that doesn't serve you or the ones you love, you can take back your power by setting an intentional boundary, or, as I like to call it, a fire wall.

My own burning ritual was how I owned my choice to go on my book tour. I made a conscious choice to turn down the noise that said, *I feel guilty because I am leaving my family . . . [blah, blah, blah]* and reframed it: *I'm making the choice to leave for two weeks because I believe that I have an important message and a unique skill set to help other women that I wholeheartedly intend to share. End of story and bon voyage.*

And guess what? My boundary held. In fact, as my two weeks away were coming to a close, I had the inspired idea, *Maybe I'll stay just a few days longer to explore the town.* My tour had culminated in Davos, Switzerland, and while attending the World Economic Forum was an empowering, never-forget, optimal experience, I hadn't really had time to leave the hotel or the convention floor. Shouldn't I take at least a peek at the iconic Swiss countryside? I hadn't invested in a new puffer coat with a faux fur hood for nothing. I called Seth and presented my plan to delay my flight. He hesitated. "Really, another few days?" Then, he followed with an automatic serving of mom guilt: "You know, your kids really miss you."

I checked in with my heart. I missed them, too. I checked in with my gut. Were two more days away going to make or break my family? Not likely. Their needs were important, but they didn't hold a permanent position in the hierarchy of needs. I checked in with my feelings. Noticeably, I didn't feel that old familiar feeling of guilt. I actually tried to conjure it up, and I couldn't. I said happily to Seth, "Sorry, not going to work this time. Remember, you saw me burning stuff in the backyard before I left. That was my guilt and shame. You can't use them against me anymore."

Seth laughed good-naturedly. "Well, then, that proves it. You really are a witch."

"A *good* witch," I tossed back.

My own journey has taught me that the very thing that I once feared—that asserting boundaries would blow up my marriage— actually saved it. And now if guilt and shame rear their ugly heads (*I feel guilty because I didn't put Anna to bed tonight*), I reframe this thought (*I chose not to put Anna to bed tonight because I have an important dinner date with Jessica . . . and I'll be there to kiss Anna awake in the morning*). If that doesn't cut my guilt and shame off at the knees, I revisit my burning ritual; sometimes just striking a match to light a candle does the trick!

By giving yourself permission to make intentional choices about how you live your life, you are building a fire wall, a boundary between your own time and guilt and shame. And within those protective walls, your relationships with others may also improve. Or as my next interviewee so beautifully illustrated— your relationship with yourself can reach new heights.

CONSIDER:
THE CASE OF THE INVERTED PYRAMID

I met Leslie Forde, CEO and Founder of Mom's Hierarchy of Needs, on a panel that addressed the increased mental load for women during COVID. I was instantly taken by Forde's approach to alleviating it, which is to flip Maslow's hierarchy of needs on its head. As Forde has reimagined it, the Mom's hierarchy of needs prioritizes self-care and personal interests because, Forde explained, "what happens for a lot of mothers, as it did for me, is if you spend too much time at the bottom of the pyramid prioritizing your children's health and well-being and all the responsibilities of the household, you can start to lose your physical health. My research showed that many women who live at the bottom of the hierarchy reported ongoing signs of anxiety and depression, which are much more prevalent in women. And my studies show that it's creating a mental health crisis."

Forde began her own journey up the pyramid after the birth of her second child, when, she said, "I crashed. I was exhausted, becoming depressed, and losing what made me *me*. I was becoming a 'gray' version of myself."

Forde understood that she needed to make a dramatic shift in her life or her health would continue to suffer, and it started with "taking better care of myself, allowing myself to take a walk at lunchtime instead of powering through one hundred emails."

From that first step forward, Forde describes a "ruthless intentionality" and commitment to caring for herself and valuing her own time, which spurred her on to help other women also create that space for themselves. "Once I started digging into the neuroscience of stress and talking with other women, it was so clear how mothers specifically are celebrated for the self-sacrifice moments down at the bottom of the pyramid and shamed for doing things at the top like learning, pursuing interests, and having fun—everything that feeds our mental, emotional, and physical well-being."

Forde cautioned, "And we're never going to rise to the top if we continue to assume responsibility for everything at the bottom and feel guilty when we do take tiny scraps of discretionary time for ourselves. *And*," Forde further emphasized, "women most certainly will not get into 'flow' if we continue to let our time be chopped up into little scraps, all day long, all year long, all decade long. You'll never evolve your bright ideas or be able to pursue whatever interests are percolating for you unless you have uninterrupted, guilt-free time."

Yes! When you give yourself permission to reclaim your finite space and time, when you give yourself permission to turn down or turn away from guilt, you're afforded mental space, allowing you to get into your own version of flow.

"Letting go of what no longer serves me has created so much space in my life for what [I'm] meant to be," said Melissa, friend and Uni, and founder of Melissa Wood Health. "After going nonstop and giving everything I have in every direction possible, I hit a wall. I'm getting so clear with my yesses and even clearer with my nos. [I realized] if you're not giving to yourself first and foremost, you'll have nothing else left to give."

I will not feel guilty about how I choose to spend my time. I will assert space and time for me.

Onward! The path forward to the promised land of Unicorn Space is yours when you commit to reframing how you value your time and then intentionally reprioritize uninterrupted time for *you*. Strike down the internal and often self-perpetuating interruptions of guilt and shame that compromise your choices and block your creative flow. Preserve personal time and space by saying no and, if need be, by striking a match.

ASK YOURSELF: IN THE ABSENCE OF GUILT AND SHAME, HOW MIGHT I FEEL?

Complete the sentence: When I choose to spend my time doing [insert your Unicorn Space], I feel:

- *Proud*
- *Accomplished*
- *Fulfilled*
- *Gratified*
- *Content*
- *Delighted*
- *Respected*
- *Worthy*

Repeat once a day: "I will not feel guilty or feel shamed about how I choose to spend my time."

6

RULE #3—
Permission to Use Your Voice

//

How to Ask for the Creative Time You Require

WHAT'S YOUR LINE?

I would engage in meaningful activities that make me happy beyond my role as partner, parent, and professional, but . . .

- ○ I don't have any "extra" time for me. (Still hung up by the clock? Turn back to chapter 4.)
- ○ I feel guilty taking time away from my other responsibilities—work, kids, the household. (Still stuck on the "shoulds"? Turn back to chapter 5.)
- ○ I've given myself permission to be unavailable and to burn guilt and shame, but I'm getting pushback from my partner.

- "When my partner hears, 'I need free time to myself,' they just tune me out."
- "She resents the time I want for me."
- "He doesn't get it. He doesn't get *me*. I feel dismissed."
- "They flat out say no!"

○ When I assert my desire/need/right to time for *me*, it comes out the wrong way.

- "Once I start talking, it turns into yelling."
- "Before long, we're in a big fight."
- "I'm not even sure what to ask for."
- "Sometimes, it feels easier not to bring it up."
- "I don't know what to ask for, so I stay silent."
- "I finally asked for 'me time' when I asked for a divorce."

Does miscommunication, or a lack of communication, prevent you from pursuing a life beyond the Three P's? Do any of the aforementioned narratives rob you of the space and time to do your thing? Using your voice to assert your right to a more creative life is essential and *how* you voice it is key.

ASKING FOR IT

I stopped by my friend Bianca's house one Sunday morning to catch up on the week. As we sat at her family-size kitchen table, swapping stories about raising young kids and juggling our professional lives, her husband, Steve, trotted downstairs and breezed into the kitchen wearing shorts, running shoes, and earbuds. He waved a courtesy "morning," and as he filled up his water bottle at the sink, Bianca leaned in and whispered, "He's training for a marathon, and Sunday mornings are his 'long runs,'" she punctuated with an eye roll, "which means I'll be left alone with the kids all day."

Steve popped out his earbuds and whirled around. "I heard that. And I won't be gone *all day*. I'll be home this afternoon. Did you mention to Eve that you were out late last night while I was home with the kids?"

"It was my best friend's fortieth birthday," Bianca shot back, "and I was only out for two hours. Plus, I ordered you guys DoorDash and queued up a movie before I left!"

"Well, that was your choice," snapped Steve. "The deal is that Sundays are my time to run and it takes as long as it takes."

"Oh, I'm sorry," Bianca snapped back with not a hint of apology, "but when did *we* make this deal?"

Back and forth the sparks flew over the issue of "free time." I slunk down in my seat and waited it out. Finally, after Steve charged out the back door with a slam, Bianca sputtered, "Every Sunday it goes this way. We always end up fighting. We just can't communicate." As I drained my coffee mug and readied to leave Bianca's kitchen before I got in the middle of another heated exchange, I thought to myself, *Well, actually, you are communicating. Just not effectively.*

ARE YOU MISCOMMUNICATING?

"You are the human equivalent of nails on a chalkboard." This is how my husband, Seth, used to describe my communication style. And he was right. My tone could be harsh. *I'm busy! What do you want? Don't interrupt me. I said, I'm B-U-S-Y.* Did I get the time and space I needed? No (refer back to "The Case of the 'Unavailable' Post-it" [page 68] as evidence of my failed communication attempts). My sharp commands more often fell on unlistening ears, and I continued to suffer interruptions and frustration until I shifted my communication style.

Many women in my growing Uni coalition confided that they "can't communicate" their longing for uninterrupted space and time in a way that generates their desired outcome. "It's too triggering," confessed Jakki. I have no doubt this is true. Many of us don't communicate in a way that produces a positive result. But this isn't because you *can't* communicate. When you yell, storm out of the room, or silently seethe, you *are* communicating . . . by miscommunicating.

POP QUIZ
What's Your Communication Style?

Do any of these communication methods sound familiar? In the spirit of the popular *Newlywed Game* show, in the heat of an argument how would you and your partner describe each other?

- *Long-winded:* You're talking and no one's listening. Or no one's responding because you're still talking. "And just one more thing . . ." Your one-sided monologues suck all the air out of the room.
- *Sharp commands, sir:* Your drill-sergeant tone and delivery doesn't rally the troops. "Stop interrupting!" "Close the door behind you!"

- **Bad timing:** *Your grievances are ill-timed. "I know it's late and you have to get up early, but we need to talk—now." Additionally, your requests for "me time" are poorly timed. "I signed up for a tennis tournament today. It starts in twenty minutes—okay if I leave the kids with you? Thanks—bye!"*

- **Toxic word choice:** *"Are you f*cking insane? You're playing tennis—again?"*

- **Verbal assassin:** *Meant-to-hurt words said in a kind, measured tone. "Oh, honey, did you ever expect that you'd become the worst father of all time and choose yourself over everyone else?"*

- **All or nothing:** *"You* always *take time for yourself. You* never *think about me."*

- **Dredging up the past:** *"This is just like the last time you left us for the entire weekend."*

- **Boiling over:** *"I didn't say anything. I wasn't going to say anything, and now [screaming] I'm really pissed."*

- **Already boiled:** *"That's it. [screaming and crying] I'm out."*

- **Avoidance:** *Rather than risk a fight, you shy away, sit in silence, put in your earbuds, sneak out, or act independently. "Who needs to talk when I can text, 'Don't wait up. I'll be home late.'" Or "Why bother asking if they're just going to say no or try to talk me out of it? I'll just do what I want."*

- **Dismissal:** *"No."*

Passive-aggressive, all-or-nothing comments, bad timing, loud demands and accusations, dismissing, and avoiding are how many of us are communicating with our partners. "When I hear people say things like, 'He always . . .' or 'She never . . .' I can tell that demonizing is happening—each person sees their partner as the opposition . . . and when a partner demonizes the other and holds resentments against the other for years, it creates a very unstable marriage," writes Susan Pease Gadoua in the *Newsweek* article "I Work with Couples about to Divorce."

"Avoidance is [also] an exceedingly common response to conflicts today," writes William Ury, PhD, in *The Power of a Positive No.* "Because we are afraid of offending others and drawing their anger and disapproval, we say nothing, hoping that the problem will go away even though we know it will not. . . . Avoidance can be costly not only to our personal health. . . . Avoidance . . . is deadening."

Psychologist Jennifer Petriglieri, PhD, associate professor at INSEAD and the author of *Couples That Work,* said to me, "All couples sometimes communicate in negative ways—contempt, criticism, defensiveness, and stonewalling, what the Gottman Institute call 'The Four Horsemen' in conflict discussions. None of us is perfect," Petriglieri continued, "but what many psychologists find important is not whether we are communicating in negative ways but the ratio of negative to positive."

"I can't take it. I want out of my marriage," sputter-cried my friend Kelly one morning over coffee.

"Hold on, back up. What happened?" I implored.

"It's the same thing over and over. He gets annoyed and walks away, and I get quiet and resentful. I think it's over."

"Maybe you need to talk?" I offered.

"We can't," she said flatly.

Kelly's desire to leave her partner over unspoken grievances sounds extreme, but she is not alone. I've met many women who'd rather ask for a divorce than directly ask for what they need to feel fulfilled in their marriage. And I can't tell you the number of times that I've asked people—many in leadership and power positions—how they communicate with their partners at home, who say: "We don't talk." And countless more take even more passive-aggressive action. Instead of speaking *to* their partners, they speak *about* them (and not politely) on online forums.

"If speaking to your spouse—the person with whom you have a problem—isn't a tool in your toolbox, it needs to be," advises Susan Pease Gadoua. Agreed! We live in a society where meditating alone in a quiet room is more normalized and accepted as a daily practice than communicating directly with the people we share four walls and a bathroom. That needs to change. And we can resuscitate healthy dialogue with our partners/roommates/colleagues/loved ones by clearly communicating our wants and needs. Yep, I'm talking about direct, honest talk. The kind that author Brené Brown, champion of exposing the naked truth, espouses, when she says, "You fully embrace your vulnerability and allow yourself to be seen."

CAUTION AHEAD!

The gates to the promised land of Unicorn Space, where you will pass through the Three C's (curiosity to connection to completion) will remain closed until you give yourself permission to use your voice to clearly assert time and space for yourself. If you're reluctant, recognize that you are likely already communicating, if even only nonverbally. It's time to step out of the realm of the unspoken and deal with the people in your life head-on. Consider the marching order of Tiffany Dufu, founder of the Cru and author of *Drop the Ball*: "If you want something you've never had before, you'll have to do something you've never done before in order to get it."

LOOK FOR A WIN-WIN SOLUTION

Throughout my years working as a professional mediator, I've learned that communication is one of the most important practices of your life because practice makes progress. Over the years, I've borrowed from experts and developed a few tried-and-true tricks of my own that produce positive progress for all parties involved. With respect to creating individual time and space to feed your unicorn, the first thing I ask people to imagine and set for themselves is a *non*-zero-sum goal. Most of us are familiar with the zero-sum game where one person's gain is equivalent to another's loss. As an example, when Steve takes four hours on Sunday morning for his marathon training, Bianca regards this as minus four hours for her. Meaning, his gain is her loss; his time to engage in activities that fill him up means Bianca has even less time to fill her own bucket.

If this is how you and your partner similarly keep score, it is 100 percent guaranteed that one of you will continue to come up short and, in most hetero cisgender partnerships that I've observed, it's the woman who predominantly loses. So then, the first important step toward arriving at an intersection where you and your partner both get what you want is by shifting your communication style away from competition (zero-sum) and toward collaboration (non-zero-sum). In other words, you must work as a team.

"In my work, when couples realize that they've been engaging in a zero-sum dynamic—this is the breakthrough moment," said Jennifer Petriglieri. "They finally recognize that this shared dynamic is not about what you did to *me*, but what we've done to *us*."

BY INVITATION ONLY

Collaborative dialogue is by invitation only, so invite your partner to discuss the importance of your individual Unicorn Space. A minimum of two people is required for active dialogue, but one person must speak up first, so why not empower yourself to take the lead? Because this isn't always easy to do, for guidance on initiating collaborative dialogue, I reached out to my high school friend Daniel Stillman, who has the coolest job in the world. Stillman is a "conversation designer" and the author of *Good Talk: How to Design Conversations That Matter*.

"A complete invitation," he said, "is more than the dreaded, *we need to talk*. It includes a payoff, a direct benefit for both people. For example, if I say to my partner, 'I need more alone time,' this can easily sound threatening or come off like a withdrawal or rejection of my partner. But if I say, 'I'd like to talk about creating more time for me, for you, and for us,' then the couple wins. When you build a direct benefit for both people into the 'ask,' and also embed a quality that feels safe, you drive up motivation to engage."

As alternative opening lines relating specifically to Unicorn Space, Dan suggests: "I'd like to talk about what gives us both joy"; "I'd like to explore what will make us feel more fulfilled"; or, more pragmatically, "I'd like to talk about ways that we can work *together* so that we both have more time and space to pursue interests and activities outside our jobs and our roles as parents."

Do you see how Dan's openers are "both" statements that invite your partner into the conversation? "Think about the arc of your invitation and include a payoff," he underscores. "'We'll *both* get what we want. We will *both* be happier.' That's your non-zero-sum game."

When crafting your invitation, Dan also suggests, "The way to get your foot in the door versus the door in your face is to desensitize your tone. Invite your partner to the conversation in a nonchalant, nonplussed, easygoing way. It's not WE NEED TO TALK! Rather, try a relaxed, 'Hey, can we carve out some time later, when it works for you, to talk about [fill in the blank]. Are you up for that?'"

Lisa Damour, PhD, psychologist and bestselling author, supports this strategy. She shared with me, "Communication is about the lyrics (the words we say) and the tune (how we say them). When it's time to discuss potentially upsetting topics, we can often be most helpful if our lyrics are clear and direct, while our tune is calm, warm, and reassuring."

What Damour and Dan are touching on here is a communication strategy I've used as a mediator for over a decade, and I cannot count the times I have seen it both make and break relationships. In my own words, the strategy I employ is: *No feedback in the moment.* In an effort to genuinely engage your partner with the right lyrics and tune, that often means holding your tongue and . . . waiting for it.

WAIT FOR IT

When it comes to communicating in the spirit of collaboration, timing really is everything. Whether it's with your partner, a roommate, or your employer, I recommend waiting until emotion is low and cognition is high. What do I mean by that? Here's an all-too-familiar example of how the reverse plays out between couples—your partner asks you if it's okay to leave the house in twenty minutes to play tennis with his buddies as your toddler's having a meltdown in the middle of the kitchen floor and you haven't yet had a shower. You think to yourself: *I swear to all that's* holy, *if he walks out that door, I will change the locks while he is gone.* This type of highly stressed moment can easily lead to what behavioral economist Dan Ariely calls "emotional cascades," which he described to me as when you make an emotional decision that reverberates and can often have unintended consequences.

Professor and neuroscientist Darby Saxbe explained this further on a call: "I've studied 'stress contagion'—how couples can amp up each other's stress hormones over time. When couples fire each other up rather than help each other cool down, conflicts can quickly escalate and get out of hand. We start reacting rather than being calm enough to listen to each other." As a result, this cascade effect lowers long-term marital satisfaction, according to a new study by Daniel Carlson, associate professor of family, health, and public policy at the University of Utah. To sum it up: To avoid being locked out of your house today—and into the future—pregame when emotion is low. This is the optimal time to ask your partner for the afternoon "off."

Over the years, I've worked hard on engaging Seth in low-emotion, high-cognition dialogue. Today, when I feel the need to voice a boundary so that I can dig into my writing or turn up the volume and dance, instead of metaphorically scratching my nails on a chalkboard—I NEED ALONE TIME!—I'll hold my tongue and wait for a time when we can calmly sit down and communicate with ease. As I said earlier, effectively setting boundaries is not barking demands or threatening divorce. Rather, to guard your space and time, invite your partner to communicate within a safe container where you both can speak and be heard.

CREATE A CONTAINER

Quiet easy time to engage our partners in collaborative, thoughtful dialogue. In what dreamy world does this exist? Just like Unicorn Space, it will not magically appear, so in this instance, *don't* wait for it. You must create space to engage by designing a "communication container," a prescheduled time and place where you and your partner can safely and respectfully assert your boundaries. Seth and I check in nightly (yes, every night) after the dinner dishes are done and the kids are in bed. We sit at the kitchen counter and, more frequently than I'd like to admit, we enjoy a pint of ice cream (and sometimes, one for each of us!). We discuss what's working in our household and what's not and how we can more efficiently balance the division of labor between us so that we each have time and space for our individual pursuits. Through much trial and error and too many calories to count, we've discovered that our nightly deep (but short) dive is the optimal time for us to connect, align our schedules, and collaborate in the spirit of creativity. And although it sounds counterintuitive, communicating within a container, which for us is defined by a pint of Ben & Jerry's Imagine Whirled Peace, expands and deepens our connection. We wait to talk within a specific time frame and we connect more than ever before. Pretty cool, right? What's your "communication container"? Not sure you have one? There are only five ingredients that I outline below.

> Communicating within a container expands and deepens connection.

SET A SCHEDULE AND STICK TO IT

Whether it's daily or once a week, prioritize your check-in like it's the next episode of your favorite must-not-miss show. I'm not kidding—do not skip it! Based on conversations I've had with couples all over the world, those who make regular time to come together and discuss their Unicorn Space report higher connectivity. In fact, it's one of the chief observations I had of relationship longevity and individual happiness. Conversely, I found that couples who skip regular check-ins report that they revert back to old patterns of miscommunication and the negative cascade effect that goes along with it.

Many couples report that a nightly check-in is the best time to discuss their individual pursuits, because this type of ritual fosters intimacy and focused attention on each other. Other couples like to check in over Sunday brunch, at the dog park, or on Friday nights when the kiddos are occupied with a movie. The setting doesn't matter, as long as you intentionally set aside or design an optimal time for you and your partner to connect and align your schedule. Once your check-in is set, then the pressure to initiate conversation is lifted off you both. If it's on the calendar, then no one has to say, *"We need to talk."*

Tip! Ritualize it. Ideally, schedule your check-in when you and your partner are free of distractions (when emotion is low and cognition is high), and at a time that can be easily replicated week after week, or more than once a week if desired.

PRE-NEGOTIATE YOUR CREATIVE SPACE AND TIME

Once again: you won't *find* untouchable space and time for pursuits beyond the Three P's—you have to assert and create it. During check-in, pre-negotiate or renegotiate the division of labor and childcare in your home so that you and your partner can both schedule time for Unicorn Space. Use this time to talk about what's working and what's not. Lead with something positive and then shift the conversation toward areas that need rebalancing. Negotiate in the spirit of collaboration until you achieve what feels reasonable and fair. Note: this is a prime time to "customize your defaults." That is, negotiate in advance which household and childcare tasks you are individually responsible for. By customizing your "who does what," no one becomes the default dishwasher, carpool driver, or dog walker, and you both can enjoy your allotted, uninterrupted time and space to do your thing. In my household, I am responsible for breakfast and getting the kids dressed and off to school, and then Seth assumes full ownership of all things kid-related when school gets out, including driving both our boys to their separate extracurricular sports activities. (Honestly, I feel like I have the better end of the bargain on this one, but Seth loves sports, so he considers it a win for him.)

Jonathan Finkelstein, founder and CEO of Credly, shared in *Fast Company*, "When my husband, Andy, and I decided to become parents, there were lots of eyeballs on us but no societal playbook to follow. [We heard] questions such as 'With two dads, which one of you will stay home after the baby is born?' (which for some translated to 'Which one of you is the mom?'). . . . We saw a chance to help move past a conversation dominated by the archaic maternity-leave playbook, which has perpetuated bias against women in the workplace and permitted men to operate under lower expectations."

His comments about same-sex parental responsibilities in the context of "customizing defaults" piqued my interest, so I reached out for an interview.

"Making the choice to have a child meant having a lot of internal conversations," he told me over Zoom. "For starters, as two men, how will we bring a baby into our life? How will we parent coequally? Planning to become parents led to discussions about time equity in the home—learning to share parental responsibilities, navigating our respective parental leaves from work, and discovering how to create new space for doing things individually and as a family."

> Pre-negotiate untouchable space and time.
> Otherwise, it will remain a fairy tale.

MIND YOUR TONE AND LISTEN

Once you're face-to-face and have each other's attention, communicate in a way that inspires a positive experience—where you both feel seen, heard, and that your respective time is valued. For starters, check any passive-aggressive finger-pointing and direct accusations at the door and communicate clearly and respectfully. This may seem obvious, but the reality is that most of us engage our partners without a considerable amount of forethought or care. We just dive right in without considering how our words will be received. "When I stopped throwing f-bombs into every sentence and speaking at a pitch that could shatter glass, my partner actually started listening to me," admitted Jakki.

Communicating in a way that feels inviting rather than alienating, and that allows your partner to truly *listen,* is key. "Listening is one of the most powerful skills you can bring to a difficult conversation," offers Doug Stone in his aptly titled *Difficult Conversations: How to Discuss What Matters Most,* a *New York Times* business bestseller.

And when people feel like someone is truly listening, adds

Jonah Berger in his book *The Catalyst: How to Change Anyone's Mind,* "a sense of trust begins to form."

CLARIFY YOUR "WHY"

Beyond feeling heard (a big win in itself), your request for time and space boundaries is more likely to be accepted, even applauded, when you underscore your "why." Conversation designer Daniel Stillman cautions, "You have to know what you're asking for and *why* before you ask for it. And when you can share both your 'what' and your 'why,' this threads a conversation progressively deeper and deeper."

Case in point—when I became inspired to write this book, I imagined readers becoming similarly inspired and busting through their unique domestic, professional, cultural, and creative barriers to rediscover or uncover their creative self-expression. It was super clear to me that I needed uninterrupted space and time to craft this important message. But when I shared my idea for a second book with Seth one night over a pint of Ben & Jerry's, he said simply, "But you wrote your book already."

I put down my spoon and slowly turned to face him. "Yes, and my writing doesn't just end with *Fair Play.* I could turn the same question on you. You build companies for a living. After you built your first one, were you done?"

"Fair enough." He smiled at his own play on words. "But . . . why? Why do you want to write another book? It's a lot of work."

I threaded deeper, as Dan Stillman advises. I considered— what is my "why"? When I had my answer, I said to Seth, "Creating Fair Play has been the most exhilarating ride of my life. I've learned so much from others and connected with women all over the world who are fighting for change. This work has made me a better version of myself for me, for you, our kids, for everyone I meet. And that work is not 'done,' and I won't abandon it just because it's hard. Inspiring women to live in their full power is why I continue to write. You get it?"

"Got it." Seth smiled with affection. And guess what? He hasn't asked me since why I'm writing this book. (As you recall, requesting time and space to write was a harder ask and took more practice and more than a Post-it.)

"Your *why* is your hidden motivation for wanting something," says Greg McKeown, author of *Essentialism: The Disciplined Pursuit of Less* and host of the podcast *What's Essential*.

McKeown invited me on his show to talk about domestic rebalance, and by the end of our time together, we pivoted into the arena of "why." "If you're willing to reveal your *why*, you can talk about almost anything," he said. "It sounds so obvious, but people often skip over it. Perhaps because sharing their *why* makes them feel vulnerable."

That may be true, but when we allow ourselves to be vulnerable and set boundaries, respectfully and without apology, our partners are drawn in. "People can only meet you as deeply as you meet yourself," teaches Matt Kahn, spiritual leader and bestselling author of *Whatever Arises, Love That: A Love Revolution That Begins with You*. And this is what happened in my own relationship. When I lowered my defenses and invited Seth into my story, he met me. And the majority of couples I've interviewed report that when they unpack their "why," their partners lean in and more readily give their support to each other's Unicorn Space.

"I've yet to meet a spouse who can read minds," writes Susan Pease Gadoua in *Newsweek*, "but I've met many people who expect their partner to just know what they need. . . . Partners also need to ask a lot more questions of their mate and not assume they know more than they do. Making assumptions is where I see so many good people get into trouble."

In my mediation practice and philanthropic work and when workshopping Unicorn Space with couples, I encourage a storytelling exercise to unravel the "why." Back to marathon-runner Steve, I asked him specifically: "Tell me a story about your first race. Describe how you felt the first time you crossed the finish line. How do you feel when you're training? How would you feel if you *didn't* have time to run? How does this personal pursuit help you to weather the harder parts of your day?"

Steve's "why" was powerful and profound: "I lost my father to diabetes, so it's really important for me to stay healthy for my family."

I have to admit, Steve's answer surprised me—in a good way! Suddenly, his Sunday runs didn't seem like the selfish act Bianca had interpreted them to be. Rather, Steve's honesty and vulnerability transformed him into a sympathetic character I wanted to cheer for at the finish line.

I encouraged Steve to share his story with Bianca, and as I suspected, when he shifted the conversation from "I'm going on my Sunday run" to "*why* it's important to me to take my Sunday run," their zero-sum dynamic shifted.

"Once I understood why it was important to him to run and stay healthy for me and the kids, I resented his Sunday mornings 'off' a whole lot less. And then, when I asked for time and space for me, Steve was encouraging," Bianca told me.

EXERCISE
What Is Your "Why"?

Write down or formulate in your mind a one-line **why** or intention for creating Unicorn Space in your life.

Building time into my daily/weekly schedule for _____ _____ is valuable to me because _____ _____.

Continue to brainstorm: How do you feel when you're doing it? How would you feel if you didn't do it? How does your creative expression insulate you from less creative parts of your day? How does having or not having Unicorn Space impact other aspects of your life . . . your relationships, workspace, and productivity; your emotional, physical, and mental state? _____ _____ _____

Eventually, you will share your "why" with your partner and equally reciprocate by inviting them to share their "why" for uninterrupted space and time. Again: when you build in a payoff that benefits you both, you significantly increase your partner's (or your kids'/colleagues'/roommates') motivation to support you. Here is a sampling of "why" statements that were crafted by couples in my growing interview set.

Building time into my schedule for my Unicorn Space is valuable to me because:

- *I want to feel a deeper connection to myself and to our life together.*

- *I want us to both feel connected to something beyond our work and our home.*
- *I want to feel free to have time for me without leaving the relationship/this employment position.*
- *Having this outlet energizes me. I wake up happier, which makes me a better partner/parent/employee.*

If you're stuck on "what" you'd do with uninterrupted time and space, hold tight. Securing precious time and space is the first, important step. Filling it with the "what" is the fun and exciting work of the next chapter: "Identify a Curiosity." Until then, stay focused on your "why," even if only in a very general sense. Your "why" sets your intention, eventually leading you to your "what."

○ ○ ● ○ ○ ○ ○ ● ○ ○ ○ ○ ○ ● ○ ● ○ ○ ○ ● ○ ● ○ ○ ○ ● ○ ○ ○ ○ ● ○ ○ ○ ● ○ ○ ○

TELL YOUR STORY

The "why" is at the heart of your story. So *tell* your story. Share moments from your life that are meaningful to you. Many of us mistakenly think our families know our stories because they're "our people" or because our partners are our most intimate companions, but our loved ones often don't know our "why" until we explicitly spell it out.

Dr. Stew Friedman, management professor at the Wharton School at the University of Pennsylvania, underscores this point: "Being honest with yourself and your partner about what you care about requires considerable courage and commitment to look candidly at what you want your life to mean." And when we do this important work, something magical is evoked: our honesty and vulnerability have the power to deepen our relationships, awaken empathy, and inspire excitement on the part of our partners when they understand not only what fulfills us but also *why*.

Permission Slip

I grant myself permission to
use my voice and tell my story.

—signed by: ME

Simon Sinek, business speaker and author of *Start with Why: How Great Leaders Inspire Everyone to Take Action*, encourages "thinking from the inside out" because, he says, "People don't buy what you do, they buy why you do it." To inspire starts with the clarity of "why," and Sinek asserts that the most inspired leaders and organizations all act from this place. And I'd argue that the most inspired partnerships also originate from the inside out.

STICK TO YOUR OWN STORY

So tell your story and resist telling the story you tell yourself about your partner. Or the story you think your partner tells about you. Wait—what? Let's unravel this. In my interviews, I uncovered two leading reasons for why we tell stories, often only in our heads, about our partners and other people in our lives. One is to avoid disappointment (they could say no) and the other is to avoid a difficult conversation (I don't know what to ask for/how to ask/we end up in a fight). I've heard many people tell stories like this:

○ They will never go for this, so why bother asking?

○ My partner won't pick up the slack in the house so that I can journal for an hour in the morning. So why ask?

○ My boss would never let me leave early for a pottery class.

○ My kids can't leave me alone for five minutes, so I don't even try.

○ I can just imagine the reaction if I said, "I'm taking the night off to watercolor."

○ I can just hear them now . . .

So many of us are telling stories about why our partners/ children/friends/employers won't accommodate or respect our desire for uninterrupted time and space without actually testing if these story lines are true. The unfortunate result: we resent our partners/children/friends/employers unfairly. Worse, we don't get what we want.

Daniel Stillman challenges, "Rather than marinate on assumptions and the worst-case scenario, how about considering another possibility, the best-case scenario? *What if I get what I want?*" And what's the most effective way to get what we want from the most important people in our lives? Stillman suggests: just tell them what you need. Conversely, he says, the best way to understand what other people want is to just ask them.

Dr. Stew Friedman takes Stillman's prompt a step further. He says, "In my research and consulting with working families, what many people discover is that they don't know their partners as well as they think they do, so I encourage dialogue that addresses this, such as—*Honey, these are the things that I think are most important to you. Do I have it right? I recognize that I don't really know what you're really thinking. Here's what*

I think you're thinking. What am I missing? Can you give me more clarity and detail?"

If you're reluctant to ask for or assert your desire for more space and time for *you*, consider the high likelihood that you're telling stories to yourself about how your partner/child/ friend/employer will react or behave in a negative way (that are probably false!). Challenge these story lines and use your voice instead. Bravely ask for what you need without apology, and assume you'll get it.

CONSIDER:
THE CASE OF HONALEE

A week after my friend Kelly considered leaving her marriage, she sent me this text: "You and Puff the Magic Dragon may be on to something."

Curious, I asked her to meet for a quick walk. As we rounded our neighborhood, she explained that she'd just watched the movie *Puff the Magic Dragon* with her eight-year-old daughter. Kelly hadn't seen this classic animated TV special since she was a kid in the seventies, and she explained how profound it was for her to watch it now.

"You remember the basic plotline, right?" she asked me.

"I actually don't," I admitted.

Kelly elaborated, "Okay, so little Jackie Draper is the boy in the story, and he's stopped talking and using his voice, and then Puff the magic dragon appears in his room and they start a conversation, and then they go on a magical journey where they conquer fear, and Puff's magic rings reveal people's inner desires . . ."

Kelly was rambling, but she was so excited by her recount of the story that I didn't interrupt her.

Finally, she said, "By the end of the story little Jackie Draper finds his voice again and . . ." Kelly stopped in the middle of the sidewalk and turned to me teary-eyed. "That's when I realized I'm little Jackie Draper, and I have to find the courage to speak up and have hard conversations—and also be an example for my daughter to use her own voice, too."

"That's beautiful." I hugged Kelly. "It does take courage, but you can do it."

Ever since I found my voice, I can't shut up.

—SARA ERENTHAL, MULTIDISCIPLINARY ARTIST

CREATE A SOUND WALL

By giving yourself permission to use your voice to ask for what you need through telling your true-to-you story, you are asserting another important boundary to protect uninterrupted and untouchable time and space for *you*. Will this boundary always hold? No. It's a practice. Like working out or learning a new dance routine: At first, it is a challenge. . . but it gets a little easier every time you lace up your gold-glitter sneakers and start moving. (Or, in this case: it gets easier every time you assert yourself.) And like any effective workout that demands your energy, time, and continued commitment, the payoff is worth it. By exercising your voice, you just may get what you most desire.

Onward! The path forward to the promised land of Unicorn Space is yours when you commit to engaging in open, honest, and collaborative dialogue. Strike down any internal stories that silence your voice and clearly communicate your feelings and needs without apology. When you hit the proverbial sound wall, engage in a little throat-clearing (*ahem*) and reinitiate the conversation.

CONVERSATION DO'S

○ Define your "communication container."
  (Remember: your container should include the following ingredients.)
  - Check in regularly.
  - Mind your tone and *listen*.
  - Pre-negotiate your time and space.
  - Clarify your "why."
  - Tell your story.

CONVERSATION DON'TS

○ Walk out when someone else is speaking.
○ Hijack the conversation by interrupting, going off topic, or changing course.
○ Check in when you're distracted or multitasking.
○ Engage (outside the container) when emotion is high and cognition is low.
○ Make up stories about your partner.
○ Apologize for your Unicorn Space.

PART III

CULTIVATE THE THREE C'S OF CREATIVITY

Curiosity, Connection, Completion

We'll explore the Three C's of Unicorn Space in the chapters that follow: Curiosity (Chapters 7 and 8), Connection (Chapters 9 and 10), and Completion (Chapters 11 and 12).

7

Identify a Curiosity

///

How Value-Based Curiosity
Can Lead You to Your Unicorn Space

WHAT NOW?

My friend Michelle recently confided to me: "My husband and I have been rebalancing the workload at home so that we each have more time for ourselves. This is progress, except now when I do have time to spend on 'me,' I have no idea *what* to do."

"What do you mean?" I asked.

Michelle is an accomplished and interesting woman—an HR executive, a mother, and part of my growing Uni cohort.

She continued, "Just the other afternoon, I was gifted two free hours when Dan offered to take the kids to the beach. I was elated, and then as soon as they left, I sat at the kitchen counter racking my brain: *What do I like to do with free time for* me?

What are my *interests?*" She sighed as we looked at each other through the *Brady Bunch*–style boxes on our Zoom call. "As the minutes ticked by, I actually began to resent the free time and space for myself, because I felt so lost and aimless without my list of to-do's. How messed up is that?"

"Now, hold on," I said to Michelle. "It sounds like you and Dan are openly communicating about how to renegotiate the division of childcare. That *is* progress. And that's only happening because you've identified that time and space boundaries are essential to your sanity, your relationship, and your connection to self. That's your 'why.' Now comes the fun part. Filling it with the 'what.' What do you want to do with your time?"

"That's the problem, I don't know what to *do*."

"Well," I nudged, "what's an activity that fires you up? Gets you excited?"

Michelle thought about it and lit up as if she'd found her answer: "Sometimes I scroll Venmo to see how my friends are spending their money. A lot of sushi and dog sitting."

Have you lost sight of the you
underneath your lists of to-do's?

With Michelle's permission, I shared her (too good not to be true) story with Erica Keswin, bestselling author of *Bring Your Human to Work: 10 Surefire Ways to Design a Workplace That's Good for People, Great for Business, and Just Might Change the World.* Erica is a workplace strategist, sought-after speaker, and a business coach who specializes in creating a "more human" work environment, and she offered up a similar experience: "It's the one question I ask all of the guests on my podcast—what do you do in your life that makes you feel the most like you? More often than not, it stops them in their tracks. They have a really hard time answering. I once asked a highly successful CEO this very question and after an extended pause, she answered: 'Shopping?'"

"Why is that?" I wondered aloud. "Why is it so difficult for us to name not just who we love but *what* we love?"

"It's simple," Keswin told me. "We're not connecting to ourselves." But what does that even look like? And how can we start to find what we love if it's not even a question we've dared to ask ourselves for so long—if ever?

CURIOSITY BEATS PASSION

I thought more about this in the next several weeks in the context of Unicorn Space. Why is naming the "what" that makes us come alive such a difficult exercise and particularly for women? Why is the question—*What makes you feel the most like you?*—so often met with an extended pause? Why aren't we connecting to ourselves and to our passions?

Passion, I've now come to believe, is an awfully high bar to meet. If you were suddenly asked on the spot: "Quick, what are you passionate about?" I think most of us would probably freeze. But if I were to ask you: "Quick, what's your child's favorite Disney character?" or, "Where's the cheese aisle in Costco?," you would likely answer without missing a beat. I think this is because we're more connected to our caretaking and task-mastering selves . . . and also because most of us find "passionate" interest, as well as the ideas of "creativity" and what makes us "unique," to be amorphous and ambiguous concepts. We're stumbling over the words.

When I reflected on the hundreds of interviews I'd conducted to date for this project, a predominant number of people have said to me absolutely: "I'm just not creative." One woman offered definitively: "I'm very type A, structured, and practical. 'Creativity' doesn't apply to me." Assuming that semantics are a stumbling block for you, too, let's reframe the question.

What are you curious about?

WHAT IS CURIOSITY?

Yet again, *curiosity* can be an amorphous concept that's hard to define and still, many smart folks have tackled the definition. Here are a few that resonate with me:

All men by nature desire to know.

—ARISTOTLE

Curiosity starts with the itch to explore.

—IAN LESLIE, AUTHOR OF *CURIOUS*

Without a burning curiosity, a lively interest,

we are unlikely to persevere long to make a

significant new contribution.

—MIHALY CSIKSZENTMIHALYI, PSYCHOLOGIST, RESEARCHER, AND AUTHOR OF *CREATIVITY*

☆ Curiosity is like a hunger.

—ELIZABETH BONAWITZ, PROFESSOR AT HARVARD
GRADUATE SCHOOL OF EDUCATION

A desire, an itch, a burning, a hunger. I love these descriptions of curiosity because they can be applied to just about anything, really. When viewed through this lens, our curiosity can lead us to some strange new places. And our creativity to even stranger places. Mo Willems, illustrator and author of children's books, describes the unpredictability and nonlinear nature of creativity: "You don't know what it opens you up to. It's not a line from A to B. It's a line from A to strawberry pizza."

My friend Brennan Spiegel has drawn his own incongruent line, not to strawberry pizza but into the unexplored recesses of the brain. Brennan is a doctor with an insatiable curiosity for the medical power of the mind. In recent years his curiosity has led him to define an entirely new genre of medicine: VRx, a revolutionary new kind of care that uses virtual reality to treat illnesses. VRx is poised to help doctors and patients heal the body and the mind without relying on intrusive surgeries or addictive opioids. It's an exciting new frontier in health care, and I was particularly interested in how he came up with this idea and what he thinks it portends for the broader future of creativity.

We joined Brennan's family on a recent camping trip, and one evening he and I got into a deep discussion around the campfire about curiosity and creativity. I asked him, "In your own life, how do *you* define creativity?"

Without hesitation, he said, "To me creativity and curiosity drive all my scientific pursuits. Early on when I was personally experimenting with virtual reality, I had this out-of-body experience where I split apart from myself and floated up to the ceiling and looked down on my vacated body. I thought, *How is it that a computer running thousands of lines of code can so easily fool me into thinking I have abandoned my own body? How could it put my consciousness into an alternate reality?* It started as a curiosity—what can I learn from psychology or neuroscience or philosophy of mind that can have an impact on patient care? How can we combine disciplines within medicine? Are there new solutions we haven't thought of before? It was following this pure line of curiosity and asking questions that led to a series of breakthroughs in the field, and I'm so excited about how VRx is proving effective against everything, from burn injuries to stroke to PTSD."

Depending on who you talk to, medicine isn't generally categorized as "art," and Brennan emphatically challenges this. "Medicine is *my* art, and I'm so grateful to have a job that allows for creativity." Through medicine, Brennan has found his Unicorn Space.

OUR FEELINGS ARE OUR CLUES

Okay, so if we are expanding what "creativity" can be—led by curiosity rather than passion or art alone—what then does it mean to "live a creative life"? Here's the great news: creativity is not just limited to the "making" (of visual art or creative writing). It is also "developing" (a new skill set), "expanding" (your knowledge within your area of expertise), and "learning" (of advancements in your fields of interest) and more. Meaning, you don't have to pick up a paintbrush to express your creativity! Based on my ever-growing interview set, "creative living" is the active and open pursuit of self-expression in any form that piques and satisfies your curiosity. If you're curious about it, and you enjoy diving into it, any activity meaningful to you can become your Unicorn Space.

Natalie Nixon, author of *The Creativity Leap* and a creativity strategist for Fortune 500 companies, told me over Zoom coffee: "It's not that there are some people who are more creative than others. Anyone can be creative, and the first step is inquiry, which is akin to *curiosity*—you need to want to know more about something."

As Brennan perfectly exemplifies, Unicorn Space is available to both right- and left-brain people alike, so long as you're curious. It's a gift available to everyone. And even more than that, it's *imperative* to all of us for our happiness, our health, and our overall well-being. The next chapters will lead you through your own journey to redefine your Unicorn Space, and it begins with curiosity.

EXERCISE
Become Curious About Your Unicorn Space

What are you curious about? What piques your interest? What are you already a student of, formally or informally? Where would you like to channel your curiosity next? What would you like to create more time and space to explore? Begin your inquiry by brainstorming with the following questions. Jot your answers down in a separate journal or in the space provided here:

I would like more time to explore _____.

I have always wanted to know/make/develop/learn _____
_____.

What was once interesting and meaningful to me was __

_____.

I want to rediscover or get back to _____

_____.

Pause.
If your answer is "I don't know," that's okay. The unknown is a good place to start. It presents an unfettered opportunity for you to dive into your discovery. Close your eyes and imagine yourself beyond your role as a wonderful partner, parent, and/or professional. Can you reconnect with other aspects of yourself—all the other things you do, *or did*, that make you feel vibrant, interested, engaged, and alive? Keep exploring.

When doing _____ or thinking of doing _____, I feel:

- *Energized*
- *Uplifted*
- *Focused*
- *Engaged*
- *Motivated*

- *Connected*
- *Alive*
- *Content*
- *Fulfilled*
- *Happy*

° ○ ● ○ ○ ○ ○ ● ○ ○ ○ ○ ○ ○ ● ○ ○ ○ ● ○ ○ ● ○ ○ ○ ○ ○ ○ ● ○ ○ ○ ○ ○ ○ ○ ○ ○

Kennon Sheldon, PhD, professor of psychological sciences at the University of Missouri in Columbia, whose research spans the areas of well-being, motivation, self-determination theory, personality, and positive psychology, says our feelings are our "clues" when it comes to reconnection with our curiosity. I tracked down Sheldon after coming across his research in nearly every article I'd read about social psychology. Amid his busy schedule, Sheldon graciously gave me an hour of his time to talk about identifying our curiosities.

"Knowing 'what' to want can be hard," he acknowledged, "because our own narrative is often fooled by the cultural narrative. We get confused by what society is telling us to 'do.' But a deeper part of you is talking to you . . . if you will listen. Because of a variety of societal factors, women tend to be very insightful but sometimes lack the courage to listen to the clues.

"The way to know if you've landed on your 'what,'" Sheldon continued, "is by gauging the feeling it gives you. If you feel happy, engaged, pulled into a flow state, that's your *clue* that you're on the right track."

This was such a big recognition moment for me. It was the reverse of what I'd heard so many times in my life, that happiness should be the end goal. But what Sheldon was saying made so much more sense. Let happiness serve as the "clue" that you're on the right track toward your "what."

> Happiness is the clue that you're on the right track!

As you continue to explore your curiosities, pay attention to the feelings that rise up (thinking about X makes me feel Y). "For me, curiosity began by unpacking the moments I'd felt my best," shared Robin Arzón, author of *Shut Up and Run: How to Get Up, Lace Up, and Sweat with Swagger*, who left behind a successful law career to embark on new adventures in the health and wellness space and has since reinvented herself into an avid ultra-marathoner and renowned fitness coach.

We caught up over coffee to discuss curiosity and the arrival of her first baby.

"Looking back on that time when I was wondering where to take my life next, I finally realized that I felt my happiest when I was running or when I was working on my personal blog, and *not* when I was writing legal briefs," she emphasized with a wink. "I also started to get curious about when I felt other feelings like jealousy. Like, I'm feeling jealous of my colleague's leadership qualities. I want to embody her confidence. Or, I'm jealous that my friend has the freedom to engage in her passion. I want that freedom, too. Jealousy was a whisper that once I started listening to it became a big clue. Those whispers told me where I wanted to go and what I wanted to do next, and eventually I created a new life from whispers that became roars."

Your feelings are your clues. As you explore them, I encourage you to sideline any doubts or concerns that pop in with unsolicited advice, alerting you to what's "reasonable" and "acceptable" or when and how you'll actually pursue your curiosity. Quiet this voice. It will distract and lead you away from creating valuable time and space for *you*. For now, listen to the whispers. Give yourself permission to be curious.

Permission Slip

I grant myself permission
to be curious.

—signed by: ME

TAKE A BRAIN BREAK

You will need to assert a boundary between you and your work/household/family for your exploration. If you're like the majority of women who juggle nearly two-thirds of the work required to run a home and a family, it will be difficult, if not impossible, to become inspired when you're busy problem-solving one urgent task after another, with no physical or mental space in between. For uninterrupted introspection, as discussed in chapter 4, you must create a boundary that allows you to get quiet so your curiosity may wander free.

Professor Barbara Oakley, PhD, has studied this concept of brain modality, and she identifies the importance of "diffused thinking," which gives our brains an opportunity to subconsciously and creatively problem solve. Once your time and space are yours alone (if only for ten minutes before someone bursts through the door you forgot to lock), intentionally downshift to diffuse-mode thinking. In other words: backburner your to-do list to create space for unfocused curiosity.

In their article "Creativity's Role in Everyday Life," scholars Katherine N. Cotter, Alexander P. Christensen, and Paul J. Silvia point out that "both landmark creative works and common creative acts are usually situated in their creators' complex, idiosyncratic, and utterly ordinary environments ... bouncing around ideas in a café, letting their mind wander while walking through the woods, or doodling on a sketch pad kept by the toilet."

I laughed when I read their creative bathroom solution because a friend had just given me a waterproof notepad (one that you can write on in the shower—really!), with the following product description: "Don't let your great idea go down the drain! Capture every clever thought, brilliant solution, or potentially life-changing idea that comes to you when you least expect it—in the shower!"

BUILD ON YOUR VALUES

Once you've identified a curiosity, a clue that points you in the direction of your Unicorn Space, then it is super-duper important that you align your "what" with your values. I lead with value inquiry when advising family foundations, and it yields extremely insightful results. So even if you know what curiosity you wish to make time and space to pursue, DO NOT SKIP this step; it's a critical piece of self-inquiry. (Sorry for the ALL CAPS, but for real, it's important!)

Our values are what we hold to be of the greatest personal importance and worth. And they vary wildly from person to person. Although seldom talked about, our values show up in everything we think, say, and do. They directly influence our lives—motivating, acting, and directing. They also can inform our curiosities.

Our values can point us in the direction of curiosities that, if we pursue and actively engage in them, have the potential to fill us up. As my cousin Jessica reflected on her own Unicorn Space journey, "How can I truly live if my bucket is empty?" To which I responded, "So let's fill that bucket of yours with new curiosities based on your values."

Many of our deepest-set values we've inherited from our families of origin, so this can also be a good start of inquiry. Ask yourself: What did my parent(s) value? Do I value that, too? A colleague of mine grew up with parents who were newspaper journalists who put a high value on free speech. As an adult, she's also made it her life's work to give people a voice through podcasting, because she holds a congruent value. In other families, it's a different story. There may be things that your family stands for that do *not* ring true to you, and there will be values that you recognize aren't worth adopting in your own life. Listen to that voice, too. Dr. Stew Friedman validates these layered emotions. He said to me, "This is where people can struggle. If standing up for the values that matter most to you means changing from what your parents taught you, that can be painful."

In doing research for this book, I read nearly every book on creativity I could get my hands on. In this space, a popular prompt for identifying your "curiosities" is to lead you back to what you embraced as a child. What did you love when you were younger? What did you do for play? For a lot of people, this is helpful, and for others it isn't. For me, it's a mixed bag. I had some awesome experiences as a young kid, like traveling to DC with my mom to march for equal rights, but there was some trauma in my early years, too, that I don't want to replicate today. If looking backward to your past doesn't motivate you in the present, focus instead on the values you, and you alone, hold today. They are another clue that will point you in the direction of what and where you want to go *next*.

∘∘∘∘∘∘∘∘∘∘∘∘∘∘∘∘∘∘ ✏️ ∘∘∘∘∘∘∘∘∘∘∘∘∘∘∘∘∘∘

EXERCISE
What *Do* I Value?

What do you value? This exercise may help you figure it out. (Note: This is a composite list of values from Job Crafting, created by the Ross School of Business at the University of Michigan; Professor Martin Seligman and Chris Peterson's twenty-four character strengths; the 21/64 philanthropic group; and from my own consulting practice.) When you glance down at the checklist, pay attention to which values especially resonate with you. After you review the list, circle your top three and cross out your bottom three values. Mark them here or write them down in a journal or on a separate piece of paper. You likely have more than three "top" values. Circle those that you most identify with today, and try not to overthink it!

144

VALUES CHECKLIST

Circle your top three values.
Cross out three values you could do without.

 Free Values

Abundance	Building	Creativity	Entertainment	Freedom
Acceptance	Care	Cultivation	Equality	Friendship
Access	Challenge	Curiosity	Equity	Fulfillment
Accountability	Civic Engagement	Decisiveness	Elegance	Fun
Achievement	Communication	Democracy	Exploration	Futurism
Adaptability	Community	Dependability	Expression	Generosity
Adventure	Compassion	Deservedness	Fairness	Giving Back
Aesthetic	Competence	Devotion	Faith	Grace
Ambition	Completion	Discipline	Family	Gratitude
Authenticity	Connection	Discovery	Flexibility	Grit
Autonomy	Conservation	Drive	Flow	Growth
Beauty	Consistency	Education	Focus	Hard Work
Boldness	Courage	Enjoyment	Forgiveness	Harmony

Healing	Leadership	Pleasure	Routine	Systemization
Health	Learning	Power	Rule Breaking	Teamwork
Honor	Legacy	Practicality	Rule Following	Thoughtfulness
Honesty	Listening	Privacy	Security	Timeliness
Hygge	Love	Problem Solving	Self-Awareness	Tolerance
Humor	Loyalty	Productivity	Self-Expression	Touch
Identity	Mastery	Progress	Sharing	Tradition
Impact	Merit	Providing	Simplicity	Transparency
Independence	Mindfulness	Purpose	Skill-Building	Travel
Influence	Moderation	Quality	Socialization	Trust
Innovation	Nature	Recognition	Social Standing	Truth
Integrity	Obligation	Reliability	Solitude	Understanding
Intelligence	Optimism	Reputation	Spirituality	Unity
Interest	Organization	Resilience	Spontaneity	Variety
Journey	Ownership	Respect	Stability	Vision
Joy	Passion	Responsibility	Stewardship	Wealth
Justice	Personal Growth	Rigor	Strength	Wellness
Kindness	Perspective	Risk-Taking	Support	Wisdom
Knowledge	Play	Romance	Sustainability	Wonder

ASK YOURSELF

- *What are my top three values at this stage in my life?*
- *What are my bottom three values at this stage in my life?*

Your top three values are your **motivating** values. They inform a present-day curiosity that can *motivate you into the future.* For example, after enjoying yet another delicious meal prepared by her mother, my friend and fellow Uni Tiffany confided in me: *What's going to happen one day if, God forbid, something should happen to my mother and all her recipes are lost?* I suggested she do the values exercise, and when she realized her top values revolved around family traditions, storytelling, and sharing through food, she and her sister began deconstructing and documenting the ingredients of their mother's most prized Chinese and Taiwanese dishes.

"We started off just collecting and writing them down for us, and then we were motivated forward. We thought, why not produce an actual cookbook with beautiful photography that really celebrates Mom's dynamic heritage and combines two unique regions of recipes that we share with people outside our own family?"

Do you see how Tiffany's top values motivated her forward to create something new and meaningful?

When I examined my own most deeply held values in this exercise, this is what I jotted down in my journal:

- ○ Education and lifelong learning
- ○ Fairness and justice
- ○ Creating community

I reflected on different moments and memories from my life that were driven by my values, and my mind backtracked to the story I just recounted—the one about me at age nine, boarding a Greyhound bus with my mom, Terry, and heading to Washington, DC, to march for equal rights, eat a brown bag lunch at the National Mall, and then reboard the bus back to

New York City the same day. Another year, Mom and I chanted for civil rights. And another, worker justice. This annual birthday tradition was inspired by my mother's motivating values, and after I adopted them as my own, they became a throughline into my adult life, influencing many of my curiosities and subsequent actions. For example, because I value fairness, I became curious about systemic domestic inequity, which then evolved into an all-out obsession with gender justice causes that inspired me to write my first book, *Fair Play*. Because I value community, my Unicorn Space is to help and inspire a growing community of Unis to explore their value-based curiosities and discover *their* Unicorn Space.

Your bottom three values are those that either don't resonate with you at all or, as my observations revealed, point to values that may have *once* prompted you but that now no longer motivate you to move forward. For example, one of my bottom three values is "obligation," which by definition means a commitment to fulfill a duty or a promise. While I do believe this value holds merit, it's no longer driving me. Ever since my husband and I rebalanced our domestic workload so that we share household and parental duties and value each other's time more fairly, this value is less relevant in my day-to-day life. To put it simply: I no longer feel obligated to pick up everyone's shit while single-handedly keeping the house from burning down.

My friends Niall and Emily, who are also on their respective Unicorn Space journeys, mutually agreed that "tradition" is in their bottom three values, because they both want to break from the traditional roles they observed in their parents. "My mom was the 'she-fault parent' who did it all and had no creative time for herself, while my dad definitely took a back-seat role in parenting. We're working on creating our own traditions that don't default to traditional roles and imbalances we observed in the households we grew up in, which means rethinking, redefining, and implementing other values that *work* for us," shared Emily.

Hone your curiosity through your values.

CONSIDER:
THE CASE OF THE UNIDENTIFIED STYLIST

At a recent backyard lunch, this line of value-based inquiry helped my friend Sheila identify her "what," something she was already doing, yet not attuned to. I was catching up with my friends Masha and Gina over iced tea when Sheila sauntered in a full fifteen minutes behind everyone else, as is her habit.

"Sorry I'm late." She flashed a smile of apology and hurried into a seat in the sun. "I just couldn't get it together this morning."

We looked at Sheila and smiled back, each of us aware of what the other was thinking: *Sheila will never be on time, but she will always look put-together.* While the three of us had casually shown up in leggings, stressed T-shirts, and baseball caps, Sheila was clean and coiffed, wearing a tailored vintage getup and adorned with accessories that matched the hardware on her shoes.

After Gina had served us a nice salad, the conversation turned to husbands, kids, and aspirational exercise.

Sheila dished first: "On my run this morning I found myself thinking: *Maybe I should have another kid.*"

"Um"—Gina side-eyed to me and Masha—"are you sure?"

"Not really, but I'm really good at being a mom and pushing my kids to excel," Sheila said. "Do what you're good at, right?"

I recalled the sage words of Tovah Klein, PhD, author of *How Toddlers Thrive*. When I'd interviewed her for *Fair Play*, she'd said, "Don't let your passion be the perfection of your children. Because when you solely define yourself in relation to another, it's not enough."

"You're also good at *other* things," I returned to Sheila.

Just as the words left my mouth, I regretted the indignancy in my tone, but come on—how many times had this group of friends candidly discussed the merits of extending ourselves beyond the roles we play at home? Again, the feminist cry of Betty Friedan echoed in my mind: "A woman cannot find her identity through others—her husband, her children . . ."

I quieted Betty's bold assertions and added carefully, "I don't mean to diminish that motherhood is meaningful and a great source of pride, but there can be more. We get to be more than one thing."

I said this not just to Sheila but as a reminder to myself, to all of us sitting at the table who juggle jobs, kids, and partners. Gratefully, Sheila didn't take offense. She was cool about it, curious even.

"Okay," she challenged, "like what other things?"

I recognized this as an opportunity to test how Sheila's motivating values may direct her toward other aspects of herself to actively pursue. "Let's back into this question," I suggested. "Beyond being an awesome mom, what other values are important to you? All of us at the table value care; that's a given. But what else do *you* value? For me, I grew up valuing justice issues because of the influence of my mom. That's a driving value for me, but that may not be one of yours. When you think of your unique-to-you values, which ones rise to the top?"

Sheila paused and looked back at me, doubtful. "This feels hard to answer."

"I think I know!" Gina jumped in, waving her hand. "Can I give you a clue?"

"Go for it," Sheila sighed with relief.

"Well, for starters," Gina said, gesturing to Sheila's outward presentation, "you're the most put-together woman I know."

"Totally," chimed in Masha. "You could be in *Vogue* with your knack for pairing consignment with high fashion."

"Thanks." Sheila smiled with a mix of appreciation and modesty. "But you know I shop the sale endcaps at Target and borrow my daughter's clothes."

"Exactly." I leaned in enthusiastically. "Found fashion is your *thing*. Transforming an outfit or a dining room comes easy to you because"—I practically jumped out of my seat—"you value beauty! You see the world through a special lens, and because of that, your outfits, your home, your garden—everything you touch—always looks beautiful. Do you see how this value naturally influences your interests?"

Sheila tilted her head in consideration. "Yes, I see what you mean, but what am I supposed to do with that?"

"You're already doing it," I practically shouted. "Give yourself permission to *do more*."

> You know how every once in a while, you do
> something and the little voice inside says,
> *There, that's it*. Do more of that.

—JACOB NORDBY, AUTHOR OF *THE CREATIVE CURE*

"Sometimes I feel like I've lost or forgotten myself," Sheila confided to me separately after our backyard lunch, "and it's been hard to find myself, let alone creatively express myself again, after 'wife-ing' and parenting for so many years. It's amazing the boxes we put ourselves in." She gave my arm a squeeze. "I'm grateful to have friends who tell me the truth and help *me* to remember who I am."

Our friends often see us more clearly than we see ourselves, so soliciting their input can help with identifying how your deeply held and perhaps unconscious values inform your curiosities. To do that, the exercise below takes inspiration from Tim Wilson, author of *Strangers to Ourselves: Discovering the Adaptive Unconscious*, whose psychological research suggests there are a variety of internal and external pathways to increase our self-knowledge. Asking friends who have a deep sense of knowing you is one such pathway.

EXERCISE
Ask the Audience

Borrowed from the popular game show *Who Wants to Be a Millionaire* and from Wilson's research, this exercise serves to be your lifeline back to you. Gather an intimate group of trusted friends (your audience) or simply phone a friend and solicit their honest and loving insights.

Tip! When considering your audience, choose friends who want the best for you and who won't beat you up, even unintentionally. Just as important is leaving out friends who love and admire you but whose judgment and guidance might be clouded by their own baggage, however innocent.

If that little voice in your head tells you they are not prepared to be generous, leave them off the list. Additionally, do not engage your spouse or partner in this exercise (don't worry—they come into play in chapter 11). The most well-intentioned partner may unintentionally say the wrong thing (*When I think of you today, I see a great mom*) or say it in the wrong way (*When we first met, you were* so *curious about everything . . .*) and before you know it, you may become discouraged, resentful, or—worst of all—resigned to the status quo.

Ask your audience to write down their answers. No sharing until the end.

- *When you think of me today and how I choose to live my life, what values motivate me?*
- *When you think of me today, or over the course of our friendship, what curiosity/skill/talent/activity/ environment have you noticed makes me come alive?*
- *What are three things you suggest I should do more of, given the values you picked for me?*
- *If money were no object, what should I consider giving myself "permission" to do more of?*

Once you've asked the questions that feel relevant to you, welcome feedback. Is there a description of you that deeply resonates or sparks a new curiosity? Have your friends given you an idea for what you'd like to pursue next? Have they suggested an aspect of how you identify with yourself that you'd like to reawaken or discover?

MAKE A CREATIVITY COMMITMENT

The Creativity Commitment is a spin on the traditional mission statement used by many organizations to summarize their values and define the goal of their operations. In the context of identifying your Unicorn Space, this exercise clarifies your "what" and then puts you on a path toward achieving it. After all, curiosity is only the starting point. Connection is the midpoint, and completion is the goal. Your **Creativity Commitment** will also help keep you accountable and provide you with a road map to refer back to should you need to course correct in the future.

Here's mine:

My name is Eve Rodsky. My motivating values include justice and fairness, education and lifelong learning, and creating community. Today and moving forward, I give myself permission to live by my values. I allow my values to inform my day-to-day curiosities, some of which are building a community of women who feel permitted to pursue a life beyond the Three P's. I am committed to explore deeper and pursue activities and interests that are in alignment with my values, one of which is interviewing people all over the world on the subject of creativity and building community around it. When I align my values with my creative pursuits, I arrive in my Unicorn Space.

Your turn. Either here, in a separate journal entry, or even in the form of an email to a friend, make a **Creativity Commitment** in writing. (Hold on to it! You will continue to return to and build on your commitment throughout the following chapters.)

My name is _____. My motivating values include _____. Today and moving
forward, I give myself permission to live by my values.
I allow my values to inform my day-to-day curiosities,
some of which are _____. I am com-
mitted to explore deeper and pursue activities and interests that are in alignment with my values. When I align
my values with my creative pursuits, I arrive in my Unicorn Space.

Expanding again on the definition of what it means to live a
creative life—it is the active and open pursuit of self-expression
in any form that piques and satisfies your curiosity, and that
aligns with your most deeply held values. Which leads us to a
further distinction that I'm frequently asked to make . . .

CAN MY JOB BE MY UNICORN SPACE?

In other words, if your values are reflected in your for-pay
work, can your job double as your "creativity"? The fastest
route to this answer is by way of another question: If money
were not a motivator, would you still do it? If it didn't reward
you at all financially or with external praise, would you still
make time and space to actively pursue it?

If your answer is no, then whatever provides you with a
paycheck is presumably not your Unicorn Space. Even if your
for-pay work is deeply satisfying, but money and external vali-
dation are driving components, then it likely doesn't qualify as
100 percent Unicorn Space.

Now, if your for-pay work does deliver a Category 5 storm of
passion to your life and payment for doing it feels like a bonus
check, congratulations! "Your vocation is your avocation," my

twelve-year-old son, Zach, proudly distinguished after acing his vocabulary test. Still, I'd argue that even people who passionately love their job need to cultivate other curiosities and enthusiasms, or risk becoming burned out (hence my return to dancing).

In my continued search for people who were actively cultivating their curiosities, I stumbled upon Kabir Sehgal, who in the spring of 2020 created a nightly Quarantine Concert Series on Facebook featuring musicians and music from all over the world. I was quickly drawn in by this free series that emanated so much beauty in such a hard time. Curious to learn more about him, I googled Sehgal and found a piece he'd written in the *Harvard Business Review*, "Why You Should Have (at Least) Two Careers." I discovered that Sehgal's gig on Facebook was an extension of his work as a composer and a record producer, alongside his day job as a corporate strategist. An impressive résumé! In the article he writes, "It wasn't money that motivated me to become a producer in the first place. It was my passion for jazz and classical music." I tracked him down and he easily reiterated on our Zoom coffee date, "I still don't [produce albums] for the money because making music, something that is everlasting, is reward enough for me."

I wanted to test my thesis that our values point us in the direction of our deepest curiosities. I asked Sehgal if he would indulge me, and he agreed he would.

I asked, "What are your top values?" He enthusiastically replied, "My values are making connections and supporting creativity. During quarantine, I became curious about what music we could create remotely, and since I saw so many talented musicians out of work, I thought, *Why not try to create something beautiful that could reach people in their homes?*"

Granted, not everyone has the capital or the resources to

launch a second career like Sehgal, and he acknowledges this, while also emphasizing that curiosity is available to everyone. "When you follow your curiosities," he said, "you will bring passion to whatever you do, which will leave you more fulfilled."

UNICORN SPACE AND FINANCIAL PRIVILEGE

Ironically, I found that those in my interview set that identified as having more financial privilege typically had a *harder* time tapping into their creativity, whereas those whom I spoke to with fewer resources were *more* likely to have Unicorn Space in their lives.

Marc Bamuthi Joseph, spoken word artist and artistic director of social impact at the Kennedy Center, offers an explanation for this: "Money is often regarded as our only form of capital, whereas for communities who don't have wealth or the traditional forms of capital, we are mistakenly overlooking the power of creative capital."

CONSIDER:
THE CASE OF THE NEW CHAPTER

One night, Katrina Medina was reading a story to her two-year-old son that stopped her husband, Mario, in his tracks. He stood in the bedroom doorway listening to her with a look that was a combination of delight with inspired insight.

Kat stopped reading, "What? Why are you looking at me that way?"

"I just had a thought." He smiled. "You should record audio-books."

Kat laughed. "That's random. What makes you say that?"

"I don't know, it just hit me the way you were reading that book. It's like you do more than read the words. You tell stories. And," he added, "your voice is beautiful."

Kat appreciated her husband's compliment, and it was true, she told me, that she'd always had not just a love, but a passion and wonder for storytelling. "Snuggling up with and reading to my son is the favorite part of my day, but," she relented, "I already had a full-time job at Sam's Club in the cashiers' department and I didn't know the first thing about reading audiobooks."

Still, her husband's words sparked an idea. Kat became curious. "I started to look around at all the books lining my shelves. I thought about how much I loved knowledge and storytelling and being transported to another place. I thought, *Maybe I should look into this.*"

Kat followed her curiosity.

"I was a little hesitant at first," she admitted. "But I found a cheap microphone on clearance and borrowed my husband's laptop. I created a profile on a website for authors and narrators, and then I just went for it. I recorded a voice sample from the book *Princesses Behaving Badly.*" She laughed. "It wasn't perfect. The sound quality could have been better." But Kat took a chance anyway and hit Upload.

Kat was shocked when *within a week* she was contacted for an audition. Soon after that, she was offered her first paid contract. "I couldn't believe it. When I got the email that I'd been offered a contract, my heart literally stopped. I thought, even if this doesn't take off, I've already made a mark. I actually did it!"

After recording more than forty audiobooks, many in the evenings after her son went to bed, Kat felt confident enough to leave her job at Sam's Club to pursue voice recording full-time. To celebrate this decision, she got a tattoo: *She reads books as one would breathe air.*

"My mom freaked when I left my job and really freaked when I got a tattoo." Kat laughed. "She said to me: 'But, Kat, what if you stop doing this?' I told her, 'Mom, it doesn't matter. My voice is already out there. And that can't be taken away from me.'"

When I asked Kat if following her husband's hunch had paid off, she didn't hesitate. "I doubt it'll ever make me rich, but I'm happy."

IT'S NOT TOO LATE

"When you are thriving, creating, and living in an optimal way that is in concordance with your unique potential, happiness is the side effect," reiterated professor of psychological sciences Kennon Sheldon, PhD, when I shared with him Kat's story. "Rather than making happiness the goal," he said, "we should each go after that thing that taps into our values, what is meaningful and fulfilling to *you*. And the way to know if you're succeeding is that you feel happy."

What I love about Kat's journey toward a new career (that also happens to be her Unicorn Space—it *can* happen!) is that not only did she give herself permission to follow her curiosities; she also found the courage to begin again. To reinvent an aspect of her identity based on her motivating values. And along her journey, she wrote a new story about herself: I am a mother, a partner, a narrator, a storyteller, and I have a unique voice I want to share with others. How cool and expansive is that? "That's what I call living fully in all parts of you," offered Dr. Amber Thornton, host of *The Balanced Working Mama* podcast.

In today's culture, it is still highly subversive for women to deviate from the traditional roles, to expand beyond the Three P's and follow a whim, a calling, a curiosity—like, say, becoming a voice narrator with an on-clearance microphone after you put your kids to bed. Women: We get to be more than our roles. We get to be more than one thing. We get to define ourselves in any number of ways. An entrepreneur *and* an artist. A parent *and* a performer. An accountant *and* an athlete. Marci Alboher, vice president at Encore.org and author of *One Person/Multiple Careers: The Original Guide to the Slash Career*, found that individuals with fulfilling lives are those that include "slashes." For example, instead of identifying as a firefighter or a chef or as a mom or a photographer, it's when an individual defines themselves as firefighter/chef or mom/photographer that they are able to integrate their multiple passions, talents, and interests and live a fully expressed life.

"It's never too late to embrace new things," wrote Lisa on LinkedIn. Lisa's a California supervising attorney and a colleague of mine. "I started learning to paint at forty-four. Will I ever be good at it? Who knows? I enjoy doing it, and I want to learn. Half the time my paintings don't look the way I want. Often the colors I mix turn into mud. Is it frustrating when I can't do it as well as I would like to? Yes. But I am getting better. And if I hadn't started learning to paint at forty-four because I thought I was too old, where would I be now? I'd still be forty-six, but I wouldn't know how to paint at all. I've finally realized you don't do things to be good at them. You do them to do them."

"I was told I couldn't do art at a young age," echoed my friend Sarah Lacy, founder of Chairman Mom, an online community for working mothers. "Maybe it wasn't the role I was expected to play in my family. Maybe it was that I just had more interests that got nurtured instead. Whatever, a voice got lodged in my head that said I wasn't an artist. And I believed it until I was in my midforties! I've recently ordered a monthly sketch box and a watercolor kit. I've been excitedly shoving artwork in my family's face. My son said, 'I don't think Dad could do that well.' And Dad has an MFA! I am curious to see how much talent is really inside me that went nearly a lifetime going totally unexplored!"

Both Lisa and Sarah are exploring their curiosity with paints and color, but again, you don't have to be "artsy" to live a creative life. Remember how my friend Brennan's mind-tripping medicine is his Unicorn Space? Your version of creativity has no boundaries. So, ask yourself: What curiosities and talents lie inside me that haven't yet been explored? Furthermore, what stories am I telling myself about my abilities . . . that aren't likely true? What old stories can I retire about myself to create new, exciting stories?

> Give yourself permission to edit and sometimes completely rewrite your story at any stage, age, or page of your life.

Someone who knows a lot about turning the page and starting a new chapter is Robert Jones Jr., whose stunning novel

The Prophets debuted the year he turned fifty. We happen to share a publisher, so I tracked him down for an interview and felt fortunate to share twenty minutes of his time. When I asked him about retiring old stories to create new ones, he said, "I thought I 'missed my shot' based on an imaginary timeline that I dreamed up when I was younger about where I would and should be in life by X date—and the misinformed story I've been telling myself for a long time about accomplishments being determined by how young you are when you achieve them. If you, too, are dealing with shame or fear because your life didn't turn out precisely in the manner or order you planned, it is not too late."

I resonate so much with Jones's honesty. When I embarked on a new career at forty, I was terrified. I worried that it was too late to pursue something that was a long shot, but as my colleague Lisa discovered, if I hadn't made the daring leap from my legal profession into the publishing world, I wouldn't now be writing about Unicorn Space at age forty-four. And I like Kat Medina, I reached a goal that, despite whatever happens next, can never be taken away from me.

Jones continued, "My testimony is that your goal and your purpose are waiting on you and they don't care how long it takes you to realize them; they just want you to not give up on them. They want very badly to meet you, welcome you . . . They have no judgment of you, your path, your errors, your wrong turns, your stumbles, your pace, or your journey."

What happens when *you* regard your Unicorn Space as something that wants to meet you? That there is no such thing as "too late." But rather, you can turn the page and be welcomed at any time. No judgment. To continue on your journey through the land of curiosity, bravely confront and slay the old-age dragon that prevents you from believing you can expand beyond your roles and discover or rediscover an aspect of yourself that ignites and propels you forward. Today, put a pin in whatever stage or age you are in your life and commit to stepping forward. Turn the page from where you are now and bravely craft a new story that redefines your character and exemplifies what you most value. Isn't it time to live fully in all parts of you?

Permission Slip

I give myself permission to breathe/live/awaken/begin again. Starting today.

—signed by: ME

8

Set a Goal

Is Your Creative Ambition Audacious Enough?

CONSIDER:
THE CASE OF THE PIE LADY

Now that you have your "what" and have started a Creativity Commitment to follow your curiosity, how far do you want to take it? This is the very question Stephanie Hockersmith asked herself. Stephanie is a stay-at-home mom of two young boys with her husband, Duane, a project manager for an electrical company. She's also one of the one in one hundred people who suffer from celiac disease (an immune reaction to eating gluten). We met during my last book tour, and I looped back with her to talk about creativity—because from what I'd learned about Stephanie so far, she was a shining example of following your curiosity, unifying many interests together in a completely creative way, and in the process carving out some special Unicorn Space that allows her to share her unique talents with the world.

I asked Stephanie if she could back up and tell me how she followed her curiosity and translated it into a solid goal. She recounted, "Well, I had just gotten to the point where the repetitive tasks of home life and dealing with my health issues started to feel really stale. I was questioning myself, my life. I felt strongly that I needed *more.*"

A lover of sweets and a self-taught baker, she became curious about gluten-free baking. "It started with researching alternative flours and mixing flavors together. Just playing around, really." After some trial and error and a lot of taste testing, Stephanie turned her attention to baking pies. After some more experimentation, "I realized that I could create gluten-free pastry that was just as delicious as 'regular' pie."

Her audience of taste testers enthusiastically agreed. "My husband, Duane, and my boys loved them!" Stephanie's biggest supporter and fan, Duane urged her to enter a local pie-baking competition. As someone who often felt left out when it came around to dessert, Stephanie loved the idea of providing a delicious alternative for others like her who suffered from celiac disease. She decided to act on the prompt . . . with one little twist.

"I entered my gluten-free pie against the regular pies without telling the judges," Stephanie said slyly.

"And what was their reaction?" I asked, wondering if Stephanie's gluten-free impostor stood out from the rest.

"Of over fifty pie entries in the local competition, I won first place! When they announced my name, I felt like I was having an out-of-body experience. I looked out at the crowd, searching for my husband, Duane. The look on his face is one I will never forget. He was so happy for me."

The following year, Stephanie entered another gluten-free pie and won again. Encouraged by two landslide wins, she dared to do more to turn up the sweetness in her life. "As a stay-at-home mom with a kitchen that's always a mess and kids running around, reading and baking are the two activities that keep me sane." She laughed. So Stephanie mixed her two passions to create something completely new: delicious, gluten-free pies inspired by her favorite books. "Basically, I started 'baking' the books I love, because I believe delicious food and good books bring people together." (Note: one of Stephanie's top three values is *connection*.) Inspired by the novel her book group was reading, Stephanie set a new goal to create a recipe and design that matched the book's cover.

"I'd never defined myself as an 'artistic' person, but I tried it anyway. Duane and the boys encouraged me. Hearing them say, 'Momma, that is so beautiful,' filled me with a sense of personal success I'd been craving. They were proud of me and, maybe more importantly, I was proud of me, too."

Did Stephanie stop there? No, she leveled up again with new, more deliciously ambitious goals. She started her own Instagram account, @pieladybooks, to share her love of books and pie, and it was quickly followed by authors, publishers, libraries, fellow book lovers, and bakers.

"Again, I was shocked by the response." Since re-creating *The Smallest Part* by Amy Harmon, Stephanie has designed pies featuring many of her favorite quotes, like "Pilates? Oh, heavens, no. I thought you said 'Pie and Lattes,'" and titles like Austin Channing Brown's *I'm Still Here*.

When I spoke with her recently, we were both freaking out about her appearance on *Good Morning America*. Really, there's no stopping this woman! She continues to set incremental goals that keep her in a state of open and active pursuit.

"The creative process is so hugely satisfying," she said. "It gives me such a high. Like breathing! And I just want to keep moving forward."

Like breathing. Remember when Kat Medina similarly compared her Unicorn Space to breathing air? And Melody described herself as being brought back to life? Are you starting to notice a theme here?

THE REMIX

Once you identify a value-based curiosity (your "what"), take it as far as your imagination will go. Don't rule anything out. Really, not anything. Believe past the limitation of possibility. Get illogical. Think BIG. Think audacious. In the business management and leadership space, Jim Collins, researcher, adviser, and coauthor of the bestselling book *Built to Last*, is famous for his BHAG framework (pronounced *bee-hog*, short for "Big Hairy Audacious Goal"). He posits that the most successful companies and organizations don't merely have goals. They set their vision on big, bold, energizing challenges, like flying to the moon and unlocking the world's knowledge. As you consider your own version of mind and space exploration, take inspiration from Abigail Edgecliffe-Johnson, who followed her curiosity for confection in an entirely different direction. She calls herself a "confectionary roboticist" and an "engineer of joy" who builds interactive cakes that are also edible.

Abigail studied medical anthropology in college, dedicated ten years to research as a postgraduate, and received her PhD in anthropology and sociomedical sciences. But after the birth of her second child, Abigail considered, "Okay, now what?"

Burnt out on academia, she launched a start-up toy company that like so many small businesses unfortunately collapsed during the pandemic. Not sure what to do next after coming off her loss, "I realized that the through-line was that I'd always made cakes," she told me on a call. "It was something I always enjoyed doing—since I was old enough to reach the oven and not fall in—and I did it without external input. All my life, I've tinkered, built, and made weird stuff. As an adult, building elaborate cakes had become my creative outlet."

So Abigail took all her extra toy motors and turned her attention toward the thing she always loved doing. "It started with my daughter's sixth birthday cake. She wanted it space-themed, and I decided to make a cake that reflected the entire solar system with a disco ball motor in the center that moved the planets around the cake. Then, I did one for my son that was the Death Star from *Star Wars,* with the X-wing planes flying around it. And then I made a *Minecraft* dragon cake that swept back and forth with blue and purple sprinkles coming out of the tail, and an *Exploding Kittens* cake with eyes that lit up and shot sprinkles out of the top. What can I say, it just kind of spiraled from there by adding more movement, explosives, and making them more interactive. With every cake, I challenged myself—how can I make it weirder? How can I make it better? How can I make it more fun and crazier?"

Consider *your* goal. What do you want to create in your Unicorn Space? If you already know you want to climb Mount Everest, then please, lace up your hiking boots and go right ahead. But if you're not sure how far to take your "what," a remix can be a great place to start. It can help you to reimagine a past goal or remix a few of your passions into something entirely new.

Consider how you might follow Stephanie's and Abigail's leads and remix some of your interests to create a big, hairy, audacious goal for yourself. Love of baking + love of books = pie lady books (Stephanie). Love of baking + love of building weird, crazy stuff = confectionary roboticist (Abigail). To carry the baking metaphor one step further, how can you mix up a few of your favorite tastes to create a new batter?

Zoe, my longtime friend and a Uni, said to me on a walk, "I made a mental list of some of my favorite loves and new curiosities and have been wondering how I can remix them into my Unicorn Space—my love of *Sex and the City* reruns, leveling up my spice drawer, foreign travel, and antique picking. Anything here?"

"Hmmmm, let me sit with it and get back to you." I smiled.

As I considered Zoe's remix, I interviewed another two "creatives" who employ a similar goal-setting exercise.

Sari Azout's mission is to bring more creativity to tech and business, and she encourages start-ups to consider a similar remix. I caught up with Sari over Zoom from her home in Miami. She said, "I encourage people to make relational leaps by making associations and connections between previously unrelated concepts, and hopefully apply them to [something new]." Her latest project, Startupy.world, is a community-curated network for start-up knowledge created just for this type of remix.

"It's designed to take you down rabbit holes based on the context of an idea. So let's say you're interested in the future of learning and that leads you into the area of future jobs, and that leads you to what people are building in space and that, you realize, is related to embedded gaming, because, you know, the future is all about gamifying everything. Creativity truly is combinatorial. It's about remixing different ideas."

"It's interesting this word you're using, *remix*, because it means a lot to me," said Justina Blakeney, wife, mother, design personality, and creative force behind the home decor brand Jungalow. I'd read about how Blakeney mixes culture and color into her designs and tracked her down for a conversation, hoping she'd share.

"This creative process is very much at the center of a lot of what I do," she said from her eclectic home in Los Angeles, "taking different influences through my heritage and my own family, along with the experience of traveling and all the people I've encountered through my life. I've taken all that and mixed it and remixed it and brought it out through my art and design hoping to capture the imagination of my community."

EXERCISE
Part 1: What's Your Creativity Remix?

1. Jot down a few of your curiosities, interests, and influences, past and present. Don't overthink it, just start writing things down—people, places, traditions, experiences that touch or move you in some way. They need not be related. _____

_____

_____

_____

2. Now, mix them up. Can you connect some dots? Make associations? Take a creative leap between presumably unrelated interests and create something new? If you take your vision far, wild, and even weird—what's in the batter? What could you create with all the ingredients of your life? _____

_____

_____

_____

If your batter looks like a lump of nothing, let it sit. Let it rise. And come back to it later. "To me, creative [goal setting] means being proactive about finding reflection time. And there is no shortcut for that," says Azout. She's absolutely right! Give yourself permission to set time and space boundaries for this reflective exercise.

○ ○

As you allow your goal to take shape, take a trip back to the future. That is, start to formulate a story you want to tell about yourself *in the future.* Benjamin Hardy, PhD, writes in *Personality Isn't Permanent: Break Free from Self-Limiting Beliefs and Rewrite Your Story* that without having a clear future self in mind, it is difficult if not impossible to move forward. He boldly states, "You need more than a goal—you need a future identity."

Take a moment to reflect deeper. You may need to create more time and space for this future casting exercise. Close your eyes and envision your future self. In six months. A year. Five years from now. What do you see? Or more aptly, who do you *want* to see, and *where* do you want to be? Do you have a clear destination? A future identity in mind? Here's a sampling of "me in my future Unicorn Space" responses from some of the people I interviewed:

○ "My book is selling more than *Love Languages!*"
○ "I'm onstage in Vancouver giving my TED Talk."

- ○ "I'm walking the floor at Comic-Con, and people are dressed up as my characters."
- ○ "I'm directing my stage play about menopause, and it's hilarious!"
- ○ "I'm flying people to the moon." (Tricked you! That was JFK's dream, not an interviewee's.)
- ○ "I'm the MC at a Unicorn Space conference bigger than the Consumer Electronics Show where all my Unis have an exhibit space and where, during intermission, I choreograph a dance routine with Shige-boh (of the Senior Monsters), leading one hundred women onstage, celebrating creative expression without guilt or shame." (That's me.)

Your turn. Take Hardy's cue and deliberately focus on where you want your curiosity and creativity to lead you in the days, months, years ahead. Set a goal for your future self by writing it down.

EXERCISE
Part 2: What's Your Future Remix?

When you mix your curiosities, interests, and influences, past and present, and project them into the future, what's in the batter? What can you create forward into the future?

If your batter is still formless and drippy, try a trick used in improv that allows actors to imagine the impossible by utilizing the power of "Yes, and . . ." My friend Alexis Jemal, JD, LCSW, PhD, is a social worker whose Unicorn Space is storytelling to explore racism and sociocultural barriers. She encourages her students to "radically imagine" new possibilities for their lives by improvising on this popular exercise. Imagine that what is *impossible* in your life today is *possible* tomorrow with the following prompt:

Fill in the blanks: YES [I am _____], AND [I can be _____].

° °

When I did this "Future Remix" exercise in the context of setting a creative goal, it read like this:

Yes, I am Eve Rodsky, lawyer, writer, mother, daughter, wife, sister, *and* I'm building a community of creative women who no longer feel like they're drowning but who are dancing in the rain (onstage with me and Shige-boh)!

Benjamin Hardy applies a similar principle and suggests writing your future goal *in the present tense*. For example, rather than saying "I can" or "I will" become the MC at a Unicorn Space conference, say, "I am the MC at a Unicorn Space conference." Stating or writing it in the present tense, he says, "highlights the fact that you are being who you want to be, which will then inform what you do and ultimately who you become."

So, who do you want to become? Imagining who you are becoming leaves space for your authentic self to step forward. Authenticity is an important distinction, one that leads us to the next section—setting *authentic* goals. You see, not all goals are created equal, and especially not big, hairy, audacious ones.

GOAL CHECK:
IS YOUR GOAL THE RIGHT GOAL?

My friend Meghan left her career in business to raise two children and create a rich family and home life. When I interviewed her several years ago, she bravely admitted, "It's physics. Bodies in motion stay in motion. And I no longer feel *in motion*. I feel like an object at rest. My goals were climbing the corporate ladder and raising my family. I've met all those goals. What's next? How do I get back in motion when I don't know what I'm moving *toward*?"

Meghan is an epic mom, a dedicated partner, and one of the smartest women I know. It crushed me to hear her express a lack of momentum given all she's accomplished and is still capable of creating. I suggested to her that the goals she had at one time might need a remix as she, her family, and her needs change. It's okay to want something new and different!

As you move forward into that future you radically imagine for yourself, do a goal check. Ask yourself: Am I working toward the right goals for me at this time in my life? If this feels like a trick question, it's because the answer lies within another question: *What is motivating you?*

Meghan's story was particularly poignant when juxtaposed against another conversation I had right after that, one that changed the way I regard motivation. It happened unexpectedly when I was in Davos, Switzerland, attending the World Economic Forum in the aftermath of publishing my first book, *Fair Play*. After a heady panel discussion aimed at encouraging leaders to value care when setting corporate policies, I took a beat to connect with my body alongside one of the most famous dancers in popular culture—Julianne Hough of *Dancing with the Stars* fame. I popped in on her *KINRGY* demonstration of expressive fitness, and thirty minutes later, after I'd moved myself into a pool of sweat and headed back out to the conference floor with name tag in place, I actually bumped into Julianne herself on a crowded staircase. We were both heading to an event in the aptly named Female Quotient Equality Lounge (how cool is that?), so I boldly took the opportunity to introduce myself. A few months later, I interviewed her over Zoom. With all that Julianne's achieved by her early thirties, I wanted to know where this dancer turned singer turned actress turned wellness advocate and entrepreneur gets her seemingly relentless energy. I asked her, "What motivates you?"

She eagerly answered, "You know, I've done all of these amazing things—became a singer at nineteen, acted in my first movie at twenty-one, I've had a number one album. I pushed really hard to achieve these things, and then one day I realized, I've hit all my goals. And I am exhausted. I have no energy left in me."

I'd heard that one before. Julianne's sentiment reminded me so much of what my friend Meghan was experiencing—both women were reconsidering goals that they'd set for themselves and met . . . and that no longer sustained them.

"What changed?" I asked Julianne. I'd seen her at Davos dance herself into a beautiful frenzy without missing a beat. This woman had energy (and flexibility) to spare! Had she rediscovered a secret well of inspiration that we could all learn from? Turns out it wasn't anything magical like that . . . but it did validate my growing thesis that our curiosities and our values must motivate us forward—and for the right reasons.

"I realized there is a pushing motivation and a pulling motivation," she said thoughtfully. "For a long time, I was very much a pusher. My motivation was just to 'be motivated'—to go, go, go. And how do you stay motivated from that exhausting place?"

In psychological terms, Julianne is describing the difference between intrinsic and extrinsic motivation. Sonja Lyubomirsky, PhD, professor of psychology and author of *The How of Happiness: A New Approach to Getting the Life You Want*, writes, "Intrinsic goals are those that you pursue because they are inherently satisfying and meaningful to you . . . [and] no one besides yourself is rewarding you or pressuring you into such efforts. By contrast, extrinsic goals reflect more what other people approve or desire for you—for example, pursuing goals for such superficial reasons as making money . . . seeking power or fame, and bowing to manipulation and peer pressure." In other words, are you dancing because it feels good to you physically, emotionally, and perhaps spiritually, or do you dance to gain followers on TikTok?

"People usually aim for extrinsic goals," writes Lyubomirsky, "as a means to an end—for example, working hard to obtain a reward (e.g., wealth or social approval) or to avoid a punishment (e.g., shame or loss of income)." Lyubomirsky affirms that while there is nothing inherently wrong with having extrinsic goals, "they mask the pursuits more likely to deliver true and lasting happiness."

So many women I've spoken to express their disappointment after reaching extrinsic goals. My friend Meghan said, "I did all the things I was supposed to do. What our culture says we 'should' do. All the things people said would make me happiest—get married, have two-and-a-half kids, move to a good neighborhood with good schools—but I'm still not happy. I feel guilty saying this because I have so much and there is so much good there, but I feel like something's missing."

FOMM! Fear of missing me.

BIG, HAIRY, AUDACIOUS, *AUTHENTIC* GOALS
(BHAAG)

It turns out, thinking big, weird, radically, remixed, or into the future isn't enough. What I've learned by speaking to individuals in the context of Unicorn Space is that BHAG falls short. It's missing another *A*—for *authentic*. When you have a BHAAG (Big, Hairy, Audacious, *Authentic* Goal—pronounced *bee-hog*, like a piece of Swedish IKEA furniture), you become intrinsically motivated to reach it.

An authentic goal is one that is rooted in your deeply held interests and core values—Remember? Value-setting is key!—and not driven by our desire for social recognition or to gain the favor of or meet the expectations of our parents, peers, partners, or other professionals in our field.

"Not surprisingly," Lyubomirsky says about the research into goal setting and autonomy, "people are happier, healthier, and more hardworking when they are following goals that they own . . ." Discerning your authentic goals takes a bit of self-awareness and emotional intelligence, she continues, but "if you understand your guiding values and have a clear sense of your preferences and desires, you will likely instantly recognize when there's a match between you and [your goal]."

Back to Julianne. Can you guess what value motivates her forward? "My number one value is to create!" she said. Notice that she said *to* create, not *be* creative. She made it a verb, not a noun. Not surprising. Shelley Carson, author of *Your Creative Brain: Seven Steps to Maximize Imagination, Productivity, and Innovation in Your Life*, discovered that the most highly creative people are intrinsically motivated in what they do. Carson says, "They also arrange their lives so they can do more of the work they find intrinsically rewarding."

"My new goal," Julianne continued, "is to help other people feel free to create, to dream, to express themselves . . . and I've never been clearer in my life"—Julianne continued to radiate—"because [my goal] is coming from me, not from external expectations. I'm being *pulled,* and I have so much more energy and capacity to create from that place that is much more real, so much more authentic."

Are you being *pushed* by external expectations or *pulled* toward your authentic goals?

POP QUIZ
The Deserted Island Test

How do you know if your goal is authentic and aligned with your values? Ask yourself: Would I still be pursuing it on a deserted island?

Picture this: You are awarded one year to pack your bags and get the heck out of Dodge. You relocate to a remote and beautiful island, where you have the privilege of all your basic food and shelter needs met and you have unlimited supplies and access to Wi-Fi and local resources. Oh, and did I mention that your job and wages are secure, and your family is thriving back home while you're on extended vacay? (Think *Survivor* but with perfect weather and great food you don't have to share. It's a fantasy, just go with it.) Given the idyllic setting and optimal circumstances, what would you do with your time? What activities would *pull* you?

My Deserted Island goal is to (build, learn, play, design, create, write, sing, make, explore, discover...): _____

_____.

Over the years, I've asked this question of many people, and while their answers dramatically range from cross-pollinating pineapples and mangoes (the mangapple) to building outrigger canoes and studying marine life, what I've never seen make the list is:

A. Go on a crash diet
B. Get Botox
C. Drive an expensive car
D. Dress to impress (*Who?* You're the only one on the island.)
E. Make more money

Why don't these things make the list? Because they're *extrinsic* goals based, in large part, on societal expectations and cultural norms. The Deserted Island Test is designed to identify your *intrinsic* goals, those that have the power to pull you forward and toward a life that is authentic and true to *you*.

"*Make* sure that your goal reflects *your* desires, *not* the wishes of someone close to you and *not* what you think society would expect you to do. In order to achieve its full effectiveness, your goal has to come from within," similarly espouses Shelley Carson, PhD, author of *Your Creative Brain*.

Looping back to Abigail, confectionary roboticist—remember how she said that baking was something she always loved doing "without external input"? That's what I'm talking about here. She didn't take my Deserted Island Test, but she did share that when she was becoming curious about what to do post-academia, a friend of hers reminded her of a conversation they'd had years ago. Abigail recounted, "My friend said to me, 'If you could do anything, if you had all the money in the world, what would you do?' And I said, 'I would make weird shit.' That was me at twenty, and that's me now! That's the thing that brings me joy. If the thing that you're doing doesn't bring you joy, can you change that?"

> As you are living up to the expectations of who the world says you should be, you're letting your authentic self down, and that creates a vacancy in this world for you as you are.
>
> —ALEXIS JEMAL, JD, LCSW, PHD

THINK BIG, ACT SMALL

Once you have identified your "pull" or intrinsically motivated BHAAG, you will take small actionable steps forward. This isn't just my directive. While researching goal setting, I interviewed more than fifty people who identify as business and life coaches, and they all use a version of a small-step framework. Shelley Carson refers to them as mini goals toward your "main goal." The John Whitmore GROW model distinguishes between "performance" goals and "final" goals. If your final goal is to run a marathon, he uses as an example, then your performance goal would be to run thirty minutes a day.

The S.M.A.R.T. goal framework, developed by George Doran, Arthur Miller, and James Cunningham in their 1981 article "There's a S.M.A.R.T. Way to Write Management Goals and Objectives," encourages people to create goals that are specific, measurable, attainable, realistic, and timely.

I reached out again to Professor Kennon Sheldon to weigh in on this popular small-step framework. "With goal setting," he agreed, "it's important to have something big that you're striving toward that feels meaningful and authentic to you. At the same time, you want to set smaller, measurable goals on the way to the big goal so that you feel like you're making progress. That's where pursuit comes in."

He continued, "When we conducted experimental research on this approach to goal setting, we found that people who were only thinking about their 'eye on the prize' goal of completion gave up if they stumbled along the way. Whereas those people whose focus was on the smaller 'nose to the grindstone' daily goals could keep going and feel more successful."

Identifying small, attainable steps along the way to your BHAAG is a popular framework because *it works*. And there's no reason to deviate from something that's working for a lot of people across all types of disciplines. In the context of Unicorn Space, I refer to this aspect of goal setting as "leveling up," a term lifted from the video game world. I tried it out on Sheldon. I noted, if you've ever played a video game or watched kids play video games, you understand this basic concept: you don't want to die on level one! In order to keep playing, you slowly "level up" by building on what you just learned or accomplished to reach a higher goal.

As a real-life and quite literal example of leveling up, I reflected on my interview with Sandy Zimmerman, the oldest woman (at forty-two) and first mom to complete the course on

American Ninja Warrior and who hit the buzzer at the top of the nearly fifteen-foot-tall Warped Wall after rigorously competing for four seasons. When I asked Zimmerman about her own process for setting goals, she recalled her early training for the show when she was first learning how to climb the salmon ladder, a technique where you swing from a bar and then use your own body's momentum to jump the bar up to the next rung.

"In the beginning, I just hung from the bar," she said. "I didn't even *try* and move it out of its cradle. And I did that for days until I got the nerve to jump it up one rung. And then I practiced that for days until I jumped it up two rungs. I practiced that over and over until I had the courage to go up the ladder again. I took it step by step, at my own pace, one obstacle at a time."

On such a highly competitive show, I wondered if Zimmerman ever felt that her "leveling up" approach held her back.

"Absolutely not. It's a process, and some days I feel like I nail it and other days I fail epically, but to me, mistakes are great feedback. They've taught me to keep going, to 'grit it out,' and [mistakes have] helped me grow along the way. Looking back, I'm actually grateful it took me four seasons to hit the buzzer."

Professor Sonja Lyubomirsky suggests a congruent approach. "To make progress toward your higher-level goals, you must break them down into lower-level, concrete subgoals. Before you can master French cooking," she advises, "you must first learn how to braise Belgian endives. And the accomplishment of every subgoal on the way to the big goal is yet another opportunity for an emotional boost. Such lifts in joy and pride are important not only because they reinforce [feelings of] happiness but because they motivate us to continue striving."

THE S.S.S.S. YOU
(SMALL STEPS SIGNAL SERIOUSNESS)

Once you have committed to set sail as the captain of your own ship, with your BHAAG as your North Star, take small, actionable steps forward and track how you're leveling up in a succession of visible ways. For example, Brenda, a writer friend of mine, sets a daily goal of writing one thousand words. She says, "I do this intentionally, actively. No editing. I sit down and write one thousand words even if they're total garbage." Cheryl Strayed, memoirist and author of *Wild,* echoes this. "There are no guarantees to any kind of artist, but what we do know is that you won't succeed as a writer if you don't write." Putting yourself on a committed schedule will help you stay in pursuit of your BHAAG (intrinsically motivating in itself), and based on my own findings, creating a specific timeline by which you will reach the top rung (your "when"!) will keep you in active pursuit.

Permission Slip

I give myself permission to
be in active pursuit.

—signed by: ME

Being in active pursuit is the name of the game, according to Emily vanSonnenberg, UCLA professor and happiness expert. "The concept of 'static goals' can be really dangerous because most people focus on *achievement* versus *pursuit*," she cautioned in an interview. "Achievement is fleeting. Accomplishments are here and then they're gone. Being in active pursuit is a more fulfilling goal because it's an act of intentional engagement with life. What if you made pursuit your goal? And engagement with life your new milestone?"

Yes! Make engagement and active pursuit your goal, but don't sidestep the "when," because my own research showed that this is what your Unicorn Space needs to become a reality. It needs some kind of completion marker broken down into actionable steps. If you allow your BHAAG to stay parked in the dreaming or conception phase, there is a high likelihood it will fizzle, or worse, fade away completely. Absent a timeline that intrinsically motivates and pulls you forward, you also run the risk of losing valuable support. Your partner/roommate/best friend/teammate/boss is far less likely to encourage you or be willing to provide you with the time and space you need today, and in the days ahead, to take the small steps necessary to fulfill your dream. In fact, my finding was that specifically, our partners and spouses respond most poorly to our unfulfilled dreams.

"My old '74 Mustang that's been sitting in the garage for ten years is the source of many arguments between me and my partner," confided Aaron.

"I supported his restoration plans for many years and then I finally gave up," Aaron's husband said to me privately. "The reality is that he just talks about 'fixing it up and getting it back on the road,' but we know that car is never leaving the garage."

This charged reaction to unfulfilled dreams was consistent with people in nearly all interviews I conducted regarding goal setting, leading me to conclude that in order to elicit support from our best cheerleaders, we must first signal seriousness by going beyond the curiosity/idea/fantasy/dream stage and committing to those first actionable, small steps that are visible to those around us. Think about it—wouldn't you be far more inclined to make time and free up resources to support a friend's, colleague's, or your partner's interest if you somehow felt or observed their active pursuit and commitment to their goal?

Signal seriousness by taking small steps and setting an actionable timeline with a specific completion point in mind. This intentional step creates urgency to combat procrastination and will keep you in active pursuit and accountable to follow through on your commitment to achieve your goal. Again, either here or in a separate journal entry, build on your **Creativity Commitment** in writing.

> My name is _____. My motivating values include
> _____. Today and moving forward, I give myself permission to live by my values. I allow my values to inform my day-to-day curiosities, some of which are _____. I am committed to explore deeper and pursue activities and interests that are in alignment with my values, some of which are _____.
> I plan to take my open pursuit as far as _____ (think BHAAG). My first actionable, small step toward "leveling up" and reaching my goal is _____.
> My date for completing this next step is _____.
> (Remember: setting a date keeps you in active pursuit.)

PLAN TO SHARE YOUR JOURNEY WITH THE WORLD

If you're struggling with committing to a completion date (more on completion in chapter 12), reframe the question:

At what point can I share my journey with the world? If your BHAAG is to have an organic gardening show on HGTV, when can you ceremoniously share your first bounty of fresh veggies with friends and family? If your BHAAG is to converse fluently in Italian, set a date for when you'll form a conversational group that only speaks in Italian (and perhaps while enjoying Italian food and wine). If your BHAAG is to write your memoir or screenplay, put yourself on a timeline for when you will submit first-draft pages to a trusted friend or colleague to read and review them.

When you pair your goal with a "share with the world" component, when you outwardly extend and share that thing you love to do with others, my findings revealed that your Unicorn Space becomes more meaningful and purposeful, and you're more apt to continue, or even grow it.

"Yes!" enthusiastically agreed confectionary roboticist Abigail Edgecliffe-Johnson as we wrapped up our interview. "It's all about connecting with people around that thing you love to do. For me, it was finding like-minded people who have my same weird sensibility and can help me explore my weirdness. That's the through-line. Truly, what makes me feel the happiest is when I make a cake for someone and it makes them laugh or smile. I once showed up at a girlfriend's house with a really simple, sweet cake and she cried. She was so touched, so happy. And I was like, that's why I want to do this. Being an engineer of joy brings *me* joy."

So then, your ultimate goal combines authenticity with sharing. This is how that thing you do goes beyond being intrinsically motivating and becomes that much more meaningful and potentially life-changing to you and to *those around you.*

Share It with the World

//

Use Your Unicorn Space to Connect to Your Community

CONSIDER:
THE CASE OF THE DOG ON THE WALL

Lacy Freeman was working unhappily as a legal assistant. As she described it, "I spent my days in a cubicle that was zapping my soul. I went to bed late every night and got up early in the morning. There wasn't a whole lot of 'in between,' and I felt like I was just surviving my life."

When her husband, Chris, got a new job in another city as an automotive technician, Lacy found herself starting over—and looking for a new job that, she hoped, would pull her out of her depression and bring her back to life.

"We were lucky," Lacy admitted, "that things just sort of aligned for us once we got to Atlanta. I finally had a little breathing room to try something new. I knew that I wanted to be more creative, but all my life I'd heard, 'Art doesn't make money. It's not a career.'"

> All my life I'd heard,
>
> "Art doesn't make money. It's not a career."

I shared with Lacy how common this cultural message is that "creativity doesn't pay," that our self-expression must be monetized in order for creativity to be "worth" the pursuit.

"This thinking is what kept me at my desk job for so long," Lacy admitted. "I had my doubts I could, or should, do anything else. But once I was in a new city, I started trying different jobs, like teaching art camp for kids. I painted a couple of murals in the downtown area. Eventually, I made some friends in the arts community, and, over time, I realized that I was most drawn to painting. I was grateful to have this time to try different things. I do believe that when you allow yourself the time and creative space to figure out what it is you most enjoy doing, it starts to pull at you."

Paraphrasing Julianne Hough, who'd similarly described her creative journey, I mirrored back to Lacy, "When you allow your interests to 'pull' you, you have that much more capacity and inspiration to create."

Lacy said she felt undeniably pulled toward her desire to create, and she gave herself permission to pursue a Big, Hairy, Audacious, Authentic Goal as a painter. She turned a room of her new house into an art studio and started painting until she'd created so much art, she didn't have room to make more.

At that point, Lacy took another incremental step forward.

"I decided I'd try to sell some things at a local art festival," she recounted. "I was incredibly nervous. I thought, my art's not great and I've never done one of these [shows] before, but I'm going to do it anyway. I wanted to see what people thought of my work, although I was terrified that somebody was going to come into my booth and be like, 'Oh, God, this is ugly,' or 'I hate this.' But that never happened." Lacy smiled. "It still hasn't happened."

 Are you putting roadblocks on your creativity by expecting more from your art than is reasonable?

Despite a fear of failure, when Lacy shared her art with the world, she said, "I was really surprised at how supportive people were. Even if they weren't totally into the art, they were willing to spend a couple bucks on a postcard or take my card. 'Come see me again,' I told them. I realized that for a lot of people, it's the one-on-one connection with the artist that draws them into the booth. Sure, making money from my art is great, but creating things that make people smile is what makes me the happiest. And making those connections with people is what inspired me to go home and prep for the next festival."

Creating for creativity's sake and making connections with people is what motivated Lacy forward.

The paintings that people were most drawn to were her depictions of animals: giraffes, ostriches, rabbits, and llamas. "Llamas were such a 2014 thing," she recalls. "And so for the next festival, my booth was exclusively animal paintings. Nothing else. And when people came in, I'd match them to an animal. I'd ask them a couple questions about themselves and create a story about why they were more like a giraffe or a llama, and people were really getting a kick out of what their animal would be. I sold a lot of prints that year, I think because people were finding a connection to *themselves* through *my* art."

Her words reminded me of how another interviewee had described her experience singing for the first time in front of an audience: "It's now *me* connected to a bigger *we*." And this bigger-than-me connection similarly inspired Lacy to create *forward* again and *toward* a new BHAAG. Today—years since her first public art show—Lacy has a booming business as the creator of custom pet portraits for which she has a long wait list and an impressive clientele. Contrary to what she'd grown up believing—that art is not a career—Lacy has made it her full-time vocation and her Unicorn Space.

"And I'll never go back to anything else," she asserted. "I realized that if I'm not creating and making connections, I'm not happy.

"And," she said, laughing, "I'm much easier to get along with when I'm happy. Just ask my husband and my son. Really, I think if everybody could pursue and live their dreams, we would have a much happier world."

WHY SHARING MATTERS

When you pair your pursuit with a "share with the world" mindset, when you outwardly extend yourself and connect to others, the "what" you do becomes more meaningful and purposeful, and you're more apt to continue, or even grow it. If you're still foggy as to where your curiosity will lead you, by adding a sharing component, you can more clearly identify your Unicorn Space. Furthermore, your commitment to share your BHAAG with others keeps you accountable and creating forward and toward *new* goals.

I noticed it in my own life, too. The more I was connecting with people like Lacy, who weren't drowning but who were dancing in the metaphorical rain, the happier I felt and the more meaningful this book project became for me. Sharing ideas about creativity and swapping stories about how people were connecting to others through their Unicorn Space was becoming a new facet of *my* Unicorn Space. Furthermore, the majority of people I interviewed reported that when others either witnessed and observed, participated in, similarly experienced, or positively benefited from their Unicorn Space, they felt more connected to their communities. And this upped their sense that what they were "sharing" was meaningful.

MEANING MATTERS

Beyond my own research, there's a wealth of new data by leading psychologists indicating that the *pursuit of meaning*—the action of connecting and contributing to something beyond the "self" that allows you to feel directed and motivated by a community that shares similar goals—may be the true path to happiness. While seeking out studies about the power of connection, I stumbled upon an article in *The Atlantic* titled "Meaning Is Healthier Than Happiness." The writer Emily Esfahani Smith poses the following question: What is the difference between a meaningful life and a happy life? To help readers understand the distinction, Smith cited a study published in the *Proceedings of the National Academy of Sciences* (PNAS) where happiness was defined by *feeling good*. The researchers measured happiness by asking subjects questions like, "How often did you feel satisfied?" and "How often do you feel happy?" The more strongly people pointed to "hedonic well-being," or personal pleasure (like drinking a margarita on the beach), the higher they scored on happiness.

Meaning, conversely, was defined as an orientation to something bigger than the self. The researchers measured meaning by asking questions like, "How often did you feel that your life has a sense of direction or meaning to it?" and "How often did you feel that you had something to contribute to society?" Those people who oriented beyond the "self" felt more meaning in life. Having one without the other, the study concluded, leads to dissonance.

Did you get all that? The key takeaway is that you can feel happy and not have a sense of meaning. Likewise, you can have a sense of meaning in your life but not feel happy. When we spoke, Professor Laurie Santos spoke to this distinction: "When you have purpose and meaning, you're more likely to be satisfied with your life," she said. "And when you're doing things that engage your purpose and meaning, you're more likely to have positive emotions like joy."

As I relate it to Unicorn Space, the sweet spot is where meaning and happiness overlap. Happiness without meaning can feel like an empty party, and a life defined as "meaningful" because you act predominantly in service of others and sacrifice yourself is not necessarily a party on the beach, either. As these findings relate to my own life, becoming a parent has given my life more meaning, but if I'm being honest, it doesn't always make me feel *happy*. Especially when the kiddos interrupt and disrupt our family's pre-negotiated and mutually-agreed-upon time and space for Mommy (remember, no knocks on the door between nine and eleven, or else). On the other hand, what does feel meaningful and also fills me with great joy is when my dedication and enthusiasm for Unicorn

Space inspires my kids to creatively express themselves. Case in point—my nine-year-old, Ben, has begun writing his own semiautobiographical story that he hopes to publish one day (working title: *The Land of Cavemen*). And my twelve-year-old son, Zach, has taken a regular seat next to me on many Zoom panels as a Gen Z voice for gender justice. I was so proud of him on a recent call as he spoke wholeheartedly about the importance of equal opportunity for his young generation. For real! It brought tears to my eyes to witness how my deeply held values have inspired his own interests.

WHAT DRIVES *YOU* TO SHARE?

The motivation to share yourself with the world varies from person to person. I've found that most people self-identify with one of the following seven types of sharing based on their individual goals. The descriptions complement and overlap, so you may recognize yourself as the intersection of two or more types, but if you had to pick one based on your current aspiration, which one most resonates? In other words, what type of "sharing" speaks to you?

THE "SPIN-OFF" SHARE

When Uni Ashley was a young girl, she remembers her grandmother crocheting tea towels, potholders, and "traditional things for the house." Today, Ashley uses her grandmother's knitting needles to create Harry Potter dolls that she sells on Etsy and also gives to friends as baby shower gifts. She's embracing a family tradition while incorporating her own expression by literally putting her own magical spin on it.

The Spin-off share is motivated by an intrinsic desire to embrace traditions, knowledge, a skill, or a craft from a previous generation, or to impart traditions, knowledge, a skill, or a craft to a future generation. This type of share often includes the use of "transitional objects" or sacred keepsakes, like Ashley's passed-down knitting needles, which, according to Dr. Victoria Simms, PhD, President of the Simms/Mann Institute, "have the unique ability to connect generations."

Colleen Goddard, child development specialist, adds: "It is the identification and attachment to objects outside of the self—photographs, wedding bands, mementos, music, art, and culture—that define both nostalgic memorials, but more importantly, and astutely, define a state of connection and presence in the world."

My friend Nyakio Kamoche Grieco has also pulled from her past to create connection in the present. As a first-generation American of Kenyan descent, Nyakio created a skin-care product line "based on family secrets and beauty wisdom I learned from my grandmother, who was a coffee farmer, and from my grandfather, who was a medicine man."

That desire to keep family traditions alive is a strong, driving force for so many of us. Another nuance of the Spin-off share is the beautiful connection it can solidify between family members. Daisy experienced this when she signed her son up for fencing lessons to honor their Latinx heritage and became interested in the sport by sitting in on his lessons. With her son's permission, Daisy also joined the class. Now, they enjoy a shared creative outlet that has strengthened their mother-son bond while making lasting and meaningful memories.

Scott Behson, author of *The Working Dad's Survival Guide: How to Succeed at Work and at Home* and a national expert in work-family issues, wrote in the *Harvard Business Review* about carving out meaningful time together and "making memories" with his family during COVID. "My family has been baking together a lot," he wrote, and adds that developing commonality with your kids provides "unexpected opportunities for honest conversations, laying the groundwork for more adult relationships with them later on." In other words, invest in creating connections with your kids now, when they're young, to lay the groundwork for strong and lasting connections as they grow older.

Sharing motivated by the desire to Spin-off looks like:

- ○ Replicating and evolving traditions.
- ○ Starting new traditions for a new generation.
- ○ Sharing your creative expression with a loved one.
- ○ Honoring loved ones through legacy projects.

THE "SHOW UP AND SUPPORT" SHARE

Dolores recruited a bunch of her friends, including yours truly, to join her Butterfly Tribe, a movement community she created after the tragic loss of her mother to brain cancer. Her rallying cry in the Facebook group: "Remember who you are—incredibly powerful butterflies who constantly have the ability to transform." And by transform, she means by performing a ridiculous number of planks and burpees. Dolores is one ripped butterfly! I joined Dolores's group to not only support a friend but also to push myself to move more (because the truth is, I really needed to get off the couch to practice my eight counts!). The Butterflies extend all over the country and its members are connected through daily Facebook posts that encourage and inspire accountability—"Staying in motion is easier than getting in motion!" On top of that, the group also raises money for brain cancer research. Joining a community of women with a shared mission that's so much bigger than me has inspired me to take five and get up and *move*.

The Show Up and Support share is motivated by an intrinsic desire to reach the goals you set for yourself and to help others reach theirs in the process. To help you stay accountable, you might enlist a trusted friend to share your journey toward a similar goal of their own. As an additive, this allows you more time to spend together and invest in your relationship (more on the power of "spiritual friendships" in the next chapter). If you're someone who needs that extra push to show up, enrolling in a regularly scheduled class or workshop may also help keep you on track. Better yet, get three of your most motivated friends to sign up for the same class. Linda enrolled in a pastry-making class specifically to learn how to make traditional Italian tiramisu. When she served it to an enthusiastic crowd at her neighborhood supper club, two of her neighbors jumped on board and signed up for the same class with Linda the following week. Joining or creating any number of support systems (a writer's workshop, supper club, dance, exercise, or musical group, as examples) will help you to stay accountable, and it affords you built-in time to spend with other like-minded people on a regular basis.

Benjamin Hardy, PhD, writes in an aptly titled article "Accountability Partners Are Great. But 'Success' Partners Will Change Your Life" that when performance is measured, it improves; when performance is measured and reported, it improves *exponentially*. By adding an accountability partner to your life, he says, you're simply increasing your odds of success. The American Society of Training and Development supports this, too. They found that people are 65 percent more likely to meet a goal after committing to another person. Their chances of success increase to 95 percent when they build in ongoing meetings with their partners to check in on their progress. And when you have a success partner who is heavily motivated themselves, Hardy continues, "you can join forces and push each other further and further than you could ever go on your own."

Sharing motivated by the desire to Show Up and Support looks like:

- Enlisting a friend or "success partner" to join you.
- Joining a group/team/class to create accountability.
- Putting yourself and a buddy on a timeline.

THE "SERENDIPITOUS COMMUNITY" SHARE

On any given morning, countless surfers dot the waters up and down the Pacific coastline. Jesse, a seventy-year-old retired pediatrician and father of three, is one of them. He took up surfing in his forties and hasn't stopped since. I asked him what drew him to this seemingly solitary sport. "Getting away from it all and being out on the water, just me and the elements, is a great escape," he explained, and then quickly added, "but I'm never really alone. Most days, I'm sharing the ocean with other surfers. Some a few yards away, others farther down the coastline. We're all doing our own thing, but we're also a community out here. I know that someone has my back if I get into trouble and vice versa. Back on the beach, we often swap stories and encourage each other. As the oldest guy in a wetsuit"—Jesse smiled—"I've made a lot of young surfing buddies, and they draw me back to the water almost as much as the surf, itself. They keep me young!"

The Serendipitous Community share is motivated by an intrinsic desire to connect with others through your Unicorn Space, and as you maximize serendipity, you maximize a chance for authentic connection! Take it from interabled couple Cole and Charisma, who started a YouTube channel to create "a community of love." Charisma said to me, "We started our channel to show that it is possible for an able-bodied person to consider a person with disabilities. Who knows who will fall in love and what love matches may be inspired by watching us?" The Serendipitous Community share is a close cousin to the Show Up and Support share, except that your motivation to show up is primarily driven by your *own* strong yearning to make personal connections in a communal setting, one that celebrates your authenticity and values.

For Morgan, who joined my online Uni group, this meant volunteering for a political organization to meet other activists driven by similar causes. She wrote in the chat: "I started my second life as an activist by cofounding an organization called When We Show Up, which is focused on reframing and reclaiming progressive values. I'm so excited to roll up my sleeves and bring change in every way that I can."

A positive outgrowth of the Serendipitous Community share is that you often meet people you'd likely not have met outside of your everyday life. Through these unexpected or even unlikely connections, your shared experience can be "amplified in a positive way," offers Professor Laurie Santos. "The data suggests that on a very basic level, being around other people sharing a similar experience just feels good."

And beyond feeling good, sharing can be healing. Ellen McGirt, senior editor at *Fortune* magazine, shared that during the pandemic she'd become "so overwhelmed by the state of the world and my life that I felt at the end of my rope." A friend suggested to Ellen that taking on a creative practice might help. "Inspired by a stray tweet that showed the steps to successfully draw a water drop, I thought I'd try," she told me over the phone, "and it was meditative. It calmed me. And I started to feel more connected to life."

Ellen started posting her water drop drawings on Twitter, one every day, with simple messages like: *you are loved and seen.* "One thing I've learned drawing water drops is that they are filled with more light than dark. Just like me, just like you, just like the world." Creating a meaningful online community where she inspires others to similarly heal has become Ellen's Unicorn Space. "My practice has become something I share, and I love that so much."

Sometimes dancing in the rain begins with one water drop.

The healing aspect of the Serendipitous Community share came up frequently in my own research. Many interviewees and Unis pointed to their ability to repair and rebound from challenging or even traumatic events after they became part of a community. Blessing shared with our group: "I'm going to leave my current job to focus on women who are going through so much trauma due to this pandemic. I'm feeling a strong pull to connect with and empathize with other women, for their own healing, and mine. Maybe I can't solve any one person's problem, but I can acknowledge that you are not imagining your suffering, it is real."

Emma Seppälä, PhD, associate director of the Center for Compassion and Altruism Research at Stanford University, writes in *Psychology Today* that "connectedness . . . generates a positive feedback loop of social, emotional, and physical well-being. . . . People who feel more connected to others have lower rates of anxiety and depression. Moreover, studies show [that] social connection strengthens our immune system . . . helps us recover from disease faster, and may even lengthen our life."

Sharing motivated by creating Serendipitous Community looks like:

- Creating a support group/space of belonging and healing.
- Gathering with like-minded people who share similar values.
- Introducing yourself to an existing community.
- Sharing experiences to foster empathy and break common ground.
- Inspiring creativity and connection in a shared, communal space (in person or virtual).

THE "SLAY IT FORWARD" SHARE

I watched alongside my sons on TV as Rico Phillips received the Willie O'Ree Community Hero Award at the 2019 NHL Awards. I was so touched by this firefighter turned hockey coach's remarks about why it was so meaningful to him to teach low-income kids who aren't typically exposed to this expensive sport to nonetheless skate and play. His "why": he was one of those kids. As a young Black child from modest means, Phillips learned to play hockey thanks to the mentorship he received from older kids and coaches.

I reached out to him to learn more about his journey and was thrilled the day he appeared on the other end of a Zoom call. I asked him: "What motivates you?"

"There's always been a fire within me that wants to give of myself to others, through my actions and through my words," he said. Phillips says that his passion for hockey *defines* him but also motivates him to see beyond himself, moving him to make this sport available to kids who may not have thought to or cannot save for skates and equipment. "Kids who look like me don't typically have a place in hockey. I want to show them that, like me, they can be part of this community. So, the first lesson I teach them is how to fall down. Hockey is like life, sometimes you fall down, and then you get up."

The Slay It Forward share is motivated by an intrinsic desire to share your skills, knowledge, or expertise with others. Dan McAdams, the Henry Wade Rogers Professor in the Department of Psychology at Northwestern University, confirms that the most "highly generative" people, those who are motivated to contribute to *and* impact future generations, are deeply embedded in social contexts that are meaningful to them and keep them meaningfully engaged.

Like Phillips, I'm most driven by this type of share. When I'm presenting onstage or simply speaking casually to others about the topics I most value, I feel like I've arrived at my intersection of happiness and meaning. For me, slaying it forward by sharing my skills with others is *my* sweet spot.

My friend Hannah feels similarly. Once a week, she volunteers as an art docent at a local elementary school and says, "I get to teach kids about art while playing with paint and glitter. What gets better than that?"

John, a professional photographer, shares his knowledge and trade through his local Boys & Girls Club. "Being there for these kids is the best part of my week," he said. "I get to share something with them that I love to do that they aren't necessarily learning at school or exposed to at home. And"—

he laughed—"they give me really honest feedback that I don't get from colleagues in my field. My photography has actually improved since taking the advice of this group of fourteen-year-olds."

For years, Los Angeles chef Diep Tran has hosted Tet, or Vietnamese New Year, parties centered on making banh chung—sticky rice cakes. In a story in *The New York Times*, Tran said, "Tet can be such a heteronormative space, and it's usually very conservative." Over the years, her teaching parties, which began at home with a small group of Vietnamese American friends, have substantially grown in size to include hundreds of women, alongside their children, sisters, and mothers, sharing stories and scooping rice into beautifully wrapped banana leaf parcels that they can take home and share with loved ones. She emphasized in the article that the purpose of the Banh Chung Collective, as she now refers to the annual party, is to create a space that builds connections among women and people of color, and affirms queer identities.

Sharing motivated by Slaying It Forward looks like:

○ Teaching and tutoring.
○ Mentoring.
○ Inspiring.
○ Relaying knowledge and skills in any variety of ways.

THE "SOUNDING BOARD" SHARE

One of Lacy's initial motivators for sharing her animal prints at a local art show was to receive critical feedback to help inform and improve her craft. "I was incredibly nervous that first show," she remembered, "but I treated it as a learning opportunity. And I really did learn a lot! The feedback I received helped me refine my art for the next show and the next after that."

The Sounding Board share is motivated by an intrinsic desire to improve your craft/skill/knowledge/expertise. In other words, sharing for feedback allows you an opportunity to level up your unicorn for the next trek of your journey. Natalie Nixon, PhD, author of *The Creativity Leap*, compared this type of share with "oxygenating your ideas, giving them air and light. They might not be on point, you may be off, but when you share your work in progress, you learn. And from there, you can return to the work, delve back in, and start again."

Many creatives of all types rely heavily on "sound boarding" their work to help them in the revision process—like Uni Tiffany, who solicits feedback from her friends and family by asking them to taste-test recipes she's developing for her cookbook. "That's how you get the insights to help you leap forward," affirmed Nixon. The Sounding Board and Slay It Forward shares easily go hand in hand; any improvements based on feedback you receive add value to whatever special gift you pay forward to others.

Sharing motivated by the desire to be or have a Sounding Board looks like:

o Welcoming constructive criticism and embracing opportunities to improve.
o Workshopping ideas and receiving feedback.
o Asking for notes.
o Forming a group "crit" or recital.
o Sharing and co-creating to build on ideas and make them better.
o A willingness to revise or course correct.

THE "SERVICE" SHARE

As I was writing this chapter, I was invited to speak on a conference panel about mental health during the pandemic with Karolina Kurkova, the supermodel turned entrepreneur. When the moderator gently nudged her to share her adventures in modeling, she elegantly pivoted: "I'd rather talk about making an impact." She went on to share with the audience that within days after her city's shelter-in-place order was issued at the onset of the pandemic, she partnered with her friend, fellow mom and designer Ashley Liemer, to create Masks for All, an initiative that produces sustainable, nonmedical cloth masks to help ensure as many people as possible can protect themselves.

"As moms," she said, "we were inspired to contribute our skills to help our communities flatten the curve while donating proceeds to Feeding America, whose work is essential to the fight against hunger."

Closer to home, my kids' soccer coach Samir Sarkar and his wife, Jen, started a fundraiser called Save the Unicorn after their son Carter was diagnosed with Sanfilippo, a rare disease. Samir said to me, "When we found out that Carter was a rare unicorn, this was the day that forever changed our family." In response, they began acting in service to other families with children suffering from genetic diseases. To date, their fundraising efforts have raised awareness and more than one million dollars on social media.

The Service share is motivated by an intrinsic desire to act generously and in service to other people and your community (as opposed to filling an obligation). This is a feel-good share already, and "serving" comes with an additional health benefit. In an article in *The New York Times* titled "Who Helps Out in a Crisis?" Femida Handy, PhD, professor of nonprofit studies at the University of Pennsylvania, found that there was one big difference between people who do service and those who aren't as generous: "They live longer," she said of the service group. She reiterated that this finding controlled for factors including health, wealth, and education. Handy explained to me on a call that "doing good and helping others actually changes you physiologically and neurologically." In other words, acting in service to others improves your mental and physical health. "It can reduce inflammation and stress and light up the same part of the brain as when we eat a lot of chocolate," she said. In research recently completed with her colleague Sara Konrath, Handy found that giving seems to have a profound impact on the body; people who do good are even rated as more attractive by strangers. "Our research actually did show that prosocial people who do good actually look good"—she smiled—"and they tend to be happier."

Sharing motivated by Service looks like:

- Volunteering and board services.
- Delivering goods and supplies.
- Organizing "give back" drives.
- Running a local charity or church group.
- Aiding with school and community fundraisers.
- Service hours at your community library, food bank, or parks.
- (Slaying It Forward counts, too.)

THE "SHOWCASE" SHARE

Scrolling through Instagram, I resonated with the comments of a woman named Kasey, who posted: "I intentionally have been sharing my poetry with friends, although I consider the works not done and previously would've kept such unfinished things to myself. In allowing others to see me 'imperfectly' I feel I have offered my loved ones a way to see me, and thus themselves, in an increasingly authentic way."

The Showcase share is a close cousin of the Sounding Board share but is less about feedback and more motivated by an intrinsic desire to share your authentic self with the world—to be seen, heard, and known for your special skills or hidden talents.

Lara Adekoya was working in the West Hollywood Nordstrom shoe department when COVID-19 hit, and overnight, she was forced to pivot her career. No one was buying stilettos in a quarantine! Rather than spend "all my time on LinkedIn trying to perfect my résumé," Adekoya said to me, she decided to truly pivot and pursue a longtime love . . . for French baking. She got to work combining her entrepreneurial spirit with her natural ability to make good connections, to launch Fleurs et Sel, a business that creates sweet treats made in small batches. "I've always loved to cook and nurture others in all ways, including food. By nature, I am someone who values human connection and sharing with others. During the early days of quarantine and the stay-at-home orders, I yearned for a way to connect with my community. Baking cookies was not only therapeutic; it became a vehicle for spreading love and bringing comfort to others, all while making quarantine a little sweeter," she explained.

I wondered if her move away from designer shoes toward brown sugar surprised anyone.

"Early on I delivered cookies to some of my loyal Nordstrom customers to reconnect during the pandemic. At first I think they were surprised when I handed them a box of chocolate chip cookies rather than a new pair of Guccis"—she laughed—"but many of those customers quickly became the solid base of my cookie community."

When we allow others to see us more fully, we appear more real and authentic, and also, in some cases, more attractive.

"I started to like my boss a lot more when our office went virtual," admitted Uni Jakki. "Suddenly, on our Zoom meeting calls I could see that my very buttoned-up manager had a vintage Singer sewing machine in the back corner of his home office. Turns out, his creative outlet is sewing costumes for our local community theater. I would have never known this about him if I hadn't seen his private, home space. My manager has made huge gains in the 'cool' department!"

Uni Zoe had a similar experience when she stumbled across her neighbor's "ugly vegetable" posts on social media. "I've lived right next door to Ed for five years," she told me over a FaceTime call from her front porch. "I've known that he does crisis PR, but I didn't know anything about this other side of him. On weekends, I see him out in his garden but didn't realize that he purposely grows 'ugly' vegetables like giant zucchini and misshapen carrots and peppers that he photographs and posts online. Apparently, #uglyvegetables is a thing, and now I know it's *Ed's thing*. Wanna see?" Zoe pointed the camera on her phone toward Ed's lawn. "Over there, do you see all those giant zucchini? You gotta love it!"

The true beauty of the Showcase share is that your Unicorn Space draws people to you, and it acts as an invitation to others to reveal their authentic selves. When you let yourself be known, when you express and share yourself outwardly with the world, you can be the source of someone else's comfort, joy, inspiration, and gain.

Sharing motivated by Showcasing looks like:

○ Hosting a house party to reveal your hidden talents.
○ Connecting to others through your special skills.
○ Surprising others with a fuller version of yourself.

IT'S ALL ABOUT CONNECTIONS

So, what's your type? What drives you to share your creative expression, your Unicorn Space, with the world? Whichever type you feel most pulled toward today (because your intrinsic motivation may change as you reach your goals and set new ones), recognize that all seven types have one thing in common: they create meaningful connections and according to author Mia Birdsong, "Creativity plus connection creates this kind of alchemy where [whatever you are creating] expands."

This got me thinking. Was there a way to reverse engineer one's Unicorn Space by identifying the intersection between one's creativity with the best community, or space, to match it? I thought back to my interview with Justina Blakeney, design personality and author of *Jungalow: Decorate Wild*, who talked enthusiastically about the importance of creating spaces that you feel connected to and that give you permission to experiment and further create.

Lightbulb moment! Once you identify a value-based curiosity that you want to actively pursue (your "what") and how far you want to take it (your "when") along with your intrinsic motivation for getting there (your "why"), then determine how and in what type of environment you plan to share it (your "where"). This is how you arrive at your Unicorn Space.

POP QUIZ
Where's Your Unicorn Space?

If you had an uninterrupted afternoon free to pursue that thing you love to do, in which environment would you most likely be doing it? (Once you have your answer, refer to the key to identify the shared community you're most drawn to.)

> **A.** At a craft store taking an archival scrapbooking class with your sister
>
> **B.** Meeting your training buddy for your Sunday long run
>
> **C.** Building communal art with your Burning Man buddies
>
> **D.** Communing with your spiritual community or leading a support group
>
> **E.** Mentoring eight-year-olds in the hockey rink
>
> **F.** Submitting early drafts of your memoir to your writing group (for the first time!)
>
> **G.** Organizing a "save the sea lions" beach cleanup
>
> **H.** Practicing for the company talent show (guess what, you can sing!)

KEY

A: Spin-off share (legacy); **B:** Show Up and Support share (accountability); **C** and **D:** Serendipitous Community share (community building) and (healing); **E:** Slay It Forward share (skills); **F:** Sounding Board share (feedback); **G:** Service share (giving back); **H:** Showcase share (to be known)

NOW, COMPLETE YOUR CREATIVITY COMMITMENT . . .

My name is _____. My motivating values include _____. Today and moving forward, I give myself permission to live by my values. I allow my values to inform my day-to-day curiosities, some of which are _____. I am committed to explore deeper and pursue activities and interests that are in alignment with my values. I plan to take my open pursuit as far as _____ (think BHAAG). My first actionable, small step toward "leveling up" and reaching my goal is _____. My date for completing this next step is _____. (Remember: setting a date keeps you in active pursuit.) The type of share that most resonates with me is _____, and the community I intend to connect with along my journey is _____.

FAQS ABOUT SHARING YOURSELF WITH THE WORLD

Before we wrap up this chapter, I want to loop back to the top three questions I'm frequently asked about sharing your Unicorn Space with the world, in case they're coming up for you, too.

Q: What does it mean to "share" yourself with the world? Does it mean posting an image of yourself crossing the Ironman finish line?

A: Not quite. Sharing your creativity is not about living your life through Instagram Stories. It's not about counting, competing, or engaging in activities just for the external praise or the bragging rights. **Purposeful sharing is intrinsically motivated.** You extend yourself outward because it's inherently satisfying and meaningful to *you*. And by sharing a special piece of yourself, those people who witness, experience, learn, or receive from you benefit in some kind of way. So then, sharing yourself with the world means inviting others into *your* world. It means sharing your unique skill set, talents, and interests. It means pursuing and unpacking your curiosities with a community of people (small or large) in a manner that allows you to contribute to something outside yourself and that fosters further connection and engagement with your community.

Q: Do I *have* to share my Unicorn Space with the world?

A: Another good question and one that I received recently from my friend Dave, a talent manager who serves as an adviser to emerging musicians and music producers. Dave's very work is to empower and enable people to share their creativity with the world, and he's got a full life of his own—a huge job at the office and another at home, where he's the primary caregiver of his daughter (along with a lot of help, as he's the first to admit!). By our cultural definition, Dave has "achieved." And yet what many people don't know is how he spends his "off hours" pursuing an intrinsically motivated goal.

Dave shared with me: "I represent creatives, so my job is

'creative,' but my true outlet for expressing myself is through my own music." Including, as it turns out, playing drums alongside his teacher, a retired jazz legend. When I asked when I could catch his next show, he smiled and shook his head. "So much of my life is in the public eye. My music is private."

I argued, "But don't you want to share your love for music with others—your friends, family, your clients?"

He considered my question and then returned, "Why can't I have something that's *just* mine?"

I told Dave that of course he could do whatever he wanted, but that what I'd learned through my own observations is that time spent on pursuits we quietly enjoy privately do not produce the same positive results as when a pursuit is shared. Of the individuals I've spoken to, those who share their creative pursuits with family, friends, their community—or the world at large—report greater happiness and meaning. I kidded with Dave, "You don't actually plan on taking your music to the grave, do you? I'm sure your daughter would love to see your killer drum solo." He laughed and reconsidered that for his upcoming milestone birthday he "might" perform for friends and family . . . and you'd better believe I'm going to follow up with Dave for an invitation.

If your dream is only about you, it's too small.

—AVA DUVERNAY, AWARD-WINNING FILM DIRECTOR

Q: What if I don't share my Unicorn Space with the world?

A: To best answer this question, I want you to consider the Case of the Almost Unpublished Bestseller.

If you have children, and even if you don't, you likely remember seeing or hearing about the mega-popular children's book *for adults* released in 2011 with the memorable title *Go the F*ck to Sleep*. As the mother of three, I can practically recite the book verbatim from memory because the naughty parent prose like "Hell no you can't go to the bathroom, you know where you can go—the f*ck to sleep!" is similar, if not nearly identical, to the language that I've used on my own kids. (Yes, I'm guilty of dropping f-bombs at bedtime.) The author of this instant number one *New York Times* bestseller that has since sold three million copies worldwide and been translated into forty languages is novelist, screenwriter, and humorist Adam Mansbach. I tracked him down via Zoom at his home in Berkeley, California.

I explained that I was writing a book about creativity and I was interested to know, "What sparked this unconventional creative project of yours . . . and were you surprised by the reaction from the world?"

Without hesitation, Mansbach answered in the uncensored fashion he's become known for: "You know, that was a project that was never really intended to be a project. It was just me f*cking around. But at the time my daughter Vivien was two [years old], and going to sleep was not high on her list of priorities. I was in Michigan, away from my family for a short stint teaching a summer writing course and living with a bunch of other writers, sharing a house together. We were just all standing around and I made a joke about writing a children's book called *Go the F*ck to Sleep*. When I got home a week or two later, I sat down one afternoon and wrote it, even though I didn't necessarily think there was an audience for it. I read it at a couple of family gatherings and got a lot of laughs [the Sounding Board share], and I pitched it to my friend Johnny, who was in independent publishing, and he thought it was funny. But when I sent it to my agent, he was like, 'This is hilarious, but there's probably no wide market for it.'

"Despite our fear that the book would only be funny to other shitty parents like us, Johnny and I decided to publish the book through his small, independent publishing house.

"Several months before it was slated to go on sale, I did a reading at a museum in Philly. I'd come straight from my daughter's third birthday party, and at the last minute, I decided to read *Go the F*ck to Sleep*. I read it to about two hundred people, and afterward, many of them asked where they could buy the book. I was like, 'Well, it hasn't even been printed yet, but you can preorder it.' So, the next morning on a whim I thought to check the Amazon preorder page, and the book was climbing in sales. By the end of the week, it was number one on Amazon. I was like, 'This shit is crazy.' One week passes, two weeks and three weeks pass, and it's firmly at number one, and it's not moving from that position, and Johnny and I are freaking out.

"When the book finally published on Father's Day, it debuted at number one on the *New York Times* bestseller list, where it stayed for over a year."

Without intending to, Mansbach had sparked a fire. His message hit a raw, sleep-deprived nerve that resonated with a large community, far beyond the "shitty parents" he'd originally thought he'd only connect with, but with many parents and soon-to-be-parents all over the world who felt similarly and enthusiastically shared his message within their own new-parent communities (the Serendipitous Community share).

"I honestly didn't have any expectations. I thought that there was an outside chance that it might have a large audience, but that wasn't something I was banking on."

What if Mansbach hadn't acted on his creative impulse? What if he hadn't actively pursued his curiosity by putting words on paper? What if he hadn't bravely shared his story with that first audience of two hundred, which has expanded across the globe and produced two bestselling sequels?

Consider Mansbach's cautionary tale and ask yourself: *If I fail to clear the path to my Unicorn Space, what am I losing? If I fail to share my Unicorn Space, what is my intimate and larger community losing?*

You. That special thing you do.

Believe past the limitation of possibility, and rest assured that there is an audience for your unique expression, whatever that is. If you're unsure what creative space you fall into, take it from Mansbach, who started a publishing revolution that's inspired other writers and artists to follow their own unconventional path. His advice: "Create spaces where none exist."

Face Your Fears

//

Connect to Others in a "Ready, Set, Go" Mindset

FEAR:
THE GREATEST ACTION INHIBITOR

I asked more than one thousand women over the course of one year—"When you think about pursuing something just for you, what presents the biggest obstacle?" My survey produced these top answers:

○ **Time.** As in, *I don't have the time.* (Flip back to chapter 4, "Permission to be Unavailable.")

○ **Uncertainty.** As in, *Beyond work, parenting, and running a household, I don't know what I'd do for myself, or what's worth sharing.* (Flip back to chapter 7, "Identify a Curiosity.")

○ **Partner support.** As in, *My partner isn't 100 percent on board.* (Flip forward to chapter 11, "Enlist Your Partner.")

○ **Fear.** As in:

- *What if I fail?*
- *Don't finish?*
- *What if my friends/colleagues/community and the crowd judge me?*
- *Or worse, reject me?*
- *What if it's too late [i.e., I'm too old] to actively pursue or start something new?*
- *What if I'm holding myself back because I don't believe I'm as good as I used to be?*
- *What if I don't meet my own expectations?*

Across the board, my interviewees named fear as one of the biggest action inhibitors to pursuing their Unicorn Space. My friend Jill summed up her own fear this way: "I will never be as good as I was in my past, so beginning again feels really scary. What if I suck? I worry that whatever I try, someone else is already doing it better. Honestly, I don't want to be at square one again."

Do you hear in Jill's voice how fear can easily lead to *inaction*, to remaining an object at rest? If you're not careful, fear will hold you in the idea phase or at the starting line indefinitely. To help us better understand how we can break through our own—often self-imposed and self-sabotaging—limitations and engage in active and new pursuits, I reached out to Vanessa Kroll Bennett, the founder of Dynamo Girl, an after-school program that tackles fear head-on by building girls' self-esteem through sports and puberty education.

CONSIDER:
THE CASE OF THE TOILET REVELATION

Bennett was working in the area of security and crisis management post 9/11 when she became pregnant with her first child and left the workforce. It wasn't a decision she took lightly. Four kids and eleven years later, she recalls one ordinary morning when her four-year-old daughter, Zion, ambled into Bennett's bathroom to find her mother sitting on the toilet.

"She looked at me and said pointedly, 'Mommy, Eden's mommy is an eye doctor. What are *you* going to be when you grow up?' I remember just staring at her as she stood there. The truth was that I had been thinking about returning to work and what that might look like, but I hadn't vocalized it. And here was Zion asking the question as if she'd gotten into my brain the way kids can magically do sometimes. I responded, 'Well, I don't know yet what I'm going to be when I grow up,' and she smiled and said gently, 'Okay, Mommy. Let me know when you know.' And with that, she walked out of the bathroom.

"What struck me at the time was the generosity in her question," remembered Bennett. "There was no judgment in her words. She didn't assume that I had already missed the boat. This tiny person believed there was still as much endless possibility for me as there was for her. I could still become a grown-up. I could still fulfill my dreams. As far as she was concerned, my life was totally open-ended."

Bennett continued, "At that time none of Zion's adult female role models had careers. Most moms she knew—outside of Eden's mommy, the eye doctor—stayed home with their kids. And for some reason, Zion just felt that there was *more for me*. And so, this got me thinking. Did I want to return to what I knew, what I'd done before? Or could I imagine a world where I could be successful doing something else? Creating something new that was just mine?"

> This tiny person believed there was still as much endless possibility for me as there was for her.

Prompted by her daughter's innocent inquiry, Bennett gave herself permission to dream. "And about four months later," Bennett continued, "Zion came back to me and asked me the question again: 'Mommy, what are you going to be when you grow up?' Here again was this little pipsqueak with her hands on her hips, as if to say, *I'm holding you accountable. What are you going to do because I expect big things of you?* She wasn't going to let me off the hook." Bennett laughed.

"This time, I had an answer for her. After considering my motivating values—honesty, empathy, and resilience—I'd landed on my next career move: using sports to help young girls find their voices and build their self-esteem. When I explained to Zion this concept for Dynamo Girl, her immediate reaction was: *How can I help?*"

Bennett credits Zion for inspiring her to create and build Dynamo Girl, and as such, she was one of ten elementary school girls who made up the pilot program. Eight years later, Zion is still a vital contributor to Bennett's successful company, now coaching classes and running workshops alongside her mother. "She was four when she asked me that question: *What are you going to be, Mom?* Now she's twelve, and the company continues to grow as she does. Already, I think she sees herself as the inheritor of Dynamo Girl, though what I keep telling her is that you don't have to take over for me. You can do or be anything. After all, she's the one who taught me that.

"I think for so many women like myself," reflected Bennett, "there's this fear of having missed all the opportunities or that it's too late. I'm not enough. I haven't done enough. I don't have the credentials. I don't have the ability. I don't have the time. I don't have the support. It's been truly the most incredible gift for my daughter to say to me: Oh, no, you're not done yet. There's more to come."

BEWARE THE TEN-YEAR FEAR GAP

Comparable to the "pay gap" that disproportionately affects women after their first child is born and grows larger with each additional child, the following trend emerged in my interviews: Those women who'd sidelined their unique talents and interests in order to focus more time and energy on their families felt the "passion gap" alongside a "fear gap" widen with each child and every passing year. Those women who'd relinquished their Unicorn Space for more than ten years felt proportionally much more reticent, and often fearful, to rediscover and reclaim it.

Dr. Sheryl Gonzalez Ziegler, author of *Mommy Burnout*, said to me, "I work with so many women who experience this gap, who, after reaching a certain point in their career or after their kids have gotten older and less dependent, they wake up one day and think, *What happened to the past decade?* When I hear women say this, I challenge them to reevaluate. If your kids or your partner or your work no longer fulfill you alone, what's your dream *today*? Not the dream from ten years ago, but your dream in the present? Take your power back by taking ownership of your past choices and own the choices that you will make moving forward."

READY. SET. GO!!!!

FEAR FRAMEWORK STEP 1:
GET *READY* WITH PREPARATION

When you become an "object at rest" for too long, your mindset can become fixed in fear. *I'm too old to try X, Y, Z. I'd be crazy to try A, B, C.* To help combat these limiting beliefs, I reached out to someone who has faced fear every single day of his career: Robert Harward, a retired United States Navy SEAL and a former Deputy Commander of the United States Central Command, who reframes apprehension this way: "Instead of telling yourself, I'd be crazy to [skydive, race a car, etc.], think of it this way—I'd be crazy *not* to [skydive, race a car, etc.]. Life is short, so put the rubber to the road." Harward loves a good metaphor, but he doesn't mince words. And I wholeheartedly agree with him—we each ought to adopt or reclaim an object in motion, "crazy not to" mindset in order to take those actionable steps forward to move us *through* fear and *toward* our next goal. Just because you haven't accomplished a skill or driven a race car *yet* does not mean that you cannot or will not reach your goal. Carol Dweck, pioneering researcher and bestselling author of *Mindset,* says that the empowering idea of "not yet" gives you a path into the future. Your "yet" is coming.

And yet . . .

Putting yourself out there, up front and on the big stage of life, can be anxiety-provoking, if not paralyzing. In conducting research for this project, I randomly surveyed one hundred people on social media and asked: What do you do in the face of fear? The resounding top answer was: Prepare.

As in:

○ Do my research.
○ Study.
○ Consult with others (who have done it before).
○ Practice over and over again.
○ Repeat affirmations/get in a good headspace.
○ Meditate and follow mindfulness exercises.
○ Allocate resources (time, money, materials, or equipment needed).

I respond deeply to the idea that preparation leads to greater effectiveness, in whatever form it takes for you. Furthermore, I've experienced firsthand that when you combine a growth mindset *with* preparation, you position yourself with a readiness that can actively tackle fear.

When I was invited by my editor to narrate the audio version of my first book, I knew I should have felt grateful for the opportunity to broadcast my message to a wider audience of audiobook consumers, but frankly, my gratitude was eclipsed by panic. As I may have mentioned, I don't like the sound of my own voice (sharp commands, *sir!*), and I just couldn't imagine a world in which I would read three hundred pages of my own words—out loud!—in a windowless, cramped sound booth with a producer listening for and, no question, flagging all my errors. *Can you read that line again? And one more time, please?*

I choked: What if I can't get past the first paragraph without messing up? What if the producer hates the sound of my voice, too? What if I'm thrown out of the booth when they realize I'm no Kat Medina?

I called my husband and unloaded, hoping he'd give me the kind of commiserative spousal permission that would enable my fear and let me off the hook. "So, I should just pass on it, right?" I said this more like a foregone conclusion than a question. Seth, my supreme advocate, didn't go for it. He said, "Don't take a pass. Dare to suck."

Wait, what? Suck?

Still on the hook for this assignment, I wanted to scream, and then go hide in a closet with a king-size bag of M&M's and stay there. Instead, I took a deep breath and flipped through my mental toolbox and pulled out two of my most trusted and reliable tools in the face of fear—a mindset of *I'm not a great narrator . . . yet.* And airtight preparation.

By nine o'clock the next morning, I was driving to Studio City for my first amateur voice-over lesson. I wandered into what looked like a poorly attended PTA meeting with folding chairs and fluorescent lighting, and where I was soon introduced to a commercial actor hoping to land the voice of Charlie, the StarKist tuna; a woman auditioning for the role of a rat in an animated kids' film; and a bleary-eyed sound engineer who had newborn twins at home. I silently acknowledged my jitters and then took my turn anyway. Around the circle we went, over and over again, reading our lines and welcoming comments (the Sounding Board share). I learned how to focus on my cadence and pacing and speak with "soft drama" and "high drama," indicated by jazz hand gestures from the tuna guy. While grueling, by the end of first day, I felt noticeably less afraid.

"You can totally do this," the woman trying out for the animated movie assured me. "At least you can speak in English. I have to pull off rodent-speak."

For five days, I went to my voice-over lesson in the morning and at night once the kids were in bed, I practiced my delivery way past midnight. By the end of the week, I felt ready. On the drive over to the recording studio, I listened to one of my favorite Billie Eilish songs to put me in a good headspace, and I entered the audio booth with my head held high. Stephanie, the producer, welcomed me with a nod at her Apple Watch. "It's going to be a long day, and we need to stay on time."

I felt my buoyancy begin to deflate. "But"—she brightened slightly—"I will be here to help you. If you stumble or skip a word, I'll flag it. Or if you need to slow down or add a smile to your voice, I'll raise my hand and jump in to coach you."

Okay, I resigned, and stepped into the audio booth, daring to suck but hoping for better. And you know what, I did pretty well! Although, had I known then that I'd be standing for eight hours in cramped shoes and with limited pee breaks, I may have foregone the voice-over lessons and just hired Kat Medina.

> If you wait for the fear to go away, the opportunity will go away, too.
>
> —LESLIE BLODGETT, CEO AND CREATOR OF BAREMINERALS AND AUTHOR OF *PRETTY GOOD ADVICE*

Preparation is a top-pocket tool that works for just about everyone, amateurs and experts alike. Take neuroanatomist and brain researcher Jill Bolte Taylor, who, I'd read, practiced her powerful TED Talk on brain recovery two hundred times in private before she delivered it onstage. Two hundred times! This psychological technique is known as "mental rehearsal," and research shows that carefully rehearsing potential fear-inducing moments before they happen can help reduce fear.

After careful preparation ahead of time, when the inevitable moments arrive—on the TED Talk stage, in the sound booth, or wherever they happen to be for you—they don't come as much of a surprise or a shock.

FEAR FRAMEWORK STEP 2:
GET *SET* WITH SPIRITUAL FRIENDSHIPS

For me, a "dare to suck" mindset in combination with preparation are very powerful devices for thwarting fear and anxiety, and I use both with regularity. Still—*caution ahead!*—it is important not to get stuck in the preparation. Do your readiness prep work and then set yourself up for your next step forward. The dictionary definition of *set* is to "put or bring into a specified state," and this is where spiritual friendships come into play. These are the friends who help to put you into an empowered, "I can face my fear" state. Now understand, your spiritual friendships aren't necessarily with people whom you've known a long time. They can, in fact, be fleeting. What's crucial about these connections is that they come into your life at the *right* time. They are those people who have your back when shit gets real, and they can appear from anywhere and everywhere—as I discovered along my voice-over journey. Who would have thought that Charlie, the StarKist tuna, would have been "my guy," the friend I needed most in that moment?

As I define them, spiritual friends are those who provide you with the uplifting and loving support you sometimes need to untangle yourself from the tentacles of self-doubt and fear that threaten to stall your movement forward. In addition to arming you with fear-busting courage, your spiritual friends encourage you to share your special talents, hidden gifts, and knowledge with the world because they truly *see* you and what you're capable of. The power of your spiritual friends is to help guide you back to your power, and along the way, these friendships can also serve as a source of great joy and meaningful connection.

Whenever I travel for work, I ask a spiritual friend to come along. Zoe, my longtime friend and Uni, is often my plus-one. I've lost track of how many queen-size hotel beds we've shared over the years.

"Why not get separate rooms or separate beds?" Seth will ask.

"Because," I say, "the research is clear that face-to-face interaction and social connectedness can be beneficial to an individual's mental and physical health. Basically, Zoe helps to keep me grounded if I start to spin out, and she always makes sure my hair looks good."

Through my own personal experience and backed by my conversations with hundreds of people, I have identified two types of spiritual friendships worth cultivating in the face of stress, anxiety, and fear:

- **Spiritual Friend #1: Sharing the Journey.** These are the friends who closely identify with your journey because they share a similar goal. They will encourage you to continually show up and share yourself with the world, especially when fear and doubt get in the way. My voice-over friends fall into this category.
- **Spiritual Friend #2: Supporting the Journey.** The second type of spiritual friend is someone who's expressing their creativity in their own unique way but who nonetheless is inspired by you and who supports your journey by either offering you loving

words of encouragement and advice, providing you with resources and connections to help you reach your goal, or giving you their valuable time.

I met Brenda Janowitz at a bookstore when I was publishing my first book. We bonded over the fact that we both started our careers as lawyers. She told me that she had always wanted to be a novelist, but external pressures had made law school a more attractive pursuit. "I dabbled in my own writing on the side," she told me over a Zoom chat a month or so later, "but I never really committed to it because—as you also know—when you're a lawyer the hours are punishing, you're always exhausted, and then you're trying to squeeze in a social life, too."

Even though Janowitz admitted she was unhappy with her career choice, she said she would have likely continued on the same path had it not been for the intervention of her best friend, Shawn Morris.

"Over the years, Shawn had heard me say things like, 'I really want to take a writing class'; 'It's too expensive'; 'I don't have the time.' . . . I always had an excuse. So, for my thirtieth birthday, she said to me: 'No more talking about writing. You're actually going to do it.' She'd organized a group gift with a bunch of my close girlfriends from college to send me to a real writing class."

Surround yourself with people who provide you with uplifting support, empower you to find and use your voice, and encourage you to share your special gifts with the world.

Janowitz recounted how touched she was by the gesture and how excited she felt at the prospect of joining a writing community. And yet: "I remember thinking: *How can I commit to this? Will I really be able to do this?*"

Shawn helped to quell some of her fears by encouraging her every step of the way (*Don't forget: writing class every Tuesday night!*) and by offering to read some of her earliest drafts. "There was something about dedicating one night a week to writing that really set me on my path," remembered Janowitz (the Show Up share). "Also, I started sending my friends pages to read to show them my progress, and we'd talk about them and laugh together, like, *aren't we so clever*" (the Sounding Board share).

Encouraged by her best friend, Janowitz kept at it—and a year later, she'd written three hundred pages and finished her first novel. Since then, she's completed and published a total of six novels and has a contract for books seven and eight on the heels of her most recent success. Looking back, she said, "I'm not sure I would have written my first book without that writing class Shawn gifted me." The permission slip to pursue her dream changed the trajectory of her life. "When I look back on the photograph of me on the night of my thirtieth birthday, I think about how dramatically my life changed from that moment. Once I started writing and self-identifying as a writer, I felt like I'd found myself again."

> There's something so wonderful about the idea
> that this may be the day your life
> will change forever.

—BRENDA JANOWITZ, AUTHOR OF *THE GRACE KELLY DRESS*

CREATE YOUR CONNECTION COALITION

My interviews revealed that spiritual friends of all forms (childhood besties, college roommates, our neighbors and children) often act as the strongest antidote to fear, giving us permission to begin again. When you think about the people in your life today, the ones you're surrounded by and routinely interact with, do they fall into this category—people who provide you with uplifting support; empower you to find and use your voice; and encourage you to share your special talents, gifts, and knowledge with the world? If you haven't already, I invite you to intentionally create a coalition of spiritual friends.

I seek out new friendships in all areas of my life. One of my oldest friends, Sarah, likes to joke that I'm a friendship hoarder. There is some truth to her allegation, but what it really comes down to is that I just like having people in my life. And since you never know where you might find your next friend, I try to keep my heart open and meet as many people as I can. Over the years, I've come to recognize that friendships have varied layers of support. For example, if I'm seeking advice about my kids, I call Lauren. If I need ideas for travel or infusing more fun into my life, I reach out to Bianca. If I want to go deep and talk about the existential meaning of life, I turn to Zoe (in our queen-size bed). I've even gone so far as to create a master list of my friendships broken down by type of support. I know this may sound super type A (guilty!).

When I started exploring the intersection of creativity, identity, and meaning that would become this book, I assembled a group of spiritual friends to join me on my journey. Many of these friends had supported me for years and have talked me off the scary ledge of book publishing many times. They are my core group, my inner circle, and they comprise the base of my Uni coalition. And with nearly every interview I've done in connection with this project, I meet more people whom I now consider spiritual friends because our goals are similarly aligned and we support one another's unique expression of creativity.

FRIENDSHIP COALITIONS CAN CHANGE

If you haven't already, designate a spiritual friend—or two or three or four—who will either metaphorically or quite literally hold your hand and keep you steady as you take steps forward and "level up" toward your goals. Think of this process as akin to building a board of directors for your business or organization, except in this case, create a coalition of spiritual friends to support you on your Unicorn Space journey. This coalition may change over time as goals are met and your journey takes a new turn. For now, given your current goal, designate who's in and who may need to be sidelined. This may sound cold, but just as important as naming those friends who are looking out for your best interests is identifying those who don't always have your back or who simply don't appreciate the goal you've set for yourself.

"When I first started thinking that I might want to do this, it was a very delicate dream," said Sandy Zimmerman, remembering back to her hesitation to first apply for *American Ninja Warrior*. "Luckily, I called up one of my best friends and I told her: 'I'm thinking about doing this really crazy thing. I know it's gonna sound nuts. It's called *American Ninja Warrior*.' And I told her how it worked. And she says, 'Sounds amazing! What can I do to help?' I remember thinking at that point, if I had gone to the wrong person, who may have said—*Sandy, you're crazy, you're never gonna hit a buzzer. You can't do that—you're a mother of three. Why did you set a goal like that?*—I honestly think my story would have ended there. It was such a defining moment to have a friend that says, *Yes, let's do it.* The support that women can give each other is so powerful."

Our dreams can be delicate, so you have to be careful with whom you share them first.

—SANDY ZIMMERMAN

Back to Janowitz—"I feel really lucky that I made my dream my work, and over the years, I've found that sometimes people don't like that you're living your dreams. Some of your friends may get mad, even, like how dare you live your dream? And I realize that this is because they're not living their dreams. My best friend, Shawn, has always been supportive, but unfortunately, I've had to let some other friendships go."

Over the years, I, too, have chosen to let some friendships go once I acknowledged that the energy they brought to the relationship wasn't supportive or uplifting. Susan Jeffers, author of *Feel the Fear . . . and Do It Anyway: Dynamic Techniques for Turning Fear, Indecision and Anger into Power, Action and Love,* suggests we ask ourselves the following question: "Are [your friends] excited about the new you that is emerging, or would they prefer the company of the old you that you are outgrowing?"

Letting friendships go can be extremely painful, especially with people you've known the majority of your life. But here's the key: realizing your dreams is so much easier and more enjoyable when you're surrounded by people who sincerely support you. Jeffers adds, "It is amazingly empowering to have the support of a strong, motivated and inspirational group of people."

IS MY PARTNER ON MY TEAM?

What if after doing an honest inventory of those people who are the best fit for your coalition, you realize your partner's actions or reactions to your goal make them eligible to be cut? In short, what do you do when your partner isn't supportive of your Unicorn Space?

The short answer: I encourage you to look outside your partnership for spiritual friends. Our partners cannot and should not be expected to be our sole support. That said, if you are partnered, their support is an important piece of the puzzle, and I'll address that at length in the next chapter. But briefly for now, my observations revealed that within our partnerships and intimate relationships, when one or both people don't feel supported or permitted to pursue a passion outside the Three P's, many of these partnerships report persistent resentment, perceived unfairness, and a lack of personal fulfillment. More bluntly, in the face of a lopsided division of Unicorn Space, the very things that make us the happiest are what our partners resent most about us. And it goes both ways. Can you imagine?

The good news is that when couples *do* engage in collaborative dialogue and prioritize more equitable time for individual pursuits, this dynamic can shift dramatically, and often quickly. Getting your partner's support is optimal and still, Professor Teresa Seeman, PhD, of UCLA, reveals a nuance for women: "Earlier in life, being married—that relationship—is really key, but as you get older, friendships become that much more important and whether or not you're married is relatively less important."

FEAR FRAMEWORK STEP 3:
GO DO IT

Armed with a dare-to-suck mindset and after preparation (ready!) and enlisting at least one spiritual friend (set!), you ought to feel ready to bust through any lingering fear-based objections that stand between you and your goal and . . . GO! Well, not so fast. Before you get going, I want to provide you with one more tactic to help you in that eleventh-hour moment when you're about to metaphorically or literally walk on stage or start your engines . . . and you freeze.

For a dose of fear-inhibiting motivation that can act as the final nudge to propel you forward toward your goal, I reached out again to Robin Arzón, who speaks publicly at Fortune 500 company events about how she fearlessly left a successful six-figure career desk job to pursue a new adventure as VP of Fitness Programming and head instructor for Peloton. We met for a quick tea before her next workout. I asked her: "What would you tell people who are at their own starting line, about to embark on a new journey, and fear stops them from stepping forward?"

Arzón smiled broadly. "I'd tell them what my mother always said to me, 'you can *do*' when you make the choice to step forward. And the other thing I encourage people to do is: remember your own superhero narrative." In other words: recall your own successes! It sounds easy, she says, but it can be surprisingly tough. "When we're stuck in inertia, afraid to take the next step forward, we so quickly forget the times that we actually *had* momentum. I find that some of the most ambitious and accomplished women don't take the time to revisit their own superhero narrative when they confronted fear in the past and moved through it. They forget about the important plot points that got them to where they are now."

Arzón calls this practice of going back to step forward "ritualizing discomfort," and she believes that it can be transferable to any goal—applying for a new job, enrolling in a class, having a difficult conversation with a boss, or enlisting your partner's support of your Unicorn Space.

"When you think, *I could never do that*, you remember back to another page in your personal story when you overcame your fear or when you failed and got up again. The practice of remembering fear and trusting your struggle makes it easier to face again and again and again, whatever your current struggle," Arzón reflected. "Mediocrity can feel much safer and comfortable, but you lose an appetite for mediocrity when you've tasted your own power." Before she dashed off for ninety minutes of heart-pumping endurance cycling, she lifted up her aquamarine tank to reveal a tattoo on her rib cage that reads, *resilient stock*.

Tap into your resilience. Your superhero narrative.

So then, the aim isn't to become fearless, but adaptable in the face of fear. Through the practice of remembering, we cultivate immediate adaptability and long-term resilience. David Smith, PhD, Associate Professor of Sociology in the College of Leadership and Ethics at the United States Naval War College and a former Navy pilot, likens the practice of ritualizing discomfort, as Arzón describes it, to "exposure therapy." When we spoke, he referred to his personal experience of being asked to jump off the ten-meter board as part of the Naval Academy's annual training.

"I'm afraid of heights," Smith admitted, "but everyone has to do it, and it's terrifying. The only solution [to overcoming that fear] is to jump off the board and then do it over and over again. All the research on overcoming anxiety shows that what you're afraid of is almost irrelevant. To get 'unafraid,' to get calm in the presence of your fear, requires repeated exposure."

EXERCISE
Create a Ritual of Discomfort

Take a moment and travel back in your mind to a time when you were afraid to do something and you did it anyway. When you exposed yourself to fear, you jumped, and you survived. Jot your memory down in a journal or in the space provided here:

I'm remembering back to a time when I felt afraid to give a speech/ask for a raise/perform onstage/quit my job/ learn a new skill, etc. Fill in the blank with your experience: *I'm remembering back to a time when I felt afraid to*_____.

I remember feeling worried/scared/embarrassed/anxious/lacking confidence, etc. Fill in the blank with your emotional experience: *At the time, I remember feeling*

_____.

In the face of fear, I remember feeling relieved/elated/ proud/full of adrenaline/powerful, etc. when I accomplished my goal. Again, fill in the blank with your emotional experience *after* you confronted your fear: *When I accomplished my goal, I remember feeling* _____. *I celebrated by doing*

_____.

Put a pin in it! The next time you feel afraid to do something, remind yourself of how you felt in the past when you confronted and moved through your fear. Imagine feeling that way again as you actively pursue your new goal.

○ ○

BACK TO THE AUDIO BOOTH

When I was invited by my editor to narrate the audio version of this book, I remembered back to how I felt after that first full day of recording my first book. My feet were tired and I was cranky from low blood sugar, but otherwise, I felt like I could fly. Truly, I was elated knowing that I had done something hard, something I was initially averse (i.e., panicked) to, and I'd survived. More than that, I'd actually enjoyed myself and made a new spiritual friend in my producer, Stephanie, who, after listening to me advocate for gender equity for three hundred pages and over three full days, shared with me her own uncensored marriage story.

So this next time around, I said yes to my editor without hesitation, and I requested that Stephanie join me for round two. I arrived at the recording studio the day of the first read, mentally prepared and in a pair of New Balance wides with a fanny pack full of snacks. I knew what to expect because I'd already been "exposed" to this experience before. I had the kind of jitters that surface before any performance or deadline, but I wasn't afraid. I was ready to GO.

CONSIDER:
THE CASE OF FAST-FORWARD MOTION

Throughout this journey, where I've met so many inspiring people who've pursued their curiosities in spite of their fears, there's probably no one who has applied this three-step ready-set-go framework more than Renée Brinkerhoff—who, at the age of fifty-six and after raising four children into young adulthood, made a surprising and dramatic life-changing turn toward race car driving. Admittedly naïve about the predominantly all-male racing sport, Brinkerhoff embarked on a heroine's journey that has now taken her through countless landscapes over twenty thousand miles and across every continent in the world. To date, her nonprofit, Valkyrie Racing, has raised nearly a half million dollars to aid at-risk women and children, with a specific focus on fighting child trafficking.

I sought out an interview with Brinkerhoff, who appeared to personify my object-in-motion metaphor. I asked her about flipping the fear of failure in pursuing your passions: "What did you stand to lose if you *failed* to pursue your dream? And what was ultimately driving you, pun intended?"

"Looking back nearly eight years ago," she said easily, "it wasn't an *I want to* but an *I have to*. I heard a voice in my head saying, *I'm going to race a car.* And in that moment, I realized I'd been telling myself this for a long time and ignoring it. I married young and started having children right away, and I loved being a mother and a wife, but all the other things I'd aspired to as a young girl—they stopped. At fifty-six, I realized that I'd been putting myself on a shelf in a box for so long and I was gone. And with that voice prompting me, I knew I had to go find myself."

"And why racing?" I had to ask.

"It could have been anything, really, flying to the moon. I just needed to do *something*."

Brinkerhoff needed adventure. And speed.

"As a young child," she continued, "I'd traveled to foreign countries with my family and loved it. Then I spent twenty-five years of married life *not* traveling, so when I heard about rally racing that isn't around a track but on country roads all over the world, I thought, *ding*, that sounds interesting."

With no prior experience, Brinkerhoff signed up for La Carrera Panamericana road race in 2013, a seven-day race dating back to 1950 that travels through two thousand miles of Mexican streets and treacherous backcountry terrain. Brinkerhoff purchased the right car, secured a navigator and a mechanic, and hit the literal road.

"And weren't you afraid?" I asked while thinking to myself, *Is this woman insane?*

"Yes," she quickly confirmed. "I was afraid of failure, afraid of the unknown, afraid of putting myself out there and what people would think of me. I had massive amounts of fear. *What if I can't drive? What if I can't do this?* And the race itself was dangerous. On the first morning of the race, someone died. Two days later, another car caught on fire. Someone went off a cliff. I thought, *This is a crazy, wild race; this is scary stuff*, but at the same time I was in a new world and the whole thing was so exciting. I determined to 'be bold,' to 'just go,' and that year, Roberto [her navigator] and I won First in Class. It was the first year in the history of the race for a woman to debut in a race and win! I realized, *wow*, you can learn a lot by just putting yourself out there, but still, I was stunned at how well we'd done."

That one bold move was the beginning of Brinkerhoff's transformation. What was meant to just be a onetime experience became a ferocious new passion. "When you get out of your comfort zone," she said, "you learn so much about yourself—your weaknesses, your strengths—and I found strength where I didn't think I had it. That was life-changing, and I had to go back and do it again.

"I encourage people to just go out there and do it. And to stop *over*thinking it or listening to people who are the naysayers. There's always going to be naysayers, right? Just close your ears and keep your goal in front of you and go for it."

Since her first La Carrera Panamericana road race in Mexico, Brinkerhoff has raced from Peking to Paris, through East Africa, the Peruvian Andes, and Tasmania, and is headed next to Antarctica. Along the way, she's gained tremendous attention and influence and continues to use her voice to speak out against and raise money to quash child trafficking (the Service share). And in nearly every country she goes, Brinkerhoff says with emotion, "Women and young girls will wait hours for us to come in. They thank us and start crying because of what we're doing in a 'man's sport.' They say things like, 'You inspire us to do something that our society or our culture says we can't. And you show us that we can; we can do it.' Meeting them is what keeps me going. Seeing the impact on other women's lives, that I can give them hope to break through their own barriers and pursue their own dreams and find their own power, makes it all worth it." (The Slay It Forward share.)

I had to ask her thirty-three-year-old daughter, Christina,

who's traveled with Brinkerhoff from the beginning and now acts in full capacity as her business partner with a focus on media: "Are you proud of your mom?"

"Oh my gosh." She smiled widely. "I watched a whole metamorphosis in my mom's life. After that first race in Mexico, I remember thinking, *So this is who she is.* It's been such a reflective process for me, where now I ask myself, *What am I going to do? What are the things that I want to go after and achieve?* Mom's given me a lot to live up to, but there's so much hope in her success because it's shown me that it's never too late. We can always transform our lives."

You can accomplish amazing things, beyond what you ever anticipated, when you put yourself out there and just try.

—RENÉE BRINKERHOFF, RACE CAR DRIVER

Enlist Your Partner

//

Use the Life-Changing Magic of Unwavering Support

CONSIDER:
THE CASE OF THE ZOMBIE PARTNER

Meet Shan Boodram, a certified sex educator, intimacy expert, and dating coach. Her popular YouTube videos showcase Boodram unabashedly instructing couples how to "evolve the hand job," among other relationship topics. We'd initially met when she and her partner, Jared, were my guests on the *In All Fairness* podcast and I felt their true love for each other. I caught up with her again after she and Jared had their first baby, specifically to ask how Jared reacts to and supports her creative profession.

Boodram smiled and offered freely, "Jared's reaction to my work can be summed up in one of his favorite phrases: 'I'm not trippin'." And what he means by that is—I acknowledge your work is a priority, it uplifts you, and I'm not competing with that. Secondly, he is genuinely fascinated by the work that I do and wants to contribute. He'll often buy me books or send me the link to a cool TED Talk that relates to my work."

"How can other partnerships emulate yours?" I asked.

"Jared's a performer in his own right," she answered thoughtfully. "He's a musician and a content creator. He does his own thing and has his own goals, and at the same time, he's happy when I excel. When he comes with me to presentations or events, for example, and sees how actively uplifted I become in front of others and *by* others, he also becomes elevated. He doesn't take an ego hit; he's proud in a way a parent would be. With Jared, I never have to dim my shine."

I wondered aloud if Boodram understood how fortunate she was to have such a supportive partner. More often, I speak to couples, or at least one partner, who reports persistent resentment.

"Oh, I'm aware," she affirmed. "My previous partner advertised himself as 'the most supportive partner,' but he really wasn't. He was jealous and threatened, and because of that, I spent and wasted a lot of my creative energy arguing and managing conflict in the relationship. It was a time suck."

Boodram warns that if you are in what she calls a "zombie relationship" with someone who consumes your precious brain space and creative space—get out.

"I talk and teach a lot about sex," Boodram continued, "but I define true intimacy as close personal and vulnerable relationships that change, challenge, and champion you, and not always in that order, and not always in equal amounts. Depending on the season of your life, a healthy, intimate relationship transitions *with you* as you seek to change and grow."

In the best of worlds, your partner will lend their uplifting support as you actively pursue your Unicorn Space and take steps toward completion and making your dreams a reality.

Notice that I said, *in the best of worlds.*

After speaking with hundreds of hetero-cis and same-sex couples of varying socioeconomic and cultural backgrounds, it's become evident to me that creating time and space for individual self-expression has the potential to positively transform our relationships, but only under certain conditions. Comfortably inhabiting one's Unicorn Space only happens if *both* partners claim the time and space to discover and nurture their unique talents and interests . . . and only if they also support each other's individual expression and growth in return.

Q: WHAT IF I'M NOT IN A PARTNERSHIP?

A: If you choose, skip this chapter, but before you do . . . understand that there's still wisdom and advice here for you, whether you're currently in a relationship or not. These findings can be applied to any intimate relationship in your life (friendships, family members, even roommates and colleagues). The "me to we" relationship takes many different forms, and however it looks for you, your partnerships can provide make-or-break support of your creative life.

WHAT'S THE HURDLE?

If you don't feel the support of your partner or feel granted the permission to pursue your individual goals, what is your biggest hurdle in the relationship? What's preventing you or your partner from living in their Unicorn Space? I asked this question to hundreds of people (including many in my Uni coalition) and was provided with varied responses, but the ever-popular toxic "time suck" message rose to the top:

- ○ "I don't have time. Of course my partner found time to tinker with their vintage car engine this weekend."
- ○ "I feel guilty taking time away from the kids, my partner, the household."
- ○ "They resent the time I want for me."
- ○ "When do I get *my* downtime?"
- ○ "My partner thinks my Unicorn Space is a waste of time."

Additionally, many couples report communication barriers that impede efforts to create time and space outside the partnership or the home:

- ○ "When they hear, 'I need time to . . . ,' they tune me out."
- ○ "They just say no."
- ○ "Before long, we're in a big fight."

Do you notice how easily we point to *our partners* as the reason for disengaging in individual pursuits? And even when people reported that they did find time for their own interests, they (and especially women) said they felt guilty for taking time away from their other responsibilities.

Why is this? We know following our curiosities and developing our own interests is good for us, and it's essential for a healthy partnership. So why is it so hard to give and receive the partner support we need for our individual self-expression? We're going to unpack a number of hurdles that get in our way, starting with anger.

CONSIDER:
THE CASE OF THE LATE-NIGHT WHITTLER

My friend Jane confided to me: "When I hear Ed whittling away in the garage working away on yet another project while I'm stuck inside making yet another family dinner, I can feel my blood start to boil. Why does he get to be out there while I'm stuck in here? I know he loves his 'tinker' time in the evenings, but it's not fair that he gets to hammer away until ten o'clock at night while I keep the household afloat. And when exactly," Jane fumed, "do I get *any* free time for myself?"

"You sound really mad," I mirrored back.

Jane cocked her head to one side and gave me a look like, *No shit.*

When I asked Jane what might be underneath her anger, she shrugged. I expanded, "Is it possible that your anger toward Ed might be something else, a disguise for fear, maybe?"

"No," she asserted. "I'm one hundred percent pissed."

"Okay," I continued gently, "but in a world where Ed continues to take time for himself and you continue to forfeit time for you, does that bring up any fear?"

Jane's defensiveness retreated and her eyes began to fill with tears. "I guess it does," she said reflectively. "In that world I'm afraid I'll become a bitter old woman who gave up *my* dreams—the things I love to do—to accommodate everyone else . . . and"—Jane hardened—"that makes me mad all over again."

ANGER = FEAR

My friend Jane is not a one-off. Many women I speak to are flat-out pissed at their partners for being the source of their rage, for denying them the time and space they desire to expand beyond their roles. Julie Young, a special education teacher and a mother of three, wrote an open letter to her husband on Reddit: "Just because I was born with a vagina, does not mean that I am responsible for 90 percent of household and childcare duties." She continued: "I am mostly angry with myself for allowing myself to get to this point of exhaustion and frustration." Julie's post was upvoted by more than eighteen thousand readers who resonated with her discontent. In a follow-up post, she wrote, "I've realized I am not alone in this."

I caught up with Dr. Sheryl Gonzalez Ziegler and asked her about the prevalent bitterness within our partnerships that I was uncovering and how it relates to Unicorn Space. "I learned early on in my professional training," Ziegler explained over a Zoom call, "that there are two primary human emotions: love and fear. Anger, resentment, guilt, sadness, frustration, bitterness—they all fall under the category of fear."

I interjected, "So when we yell at our partners, 'I'm so mad that you're out in your woodshop while I'm stuck inside making dinner for our family of four,' what we're really saying is—"

"'I'm afraid,'" Ziegler finished my sentence. "Using your example, if Jane came into my practice, I'd say, 'I can see that you're mad, but—what are you afraid of? What are you scared of?'"

"Well, that's my friend," I said, "and I did ask her that question. She's afraid of putting everyone first at the expense of herself. And I was there, too," I admitted to Ziegler. "Before I figured this stuff out for myself, I was the woman crying over a grocery list. And my fear was that I was losing my marriage, that I wasn't going to fulfill my dreams because I was drowning in a tsunami of invisible work. And that fear often came out as angry expletives directed at my husband—'F*cking help me, I'm doing everything!'"

"Imagine," Ziegler posed, "if after that low moment, you'd confided in your husband—'I'm scared of losing our marriage. I'm scared of losing myself.' So much more vulnerable and honest, right? It's a totally different conversation, and one that creates authentic connection."

ASK YOURSELF

- *What am I afraid of?*
- *What is scaring me?*
- *What is the fear underneath my anger . . . sadness . . . disappointment . . . resentment?*

"When you can get to your fear, everything becomes clear," affirmed Ziegler. "It's super easy to say, 'I'm pissed off that you left dirty dishes by the sink,' but what's underneath that?"

To answer that question, I tracked down the guy who wrote a superbly honest blog post in 2016 entitled: "She Divorced Me Because I Left Dishes by the Sink." As you can imagine, Matthew Fray's admission hit a nerve; his post received several million views and was shared via *Huffington Post*. Since his divorce and subsequent rise in unexpected popularity, Fray has reinvented himself as a relationship coach to increase awareness, intentionality, and mindfulness between couples. In many ways, his forthcoming book, aptly titled *This Is How Your Marriage Ends*, is a cautionary tale to men to "not do what I did." I caught up with Fray via Zoom and asked him, aside from leaving dishes by the sink (which, incidentally, women in my interview set name as one of the most enraging things about their partners), why does he think his marriage broke down?

"Dysfunctional, poor communication," he answered readily. "This is how good people who love each other inadvertently and accidentally hurt each other. Of course, this wasn't clear to me at first. After my marriage fell apart, I needed to take a hard look at my life and figure out what happened, and it came down to how we related to one another. Speaking for men partnered with women, there are three communication crimes we commit that, over time and often unconsciously, can lead to relationship breakdowns: one, we invalidate our partner's needs by saying things like, 'What's the big deal?' Number two, we try to correct or reframe *her* story by saying things like, 'You're wrong, it really happened this way,' and finally, we defend or justify our actions, thereby invalidating our partner's response and ensuring that in the future, we'll likely do it again and exactly in the same way."

"Looking back at your own marriage," I asked, "and after counseling hundreds of people who are struggling in their own relationships, what would you have done differently? How do you advise other couples in conflict?"

"It's simple," offered Fray. "Stop. Pause. And seek to understand what your partner needs. Rather than the snap-habit of correcting, blaming, judging, or invalidating what they say, can you instead choose curiosity? Particularly for men, when you embrace the opportunity to get to know your spouse as well as you know your profession or have mastered your favorite hobbies—"

"I prefer the term *Unicorn Space*." I smiled.

"Right," Fray affirmed with a smile in return, and continued. "If you get to know your partner as well as you know yourself, you'll be able to anticipate their needs in real time, not after the fact, when the damage is done. When we choose curiosity and seek clarity, our partners start to feel seen, heard, and validated."

Following Fray's lead, take a moment now to stop, pause, and seek to understand what you and your partner need. In the context of Unicorn Space, what type of support do you and your partner need? Permission and encouragement to take time and space for self-expression? To be heard, rather than dismissed? To understand and appreciate the fear underneath the anger? Become curious about your partner, and also consider what type of support you need.

CONSIDER:
THE CASE OF THE LITTLE BLACK DRESS

Back to my interview with Sandy Zimmerman, the first mom to hit the buzzer on the *American Ninja Warrior* television program. At one point during our conversation about big goal setting, I changed course and asked her about partner support.

"Your husband must be so proud of you," I assumed.

Zimmerman hedged. "To be honest, when I first started competing on *American Ninja Warrior*, it caused huge marital problems. Huge. I was finally doing something I felt deeply pulled to do, and it was taking a lot of my time away from my family, which my husband didn't like. Also, I was getting stronger, more confident. I was *growing*. And this was scary and intimidating to him. I remember one time in particular [during the first season], where I was going to be raffled off at some big, fancy dinner. Up until this point, I hadn't done many events. I didn't consider myself a public person, and as a PE teacher and a mom, I'm usually in sweatpants and a tank top. But for the auction, I decided to buy a nice dress. I found a beautiful black dress, and I thought, *I'm going to wear this dress and put myself out there*—even though a part of me was scared no one would bid on me!

"On the night of the event after I'd dressed and was getting ready to go, my husband looks at me and says, 'You're going to wear *that*?'" Sandy paused and took a deep breath. "That was really hard to hear. It hurt, and I realized in that moment that all the attention I was getting was threatening to him. I thought about taking it off, and then a little voice, my own voice, said: *Sandy, you look damn beautiful in this dress. You go to that event and you own the room.* And I did. I actually was the highest bid of the charity auction."

Zimmerman's story brought to mind so many women I've spoken to who have retracted permission to wear their own version of a "little black dress" upon receiving their partner's critical feedback: *You're* wearing *that? You're* doing *that? You're* feeling *that? You're* being *that?*

Zimmerman explained that this moment was a turning point in her marriage. She tearfully admitted that she thought about leaving her husband. "The big D-word came up," she whispered. "I was ready to leave, and I said to him—I am not going to be less than my best self, so you can feel better about yourself."

Her bold statement was exactly what her husband needed to hear. Upon *his* suggestion, they sought support through marriage counseling. "We've worked through some really tough stuff, and we will continue to work at it, but it's incredible the change that's happened in our marriage. He heard me, and now he's my biggest supporter, and it really can't be any other way."

At the risk of sounding like a song lyric on repeat, here I go again—learning how to effectively communicate is one of, if not *the* most important practices of your life. Or as author Mia Birdsong summed it up: "You just can't have your needs met without other people. We are fundamentally relational."

So if you haven't already, *get relational.* Invite your partner to sit down with you and discuss the importance of your Unicorn Space. Share your fears around taking personal time and space to reclaim or discover more of yourself. What do you both stand to lose? For Sandy Zimmerman, my friend Jane, and speaking for myself—we were all on the edge of losing our marriages if we didn't speak up and advocate for ourselves.

Laura Wasser, Los Angeles divorce attorney, advises: "Instead of thinking you have to leave your relationship to become the 'best' version of yourself, try to find yourself *within* the partnership. And if it doesn't work"—she winked—"then call me."

In other words: Ask for what you need.

REFRAME THE VALUE OF TIME

In terms of what you need specifically, that's between you and your partner, but allow me to make a few suggestions based on the feedback I've received from hundreds of couples on this subject.

Most important—Ask for time. Like I've said before, unless you're a mad scientist and can bend the space-time continuum, you're not going to discover free time in your already packed schedule; you have to intentionally create it. This means reframing how you value time and then committing to the goal of renegotiating and rebalancing the hours that domestic work requires between you and your partner, so that you both have time to engage in Unicorn Space.

"If neither of you have time for Unicorn Space because you've loaded each other up in different directions," offers psychologist Jennifer Petriglieri, PhD, "then the only way to release yourself is to release the other." If you haven't already, repeat the following partner oath from chapter 2: "My partner and I both deserve and *need* uninterrupted time and attention to focus on the things that we love. It is vital to our relationship longevity and our individual happiness."

The only way to release yourself
is to release the other.

—JENNIFER PETRIGLIERI, PSYCHOLOGIST AND AUTHOR

ALLOW EQUAL TIME

Release each other by allowing equal time and space to focus on the things that you each love. Discuss what your individual goals entail and require—time, space, and kid-coverage-wise (if applicable). How much uninterrupted time do you need to actively pursue your respective goals and dreams? Let's say that you want to set aside three hours a week to practice piano, and your partner proposes six hours a week to work on their oil paintings, then agree to the highest number. Mutually agree that both of you will get six hours a week for your individual pursuits, and then make an explicit plan with each other to ensure equal time. Whereas I advocate equity over fifty-fifty equality in the home, pre-negotiating equal time management for Unicorn Space is essential, because my findings show that when there is perceived unfairness in the division of individual pursuits, we resent our partners for engaging in the pursuits that make them happy. So, if your partner likes to take Saturdays "off" to play basketball while you're stuck in the grocery line, then in an effort to avoid contention and maintain marital harmony, you get to pick Sundays, or another full day during the week that goes to you.

Dr. Stephen Treat, senior therapist, pastor, and marriage counselor, remembers making an explicit agreement like this with his wife. "My wife, Elizabeth, looked straight at me one day and said, 'If I'm going to finish my PhD, I need seventeen weekends off, starting from Friday at noon through Sunday after lunch.' She'd figured it out down to the *hour*," recalled Treat with an amused smile.

"At the time," he continued, "we were raising two young boys and both of us were leading busy professional lives. I agreed to support her, and for seventeen weekends in a row, I took sole responsibility for our boys. The boys and I spent much of that time at the zoo and the science museum—to the point that I could name every animal and every exhibit in both places! It was a challenge to have them on my own, but it also provided me the time to really bond with my sons. If Elizabeth hadn't voiced a need and set a firm boundary, I'm not sure I would have naturally given her that time. In fact, I'm sure I wouldn't have. But her insistence gave me permission to rebalance my priorities between work and family life, and that balance has proved to be a gift to our entire family. For Elizabeth to have the time to focus on her degree and professional success," Treat added, "increased the overall success of our marriage."

Q: My partner and I have polar-opposite ideas about how to spend our individual time. He doesn't share my love for gardening, and I don't really understand his obsession with estate sales, and we often get in fights about whose personal time is more valuable. How can we resolve this fight?

A: Resolve this fight by agreeing to respect each other's Unicorn Space, whatever it is. It may not be how you'd spend your free time, and that's the point—it isn't *your* time we're talking about. (See more below.)

PROVIDE UNWAVERING SUPPORT

Femily, a Silicon Valley gender/equity adviser, has the kind of "you do you" symbiotic relationship with her husband most of us can only hope for. "This past Christmas/Hanukkah I went on a ten-day yoga retreat all *by myself*," she said from her home in San Francisco. "Now, I couldn't have felt as free to go had I looked at it like—I'm leaving my *family alone for the holidays*. Instead, we talk things out—I said: 'Hey, we both have this blank canvas over the holiday week where we're not working, so what do you want to do?' He had a standing plan to hang with his parents and his kids from his previous marriage; I said I craved time alone. We mutually agreed to both get what we wanted.

"I think we're so madly in love because we have separate time, space, and friendships. If you don't spell out your time as a 'blank canvas,' social norms handcuff you to 24/7 default togetherness."

Once you have time management squared away, remind yourself that your partner has more to give you than an hour off the clock. Our partners (at least, the good ones) can also be our most attentive sounding boards and our deepest sources of loving support . . . but it requires a give-and-take formula of telling each other what we need and *why*. My husband, Seth, continues to be my strongest advocate and biggest fan, which sometimes looks like being my audience of one. Recently, I asked him to take a seat as I practiced for a TED-like talk that I'd deliver on Zoom. One of my biggest fears is to appear unprepared and run out of things to say, or to be too overprepared and say too much. And there's always some anxiety that the audience will be critical of me from the start or grow bored before my talk is over. For all these reasons, I prepare, prepare, prepare, and my good husband sits through it.

However, during this particular bedroom rehearsal, Seth made an unfortunate and likely unintentional move: he pulled out his phone while I was mid-sentence. I stopped and stared at him until he registered silence where my voice had been. He slowly looked up at me.

"Is my talk that bad?" My words came out angry, but I was hurt.

"What do you mean?" He tried to recover. "You're great."

"Then why are you looking at your phone?"

"Uh," he stammered, and wisely set it down.

I explained to Seth, as no doubt countless women have also clarified for their partners many times, that when I am speaking, I want and need to be heard. "When you pull out your phone, I feel the opposite—unheard, dismissed, ignored, and"—I emphasized—"it's one of my worst fears that I'll be onstage talking and I'll look out at the audience and they'll all be scrolling Instagram or tweeting: *This talk is lame*."

"I'm sorry," Seth said again, and leaned forward. "You have my full attention."

And I felt that I did. For the next hour, Seth listened to me repeat the same lines over and over again (and with what appeared to be genuine enthusiasm), providing me with what I needed in the moment—his unwavering, cellular-free support, in addition to his care and respect. And I did the same for him when, a week later, he came to me and said, "Babe, I'm nervous about my meeting tomorrow. Can I bounce some crazy ideas off you?"

Author bell hooks writes in *The Will to Change: Men, Masculinity, and Love,* "When we give love, real love—not the emotional exchange of I will give you what you want if you give me what I want, but genuine care, commitment, knowledge, responsibility, respect, and trust—it can serve as the seductive catalyst for change."

THE SECRET SUPPORT FORMULA

When you (1) unpack your "why" and (2) courageously voice your fears, your partner is more apt to lean in and more readily offer their support.

Refer back to your "why" for creating Unicorn Space in chapter 6. *Did you write it down?* If not, try it now: Building time into my daily/weekly schedule for _____

_____ is valuable to me because

_____

_____

_____.

Consider sharing with your partner some additional details—how do you feel when you're doing it? How does your Unicorn Space insulate you from the storms of life?

How would you feel if you didn't have it? Is there some fear there? If so, explore it.

Share your "why" with your partner and equally reciprocate by inviting your partner to share their "why" for uninterrupted space and time for the things they love to do.

FIND COMPLEMENTARY SPACE

Once you and your partner have equal time and feel supported and permitted to pursue your individual goals and dreams, then what? The sky's limitless, and you and your partner will create alongside each other, complementing each other's journey as Kyle Connaughton and his wife, Katina, have done.

Kyle is a chef, and his wife, Katina, is a horticulturalist, and together they run the three-Michelin-starred SingleThread restaurant in Healdsburg, California. On a recent trip to the area to celebrate Seth's birthday, I met with the couple at their farm and asked them: "How do you complement each other's creative space?"

"We've been together since we were fifteen years old," said Kyle, "so we've traded off supporting one another. When we had our first daughter at eighteen, Katina was my support as I was working in restaurants, going through my schooling and language studies."

After the birth of their second daughter, when they were twenty-five, they moved to a rural fishing village in Japan so Kyle could learn Japanese-style cooking. There, Katina was befriended by the locals and eventually became fascinated by the farming her new neighbors practiced.

"I remember when she said, 'This is my calling!'"

With fresh insight, Katina followed her curiosity for farm life and eventually pursued sustainable agriculture and horticulture.

"Then," Kyle recalled, "it was my turn to support her." Eventually, as they both gained more knowledge and expanded their separate passions for cooking and farming, they formed a single vision where they could create alongside each other. They opened SingleThread, where, Kyle says, they rely on each other's creativity. "The menu is driven by the farm, on what Katina and her team grow and harvest, so I completely rely on her. I can't do what I do in the kitchen without her, and I'm the outlet for all her hard work. All of the energy that she's put into creating these living things, we have to transfer to the guest in a very short period of time, so she's relying on me to make sure that we cook it properly, that we showcase it well, that we've done our job. The way I think about my purpose as a chef is to translate and showcase the work Katina does."

Kyle describes their creative collaboration as a delicate balance, neither of their creative outlets more important than the other but equally significant and complementary. "Who we've become as individuals and what we do individually is so compatible. It's strengthened our relationship, and we continue to evolve together, as a chef and a farmer," he said.

"So, what's next?" I asked. "Is there a new dream beyond this dream?"

"Sometimes we'll do a gut check and ask ourselves, Why are we doing this work? Is it relevant? Does it have meaning? Does the world need what we do? And what we keep coming back to is that people are busy and need time, and we've created an opportunity where we give people permission [his word, not mine!] to take time to gather around the table with friends and family and open good wine, enjoy beautiful, delicious food, and have conversations that leave you inspired. In the future, we hope to *extend* the idea of hospitality to include spaces that help people feel more creative themselves and pursue their own dreams."

I think Kyle and Katina are on to something—a Unicorn Super-Space!

MAINTAIN YOUR SPACE

Finally, as I gathered notes for this chapter, I tracked an inclination by some couples to merge their Unicorn Spaces, in effect, claiming the same space, rather than designate a complimentary space for him- or herself as Kyle and Katina have done so beautifully. Sometimes a "merge" happens because couples are initially drawn together over a shared passion or an aligned goal. In other instances, when one partner is particularly passionate and the other is less so, the relationship can fall into the trap of the royal we.

"I often say to BJ that he stole my identity as a painter," half joked Frankie, who met his partner fifteen years ago. "We're both artists, but I was more of 'the painter' when we met. One of the things we loved to do together as a new couple was visit art museums and look for inspiration. It was a bonding experience, and BJ says I helped him rediscover his love of art and develop a passion for painting. Over the years, BJ really came into his own—to the point that *he's* now considered to be 'the painter.' In a way," said Frankie, "I feel like I've lost some of what makes me uniquely me."

When you and your partner regard Unicorn Space as a "we" activity by claiming the passion of one partner for both (with the second partner "just happy to be together"), after some time—a month, a year, a decade, or more—sacrifice rarely presents without some resentment, so beware of confusing "support" of your partner's self-expression with forfeiting your own. I was thrilled to hear from BJ and Frankie a few months after our initial interview. Frankie sent me the following email: "You really helped us both to understand the importance of Unicorn Space. I have started to paint again and am currently working on a new piece. So now again, we are both 'painters.' We both love vibrant pop art, but we each have our own distinct styles because after all, we're different people."

Both you and your partner need time and space to actively pursue that thing that makes you come alive. It can be complementary, but it has to be your own unique, creative expression because after all, there is only one *you*.

"The best partner fills the role of a 'sculptor' that allows the beautiful form to emerge," offered Brad Johnson, a professor of psychology, US Naval Academy, and a faculty associate in the Graduate School of Education at Johns Hopkins University. During our interview, Johnson shared with me a stream of social psychology from Caryl Rusbult's research called the Michelangelo phenomenon.

"Using the sculptor metaphor," Johnson said, "the most supportive partner doesn't create the other but looks to *see* the person they desire to become without preconceptions or assumptions. And then once we have an understanding of what our partners want to become, we look for ways to help them be that thing they most desire to be. The best partners create opportunities for one another to express their ideal form."

I see the person you want to become, and I

want to help you get there.

Continue the Pursuit

Why "Complete" Is Better than "Perfect"

COMPLETION IS NOT PERFECTION

Jessica and I pulled out our gold-glitter sneakers for an outdoor dance class. As cousins and dance partners who often act as sounding boards for each other, we took five and turned the conversation to Unicorn Space. Jessica said, "The good news is that now I'm in 'active pursuit.' I've been practicing like crazy for the upcoming Broadway Dance Center recital, but"—she paused doubtfully—"I think I went too far too fast and now I'm afraid I won't be able to get on that stage. I'm just not the dancer I used to be, and I don't know if I'll ever be *ready*."

"Maybe not the trained dancer you were at twenty," I gently acknowledged, "but trust me, you absolutely still have *it*. I only wish I could turn on my feet like you."

"I don't know." Jessica sighed. "What if I forget the routine and go down into the splits and pee in my leggings? Or get stuck in half splits and can't get back up?"

I couldn't help but laugh at the image, and I offered with a wink, "You could wear a diaper?" Kidding aside, I understood Jess's fear was real. Her comments reminded me of a particularly astute passage in Elizabeth Gilbert's *Big Magic: Creative Living Beyond Fear*: "Perfectionism is a particularly evil lure for women, who, I believe, hold themselves to an even higher standard of performance than do men. . . . Too many women still seem to believe that they are not allowed to put themselves forward at all, until both they and their work are perfect and beyond criticism."

This got me thinking about completion in the context of Unicorn Space. I believe strongly that perfection is not the goal, but to Jessica's point—how do we know when we're ready to hit the stage? When is a creative expression complete? What marks the finish line? Or as I asked my friend Julie, "When are we ready for the fire?"

I reached out to my friend and speaking coach Julie Burstein, who is an award-winning radio producer with a popular TED Talk called "4 Lessons in Creativity." Burstein also added "potter" to her résumé at age fifty. "This was my lifeline back to me," she said.

I called Burstein and appealed, "Completion is the last C in the Unicorn Space journey. And while it is a very important last step, it can feel extremely daunting because so many of us confuse completion with perfection. Women I've interviewed say things like, *What if it's not good enough? What if I'm not good enough?* They can become intimidated and sometimes overwhelmed by what they perceive as a too-big BHAAG. *What if I can't finish what I start? Can't follow through on my commitment to others or to myself?* Perfectionist thinking like this is what leads to dreams deferred or altogether unfulfilled, and the world just can't have any more lost dreams. So, my question to you as a potter is—"

"When is it ready for the fire?" Burstein interjected.

"Yes!" I responded eagerly.

"Pottery helped me with perfection," Burstein said, "because you can work on a piece forever, but at some point, if you want it to be more than squishy wet clay, it has to go into the kiln. It has to go into the fire. You have to let go. So one of the things you learn as a potter is to not get overly invested in any particular piece. As it relates to completion, one of my best teachers encouraged me to think of my work in terms of *creating a series.* Don't just make one thing, make one hundred of that thing. Don't just make it once, make it one hundred times. And as you throw things into the fire and continue to create a series, you take what you've learned and done well, and put it into the next piece. Creativity is a collaboration with the fire, so what comes out doesn't always look like what you thought it would. And sometimes that's the point. What I've discovered is that the pieces that crack or break or come out of the fire misshapen and not how you intended can be the most beautiful."

☆ Creativity is a collaboration with the fire. ☆

I imagined Burstein surrounded by hundreds of beautifully imperfect teacups as I fell head over heels in love with the idea of creating a series to resist perfectionism, because it can be applied to whatever you do. If you're a gardener, plant one hundred seeds. If you're a dancer, learn one hundred moves. If you're a baker, roll out one hundred pies. For the gardener, your goal is not the perfection of a single dazzling dahlia, nor is your flower bed "complete" after one spring bloom. Gardening, or anything else, can be an ongoing creative pursuit for as long as it fulfills you. When you regard your creative expression as a series, as an unfolding process of *im*perfection, you may feel more freedom to create and also more forgiving when some flowers wilt or a vase breaks. Through this lens, you may also recognize new ways to improve or evolve that thing you do in your Unicorn Space. Whatever it is you create—pottery, poems, podcasts, paintings—can you reframe completion as an unfinished series of stumbles and successes rather than a 'one and done' finished piece of perfect work?

I was so excited to share this new framework with Jessica. I called her right away. "It's not about getting to the point of perfection," I said. "When the day of the recital comes, you'll get onstage and you may easily go down into the splits, or you may not. And so what if you may pee on the floor?"

"Well, then I really would be 'finished.'" Jessica laughed.

"Whatever happens," I said, jumping back in, "it doesn't matter because this likely won't be your 'final act.' Think of completion as an ongoing process of creating—and in your case, dancing. After this recital, set another marker. Stay in active pursuit, and I'll keep dancing with you toward the next completion point."

As I reflected on my writing process, I recognized that I, too, struggle with perfectionism, wanting to make every word and every sentence shine before I deem it ready for print. Truly, if it wasn't for my editor keeping me to a production schedule, I might still be in the bottomless revision well many writers fall into. Had I continued the futile attempt to make my first book perfect, I might have missed my moment. Or more aptly, my publication date. And this book, the second in a series, may have never been written at all. At some point, whatever it is you create, it has to go into the fire. Let it go! Only then, in the release, can you continue onto the next leg of your journey.

264

> What if you wake up someday, and you're sixty-five or seventy-five, and you never got your memoir or novel written; or you didn't go swimming in warm pools and oceans all those years because your thighs were jiggly and you had a nice big tummy; or you were just so strung out on perfectionism and people-pleasing that you forgot to have a big juicy creative life, of imagination and radical stillness and staring off into space like when you were a kid? It's going to break your heart. Don't let this happen.

—ANNE LAMOTT, AUTHOR OF *BIRD BY BIRD*

FOLLOW YOUR OWN TIMELINE

In regard to perfection being a hurdle to completion, I reached out again to Robert Jones Jr., fellow author and novelist whom I'd connected with through our mutual editorial team. I wanted to know if he also struggled with "getting it perfect." I asked, When is a book, a piece of pottery, or any project *done*?

Jones nodded with recognition. "Well, you know, everyone has their own timeline, and for me, it's been a *really long* journey. I started writing my book in 2006, and I'd been rewriting and rewriting and rewriting it for thirteen years."

"After so many years," I asked, "how, then, did you finally know it was ready?"

Jones laughed. "It will never be done for *me*. I could have gone another two or three years revising, but that would keep me from moving on to what I want to write next.

"I finally realized that it was a complete project for the hands that will hold it, for the people who will read it. It was time to share it, to let it go. So, it's out of my hands now, but hopefully inspiring to others."

It may never be "done," but is it "complete" for the people with whom you intend to share it?

UNICORN SPACE IS NOT ALWAYS A JOY RIDE

Completion can be marked by when you share your creative, *imperfect* expression with the world, although as Jones candidly illustrates, arriving at the point where you feel ready to share yourself with the world can take time and involve a lot of editing. In conversation with people who are seeking a more creative life, many mistakenly assume, or simply hope, that once they're in active pursuit of their dream, it'll be a free-flowing experience marked by rainbows and magical glitter showers. That would be amazing if it were true, but it's unlikely, so let's take a moment to demystify the process of creating to a completion point. Again, pulling back the curtain of my own journey, what's real is that writing is arduous and friggin' hard work. Mihaly Csikszentmihalyi, the resonant sage of creativity, says, "The pursuit of a creative problem is rarely easy. In fact, in order for it to be enjoyable it should be hard."

Translation: enjoyable = hard.

Take a moment to digest that. I'm still churning it myself. It's a counterintuitive concept, and one I try to keep in mind when I'm rewriting the same sentence over and over again and wondering, *Is this the fun part?*

For me, the writing process starts off with a euphoric *POP!* I become flooded by a pool of exciting ideas. I become even more inspired by interesting people I interview, and then I sit down in an empty room where I sometimes spend an hour biting my nails and guzzling sweet tea as I rack my brain searching for the words to transcribe what's in my head. When, or *if* I get into a flow state during my writing hours (much of which depends on the temperament and subsequent interruptions by my children that day), I can get teary about how good I have it that I'm inhabiting my Unicorn Space. But let me be clear— these are highly perishable moments. Much of the time, I'm staring into a blank-screen abyss as the popular refrain of Dorothy Parker narrates my inner dialogue: *I hate writing, I HATE WRITING, I love having written.*

Let's not pretend here: The journey to completion is hard. It requires rigor, which by my standard definition is not synonymous with fun. Nor is it particularly flattering. The portrait of me writing is very different from the image I present onstage, on Zoom, or certainly if I were to meet you in person. At my writer's desk, I'm typically slumped over in yesterday's yoga pants with unwashed, unbrushed hair, along with a disheveled attitude to match. Similarly, when I'm practicing my dance steps, I frequently stumble. I've never been able to turn properly or gracefully. Turning is my Achilles' heel! And when I trip over my own feet my inner dialogue sounds like this: *I hate turning, I HATE TURNING, I love having danced.*

"Nobody wants to show you the hours and hours of becoming," writes Angela Duckworth, PhD, in *Grit*. "They'd rather show you the highlight of what they've become."

Susan Schuh knows something about rigor. "Even astronauts have to take the garbage out," she said to me during a Parents at NASA panel where I was a guest. Schuh is responsible for supporting astronauts on long-duration space missions, including prepping for living and working on Mars. "The general public is focused on liftoff, that extraordinary moment when astronauts are launched into space," she explained, "but getting to that point requires extreme rigor. These astronauts train for years to get to that moment." And once in orbit, in addition to their extraordinary responsibility for maintaining the space station and carrying out their specific missions (sequencing DNA in space, as just one impressive example), these extraordinary people are doing the ordinary and mundane daily life stuff of cleaning toilets, prepping meals, and (maybe not so ordinary) sleeping upright in zero gravity.

Getting to a completion marker as exceptional and wondrous as space exploration requires a tremendous amount of behind-the-scenes "becoming." And whatever it is *you* aim to create and complete on earth, the same holds true for you. Will the journey toward completion be enjoyable? Sometimes, yes. Other times, not so much. Is the path toward creative living a continuous flow state? Don't kid yourself. Depending on the day, creativity can be drudgery, a slog. But the consolation is that "wonder is found in the midst of rigor," offers Natalie Nixon, author of *The Creativity Leap*. "We can all recall the intense amount of concentration and effort it took to learn how to ride a bicycle . . . the frustration, necessary repetition, and redundant failure of falling off the bike over and over again was tedious—and frankly not fun. But my, the leap into finally getting it right, flying down the sidewalk on my banana seat without training wheels for the first time, and experiencing my block in completely new ways—that was the wonder."

The wonder, the point of completion where you bravely share your creative, imperfect expression with the world is what makes the rigorous process of prepping for orbit, getting back on the bike, and hammering out the words, again and again and again, well worth it.

REMEMBER THE SMALL STEPS

And still, most of us need small markers of completion along the way to stay motivated and pulled forward toward our BHAAG. Where you may not struggle with perfectionism, my own experience, observation, and interviews have revealed that those people who have specific completion points in mind create a much higher likelihood of staying in active pursuit and accountable to follow through on their commitment to achieve their bigger goals. Here again, I'm talking about the importance of taking those small steps and this time, in the context of completion. For Ashley, it's creating the basic shape of one of her Harry Potter dolls. That's a step toward completion. For Lacy, it's getting her canvas primed. For Tiffany, it's testing a new recipe for her cookbook. These are all steps toward completion.

Nixon reiterates, "Any goal can turn into a terrifying monster if we don't deconstruct it and break it down into digestible bits. When I'm writing, I will set a timer for twenty-five minutes, never longer than forty minutes, where I'm head down, all notifications on my laptop are turned off, and my phone is on airplane mode."

Nixon's process echoes Sonja Lyubomirsky's subgoal method: "Before you can master French cooking, you must first learn how to braise Belgian endives."

However you want to measure it—small bits, subgoals, or steps—reaching completion requires your ongoing and active pursuit or you run the risk of straying into "the graveyard of unfulfilled dreams."

My friend Amanda, who read early pages of this manuscript, coined this term. When talking about her Unicorn Space in the context of completion, she clarified, "Perfectionism isn't really my hurdle. I struggle more with staying on track, in active pursuit. Sometimes I don't get much further than the idea phase."

As an example, Amanda referenced her GoDaddy account. "I've registered for so many domain names that I haven't done anything with," she said. "I've registered for sauceboss.com that would pair sauces with your personality. Then there was dogcarwash.com, where you could get your car and your dog washed at the same time. Oh, and goodsadcards.com that puts a lighter spin on grief. I pay $10.99 a year to keep those unfulfilled dreams alive."

"All good ideas," I enthused, "and they'll likely be ripped off if I put them in the book."

Amanda laughed. "Your readers can go for it, and good on you, whoever you are, for fulfilling *my* dreams."

"But seriously," I said, "why do you think you struggle so much with moving past the idea phase?"

"I don't think I have a good strategy for staying in motion," she reflected.

"Well, this goes back to goal setting," I said, "taking small steps forward and also putting creativity habits into place that help you stay in active pursuit."

YOUR CREATIVITY HABIT

If reaching a completion point is in the everyday practice of taking small steps forward, what's yours? As an example, let's say your BHAAG is to attend Le Cordon Bleu culinary school in Paris. A small-step goal may be to learn to speak French. Now, how are you going to do that? By downloading the Babbel language app? By watching French movies with subtitles? By frequenting your local French café with the cute French waiters and learning through flirtatious immersion? There is more than one way to get to where you want to go, so it's worthy of your curiosity and exploration. What motivates you forward from one step to the next? What's your "deliberate practice," as Angela Duckworth refers to it in *Grit?* As you consider what works for you, here are a few more examples of creativity habits from some people you've already met:

Mental reframe. Competitor Sandy Zimmerman takes stock of the conversation she's having in her head. Her small-step process for reaching her goal is positive thinking. "What we tell ourselves is so powerful. And if the conversation isn't a positive one, if it's holding me back and saying, *I can't do that,* then I challenge myself to rewrite the script."

Just keep going. Author Brenda Janowitz commits to writing one thousand words every day "no matter what"—but if she misses a day, "I don't beat myself up. I just move forward. I may double down the next day or write over the weekend. I do this because for me, the part I enjoy most about writing is being *in it*. And I don't try to make it perfect or polished because I can always edit it later."

Protect and defend your time. Professor Scott Behson protects his time as he would an important business meeting, arguing that we are far more likely to follow through on a plan if we make it a set part of our schedule. "You may love knitting, but a call from work might scuttle your plan," he wrote in the *Harvard Business Review*, "but if you joined a weekly knitting circle (even on Zoom), you'll shut off your phone for that hour. If you enjoy playing basketball, don't just hope for a pick-up game every now and then—join a league at your local Y. Whatever your [pursuit], find a way to make it a regularly scheduled part of your week and then defend that time."

Experiment. "I really enjoy finishing projects," said designer Justina Blakeney, "because it allows me to move on to the next thing where I learn and grow from what I just did. I think it's important to give yourself permission to experiment. To try something new. You can't really create something you love until you know what you love. And you can't really know what it is that you love until you experiment."

Deadline driven. When she's not at the pottery wheel but instead producing radio pieces, Julie Burstein lets the ticking clock determine when a piece is complete. Deadlines drive her process. "If you're going on the air at five o'clock and you're not done by then, the piece won't air. Deadlines, both externally driven and self-imposed, helped me let go of the idea of perfect and embrace 'good enough.'"

Do any of these practices or habits resonate with you? Are you more of a Sandy, a Brenda, a Scott? A Justina, a Julie? Or someone else altogether? Identify your desired creativity habits. What keeps you in active pursuit? And in the spirit of transparency, bravely name your *least* favorable habits, the ones that you could stand to retire, such as, *I procrastinate until an external deadline looms, setting internal panic into high gear. Since I wait until the eleventh hour, I almost always self-sabotage my efforts, which means I don't complete things or I complete them poorly.*

Again, I encourage you to memorialize your insights in writing. Either here, in a separate journal entry, or by openly sharing them with a trusted friend.

My creativity habits are _____

My habits to retire are _____

CELEBRATE THE RIGOR

As you take the small steps toward completion, remember to celebrate. Ritualize your progress. Reward yourself for your rigor. "When I finish a chapter," Natalie Nixon bubbled, "I do a happy dance. Sometimes, I go so far as to break for a cupcake with a candle on top." (Since Nixon suggested it, I've instituted this ritual for myself. The sugar rush has helped incentivize me to finish chapters, imperfectly, and move on.) When we note our progress and celebrate it as its own accomplishment, we become reinvigorated to keep pushing forward. To support this finding that became a thread throughout so many of my interviews, I checked back in with Uni Darby Saxbe about the science behind ritualizing rigor. Saxbe, as you may recall, is both a neuroscientist and the lead guitarist for the Dahli Mamas.

"What I love about being in the band," she said, "is that we spend half of our practice time complaining about our kids and the second half learning and getting better. Week to week, my fingers learn new chords, I play faster and faster, and the band sounds better and better. That [process] of doing something difficult and actually seeing yourself getting better through rigor and hard work is so incredibly rewarding. And it is definitely worth celebrating."

In Saxbe's case, the *process* of learning to play a song is more rewarding to her than the *product* of performing the song. "As I learn new songs and develop my skills, I feel the intrinsic satisfaction of improving, even if no one outside the band hears us play."

"But wasn't it amazing when you finally did perform for a crowd?" I challenged.

"For sure," she admitted, "performing was a highlight, but the real sense of accomplishment came from pushing up against an obstacle—picking up my guitar again at age forty— and then moving through it. Scheduling shows was actually just a way for us to force ourselves to practice—but the jamming together was just as fun as the performances."

One stitch, brushstroke, guitar strum, and foot in front of the other. Just keep going and along the way, you may be surprised to discover alternative pathways and possibilities that lead to new interpretations of your original completion point, as it was the case for Jordan Sherer.

CONSIDER:
THE CASE OF THE HAM RADIO

Jordan Sherer is a software engineer by trade who began dabbling with ham radio in his spare time. "Ham," also known as amateur radio technology, broadcasts radio frequencies typically for the noncommercial exchange of messages from private recreation to emergency communication and alerts.

"It's a very niche technology area," said Sherer via Face-Time as I was shopping in Costco with my son Ben. "It's been around for a long time, but as technology has generally advanced, 'ham' has, too. I was drawn to it because of my love for tinkering, building things, and creating cool stuff. When I was on paternity leave with my daughter, I got really into it. I'd be feeding Charlotte in one hand and writing software with the other"—he laughed—"juggling two of my loves."

Sherer said that what started as a "weird fascination" led him in an unexpected direction. As he became more and more knowledgeable and skilled, he decided to apply for a ham broadcast license so that he could legally transmit. And then—

"I started hearing from people who were using my software, including a colonel in the United States military who wanted to use my technology in a training exercise that would allow squads to communicate from two opposing sides of a mountain in the absence of cellular reception or GPS technology."

"Come again?" I said as I threw cereal into my cart.

"Yeah, it's called Near Vertical Incident Skywave, and it basically shoots a signal up into the air and comes down on the other side. I've also had a couple of state emergency agencies wanting to use my technology as a backup system, when there are hurricanes or severe weather that could take down cell towers."

"So cool!" my son Ben interjected as he eavesdropped on our call. I had to agree. Not only did Sherer's curiosity present him with a surprise detour, but he also created something helpful and potentially lifesaving for people (the Service share).

"It's definitely been cool," Sherer admitted, "but the thing is—it didn't just happen. You have to take the small steps. For me, it started by being interested. Then I had to do the research, *small step*, and then I studied to get the license, *small step*, and then I had to experiment with the new technology, *small step*. It took me months of spending fifteen or twenty minutes at a time feeding my baby while doing a little programming. Eventually, three years later, all the small steps compounded to create new opportunities that paid dividends . . . *not* that I get paid for this," Sherer emphasized. "I don't, and I'm not doing it for the money. It's about self-fulfillment and doing something for other people. That's the definition of Unicorn Space, right?"

REIMAGINE A NEW DREAM

At some point, you will arrive at your own finish line determined by when you feel ready to share your creative, imperfect expression with the world. And once you get there, I strongly encourage you to celebrate (forget the cupcake, have a whole three layers!). And then, I challenge you to reimagine a new dream. To ask yourself, *What's next?* Finding new ways to creatively express yourself can be an open and active, lifelong pursuit. If you choose it to be, that is. When I finish this book (one more chapter to go), I plan to start on the next "series" of ideas, pages, and chapters. On and on I'll go so long as I feel I have a meaningful message to share and one that I'm also passionate about.

"That's the ignition point," says Afdhel Aziz, "when your talent meets your passion in service of others."

Aziz is a longtime friend of my husband who's made a name for himself as one of the world's leading experts in business as a force for good. He's a visionary whose consultancy, Conspiracy of Love, advises brands on how to do more good in the world, and whose upcoming book, *The Principles of Purpose*, is a call to arms for corporate leaders to take action on social and environmental issues. From my outside perspective, it appears that Aziz has not only found his ignition point but has also mastered his domain, so I was surprised when he told me that he felt ready to shift his focus.

"I'm going through a process of reimagining myself as a creative person," Aziz opened up. "I got to this point where I thought: *What do I want to do with the next twenty years of my life? Do I want to keep consulting and writing strategy decks for [clients]?* And my answer was no. And so then I asked myself, *What do I want to do next?*"

A new, unchartered dream. I was intrigued. "What do you have in mind?" I asked.

"Well, I want to challenge myself to become a better storyteller. I want to write a TV show. I want to make a documentary film, a feature film. And I realize that all of these projects are exponentially harder than what I'm doing now because in [those domains], I'm an amateur."

I wondered aloud, "What are your creativity habits? How do you plan to reach your new goals?"

"I'm working on a living document that helps me articulate what I stand for, what I truly want to do. I write down how I'm thinking about myself in the next ten years and where I want to go—not as a company, or even as a professional—just *me*."

What Aziz was describing sounded strikingly similar to

the Creativity Commitment you've been building since page 153, which clarifies your "what" and then puts you on a path toward achieving it. His future-lens approach also reminded me of Harvard psychologist Daniel Gilbert's TED Talk titled "The Psychology of Your Future Self," in which he encourages people to imagine and invest in their future self and to "never be defined by who you are right now."

As Aziz continued to talk about the investment he was making in a new personal narrative, I became excited by his creative resilience and eager for what he was going to roll out next.

He laughed. "Maybe some of it will work, some projects not so well, but I'm going to have fun figuring it out, and I will have challenged myself to hold true to my values and do what I really love doing and that will be the achievement in and of itself."

CONTINUE TO REINVEST IN YOURSELF

As you throw things into the fire and continue on your journey toward completion, remember that you are never "done." You're a work in progress. You, *yourself*, are a series. Imperfect but with the power to grow and shoot off in new directions every season or for whatever your reason. When you regard your life as a series of creative expressions rather than as one finished product, you allow new curiosities to move you. Give yourself permission to follow your curiosities, to reimagine your dream at any stage or age, to reinvent your life based on your most deeply held values, and to be in a lifelong pursuit of creativity.

Permission Slip

I give myself permission to
reimagine my dream.
To be in a lifelong pursuit of creativity.

—signed by: ME

Ever After

Leave a Creative Legacy for the World Around You

It was Friday night, and Seth and I were snuggled on the couch with the kids watching a Disney favorite, *Tangled*. For those of you who haven't seen the movie, it's loosely based on the fairy tale "Rapunzel," and in this version, the princess of long locks partners with Flynn Rider, the town thief, to make a break from her impossibly tall and solitary perch. Once on the ground, Rapunzel embarks on a journey to realize her dream—to travel to the main castle and witness the rise of the magical lantern lights that she's only gazed at from afar for eighteen years. After many run-ins with authority, near escapes, and singsongy high jinks along the way, Rapunzel and Flynn finally arrive outside the castle wall and have this wide-eyed exchange:

Rapunzel: I've been looking out of a window for eighteen years, dreaming about what I might feel like when those lights rise in the sky. What if it's not everything I dreamed it would be?

Flynn Rider: It will be.

Rapunzel: And what if it *is*? What do I do then?

Flynn Rider: Well, that's the good part, I guess. You get to go find a new dream.

It's at this emotional apex that the two characters break into a heart-swelling duet called "I See the Light" joined by Anna, my youngest, who watches the movie in her favorite princess dress and sings heartily along. As a family, we've seen this scene play out at least a dozen times, but on this particular Friday night, Ben, my nine-year-old, leaned forward with a fresh look of recognition. He turned to me. "Mom, that's what you say." After listening in on countless Zoom interviews over the past year and dropping in on my casual conversations with friends about actively pursuing their dreams and what it looks like to complete their creative journeys, Ben relayed my message back to me in no-nonsense, preadolescent terms: "You don't have to stop with one dream because, *duh*, you can always find a new dream."

"You're right." I smiled back at him cozily sandwiched in between his brother and sister on the couch. Looking at the three of them, I expanded on Ben's newfound awareness. A thought bubble appeared in my mind: staying in active pursuit of your dreams is how you create an *active, living legacy*.

Make the active pursuit of your dreams

your living legacy.

For those of us who have children, it's important that our kiddos see and experience *us* living full and actuated, meaningful and creative lives, pursuing our dreams at any age. And even if you don't have kids, it's just as important to live this message for your peers, family, friends, and others in your social sphere. By modeling an unapologetic openness to follow your curiosities, you help to normalize the everyday pursuit and expression of creativity, at any age and in whatever form it takes for you, and also to socialize every person's entitlement, whatever their circumstances, to locate and then inhabit their Unicorn Space. This is what it means to live an active legacy.

In my philanthropic role of advising people how to intentionally distribute their wealth, property, and assets in a way that most truly reflects their life and honors their memory, I routinely ask, "What is the legacy you want to leave behind?" Even in this setting where people are deliberately sitting down with and paying me to discuss their "dying wishes," many become uncomfortable and even dodge the question—*Can we talk about something else?*—and then shift the conversation to current events or sports. I've even had clients go so far as to say to me point-blank: *But I'm not going to die.* Needless to say, I've had to get creative about how I approach mortality (*Shhhhh, don't tell my clients*: no one lives forever) and what has worked to cushion the inevitable is a slight reframe. I ask instead: "What do you want to be remembered for *today*? Let's talk about your passions and interests and how you're living your life *right now*."

For those people who don't feel interested or invested in their current lives, it remains a difficult question. But for those people whose values are aligned with an active Unicorn Space, it becomes much easier to answer.

EXERCISE
What Is Your Active Legacy?

As you begin to think about your active legacy, reflect on how you're living today. Ask yourself the following questions and jot your thoughts down in a journal or in the spaces provided.

- *What curiosities and dreams am I actively pursuing?*

  _____

  _____

  _____

- *Am I living by and pursuing interests that align with my deeply held values?* _____

  _____

- *Are my current goals intrinsically motivated? Am I pursuing them because they are inherently satisfying and meaningful to me?* _____

  _____

  _____

- *What community of family, friends, peers, and beyond am I most connected with? Am I sharing my special gifts with the world?* _____

  _____

  _____

FIND LEGACY IN YOUR GIFTS

For her milestone forty-fifth birthday, Sarah's daughter secretly asked her mother's closest friends to provide a word or phrase that answered this question: *When you think of my mom, what comes to mind?* Her daughter collected all the responses and rewrote them as meaningful inscriptions on pretty strips of colored paper that she sealed in a golden box. Interestingly, many of her friends said a version of the same thing: *Sarah connects amazing women.*

When I asked Sarah if their assessment of her was in alignment with her values, she said, "Absolutely, building community and connection is at the top of my 'life list,' although it wasn't until my friends named it out that I saw it so clearly. They really helped me home in on what is most valuable to me in my life." Since receiving her golden box, Sarah has embarked on a new dream: hosting a podcast that connects women at "the sweet spot between neurotic and chill."

I returned to this idea of finding legacy in one's special gifts with Dan McAdams, professor of psychology at Northwestern University. I asked McAdams if he had any prompts to get people thinking about their active, living legacy.

"I think you have to find your gift and then you have to find the place or the space in the world that appreciates that gift. It's finding that 'match' of what you can offer and what the world wants and needs right now, and in generations to come. And sometimes this is difficult because many people feel that they've got something to offer, but they can't find the situation where it'll be appreciated or needed. For example, I'm really good at fixing VCR machines"—McAdams laughed—"but they don't exist anymore. They haven't existed for twenty years. I may be really good at fixing them, but I may need to find a different 'gift' to define my legacy."

What are the gifts you are sharing with your friends, family, and the world?

You can begin to craft your legacy in the present moment. Today. You're an active story that continues to evolve over the course of your lifetime, which means your identity is not fixed, nor is your legacy predetermined. To a significant extent, *you* get to determine *for what* and define the memory of *how* you lived your life.

If you're still unsure of the legacy you're shaping in the present, follow Sarah's lead and ask the people in your life. Revisit the "Ask the Audience" exercise on page 151, and this time, interpret their answers in the context of your living legacy.

- ○ When you think of me today and about how I choose to live my life, what values appear to be driving me, motivating me?
- ○ What are my unique gifts, and how do they fit a need in the world?
- ○ In what way has my life or my passions inspired you to dream a new dream for yourself?

Based on the answers you received from your audience, do you have a better understanding of the active, living legacy you are creating in the present moment?

CONSIDER:
THE CASE OF THE NEED-TO-BE-TOLD STORIES

Rudy Hypolite didn't need to ask the audience because his legacy projects play to packed houses and standing applause.

Hypolite, whom I reached out to through a former colleague, grew up in Trinidad. He immigrated with his family to the Boston area in the seventies, where he attended high school and was the first person in his family to go to college. Today, fifty years later and the father to two adult daughters, he works full-time as the technical supervisor for media and technology services for Harvard University's Faculty of Arts and Sciences. In his off time during summer break and on weekends, he's a documentary filmmaker, probably most known for his film *Push*, which chronicles a dysfunctional but talented high school hoops team that struggles against their circumstances: a deteriorating public school system and the turbulence of life in the greater Boston area. His most recent film, *This Ain't Normal*, goes even deeper into Hypolite's Roxbury roots, which follows five gang-involved youth in the high-impact crime neighborhoods of inner-city Boston.

"Why these particular stories?" I asked him.

"All my films deal with stories from communities of color, especially here in Boston, where I grew up around young men who became involved in gangs. I wanted to give voice to those who are normally marginalized, and who you don't hear from. People know the stories about South Boston and East Boston, the Matt Damons and the Ben Afflecks, but you don't hear about the kids in the different neighborhoods that I'm familiar with. The first ten minutes of *This Ain't Normal* is rough; it's raw. And that's intentional, because I wanted to show these young men for what they are, but as you're brought into the film, I hope to humanize [them]."

I wondered if he'd ever gotten any pushback from the community for putting such a stark spotlight on them.

Hypolite recounted when *Push* premiered at the International Film Festival in Boston. "There were so many people that showed up," he said. "The theater holds like nine hundred seats, and it was packed. They were turning people away. The film festival organizers couldn't believe the response, but I understood why. It was because [these communities] never get a chance to see their story. They felt the movie was for them."

Beyond packing seats and creating a space that, before him, didn't exist, I asked Hypolite what motivates him forward.

"Believe me, I'm not in this to make money," he said sincerely. "I often have to take money from my family to work on these projects. [My motivation] is to tell stories and hopefully stir and inspire people into action and bring about change—whether politically or educationally."

His two adult daughters take inspiration from Hypolite. Both of whom, he explained, are always heavily involved in his creative process. His youngest, Ashlee, will help him co-produce his next project on Black barbershops and hair salons, while his oldest is dedicated to education policy and helping first-generation college students (the Spin Off share).

"I'm so proud of both of them." Hypolite smiled.

"Your high value on storytelling and social justice has created an active, living legacy that your daughters are already carrying forward in their own lives," I pointed out. "Your work and your stories will continue forever."

Make taking and inspiring action
your active legacy.

Throughout my research, I've encountered time and again that the by-product for those people who have given themselves the gift of following their dreams is enhanced connection, deeper meaning, and overall happiness. And of these people living within this magical intersection, they're changing the many faces of creativity and also of what it means to make and leave your mark. Kat Medina, Lacy Freeman, Kabir Sehgal, Jordan Sherer, Rudy Hypolite, and so many others whom you've met throughout these pages shared a like-minded vision.

Living an active legacy, they say, is about—

o "Pursuing my passions."
o "Living a good story."
o "Making my family proud."
o "Manifesting my ideas in the world."
o "Creating new spaces that didn't exist."
o "Starting a conversation."
o "Showcasing beauty."
o "Being the change."
o "Inspiring future generations."

Dr. Stew Friedman challenges us to think creatively about how each of our Unicorn Spaces creates value for other people. He asks, "How can [what you do] mobilize people to come along with you to create a better tomorrow? Legacy is how you *live* and *live on* in the hearts and minds of the people who knew you."

By modeling a life well-lived, fully engaged and in active

pursuit of your dreams, you are in a position to influence the way your partner, your neighbors, your friends, and everyone else around you defines their own living legacy. By extension, if you have children, with your modeling and influence, your children will begin to follow your lead and make their own creative footprint in the world.

"Children will create if they see the adults around them creating," encourages children's author Mo Willems.

When you take all of this into account, isn't it your *obligation* to claim your Unicorn Space, to share your dream and become an active legacy maker with influence far beyond?

Bob Ballard sure thinks so. Ballard has a storied résumé, but he's most famous for discovering the *Titanic* and inspiring a new generation of explorers to embark on their own discoveries. Yeah, not too many people can add that to their LinkedIn profile! Ballard, now almost eighty years old, is still in active pursuit. He didn't stumble upon one of the most sought-after historical treasures on the planet and then put his feet up. He pivoted toward another seemingly impossible discovery—finding Amelia Earhart's plane—which he has now searched for in great earnest for years—unfortunately, as of yet, to no avail. Still, he hasn't given up.

When I spoke to Ballard, I was itching to ask him about legacy. And I didn't beat around the bush. After cursory introductions I jumped right in.

"Can you tell me what legacy means to you?" I asked.

"Exciting kids to dream their dream and *live* their dream," Ballard responded. With a literal sparkle in his eye, Ballard explained that children are his favorite audience because "every child is born a scientist. What's their first question: *Why?* They're naturally curious. I love going into middle-school classrooms and exciting them, pouring fire into their young lives. After I discovered the *Titanic*," he said, "I received six-teen thousand letters from kids asking, How can I do what you do? My answer: Believe in your dreams and passions. And don't be talked out of them."

When he was a young boy, Ballard dreamed of becoming Captain Nemo from the 1954 classic movie *20,000 Leagues Under the Sea*. "And my parents didn't laugh at my dream. I think [one of] the cruelest things a parent can do is to laugh at a child's dream, even when it's cockamamie, like mine. You have to work with it. So, my parents said, 'Tell me more about Captain Nemo,' and I did, and they said, 'That sounds like a naval officer,' and I said, 'No, it's more than that, he sees the ocean floor,' and they said, 'Well, that sounds like an oceanographer.' Guess what? I became an oceanographer *and* a naval officer. I did it, I lived my dream. And my parents encouraged me every step of the way."

"Wow," I said, tearing up. "Your dream really did come true."

Ballard leaned forward and struck a somber tone: "In many ways, yes—but it hasn't all been easy."

He delicately recounted how he lost his first son to a fatal car accident just before his son turned twenty-one, and less than two years after Ballard discovered the *Titanic*.

"That was devastating. To lose a child, and so close to man-hood. It's tough to talk about. And I was groping for something to get me through it, so when those sixteen thousand children wrote to me, I felt it was my moral obligation to respond be-cause I had just lost mine. It was at that point that I dedicated my life to children."

I was so taken aback by this sad turn in our conversation; I just stared back at him with tears in my eyes. I was grateful to Ballard for filling the silence.

"Life is full of storms that can knock you down and, in my life, I've been hammered to the deck. And what gets you up is your dream. And then you keep moving forward until you persevere and come out the other side of the storm. The good news is that the sun always does come out. You just have to survive the storm."

"And learn to dance in the rain." I smiled.

"That's right, and that's why I tell kids: Stay forever curious. Live your dream. Don't let anyone talk you out of it. And be ready to pick yourself up when you get knocked down, because anything worth having shouldn't be easy."

 Stay forever curious.

—BOB BALLARD, SCIENTIST, EXPLORER,
AND THE "REAL LIFE" CAPTAIN NEMO

In terms of having an optimal experience that can never be taken away from you, finding the *Titanic* certainly makes the top of the list. But as Ballard's heartbreaking story illustrates, getting to a completion marker as exceptional and wondrous as oceanic discovery requires a tremendous amount of rigor and, in some cases, is accompanied by great loss.

This plotline doesn't surprise Dan McAdams, who is steeped in the research of narrative identity, a person's internalized and evolving life story. Dan studies the Big Questions we each ask ourselves: *Who am I? How did I come to be? And where is my life going?*

"The narrative identities of highly generative adults have a common theme," he said during our interview. "And that's *redemption,* where you're delivered from your suffering to an enhanced state. When people are able to identify a redemptive arc in their life story or a string of little redemptive arcs of hardship or overcoming some adversity, their lives are enhanced. They tend to enjoy higher levels of mental health, functionality, overall well-being in midlife and beyond, *and* they show higher levels of generativity. They almost feel compelled or mandated, if you will, to leave a mark for future generations."

Dan is an academic rock star, and I could listen to him all day long (preferably seated in the front row of a lecture hall with an endless amount of sweet tea), but to ensure I don't lose you here, allow me to boil it down.

When you go from your own version of a bad event to a good outcome, from a low place to a high place, from an object at rest to an object in motion, from stagnation to creating something you bravely and proudly share with the world, you become a healthier, more adjusted person who can weather the next rainstorm (because you've been through a few and now have the wherewithal to throw up an umbrella and keep going). But even more than that: you become someone committed to improving the lives of others. You increase your "generativity"—your concern for, contribution to, and impact on future generations. And that, dear reader, is how you create an active and lasting legacy.

Displaying "generativity" means caring
about people besides yourself . . . that leads
to help guiding the next generation,
which often leads to a positive legacy.

—ADA CALHOUN, AUTHOR OF *WHY WE CAN'T SLEEP:*
WOMEN'S NEW MIDLIFE CRISIS

WHAT'S YOUR REDEMPTION STORY?

So, what's your redemption story? You don't think you have one? Well, let me assure you that if you've made it through this book, you have a redemption story—or at the very least, you're in the process of crafting one. It's likely unfolding right now, as you continue to seek and actively pursue ways in which to make your life more fulfilling or meaningful in some way. I don't want to presume, but I think it's safe to assume that you embarked on this journey because, to some degree, you felt less than fulfilled and wanted more, or something different.

As you consider your narrative arc, I'll share mine. My redemption story started as so many do, with a breaking point. After the birth of my three children and downscaling my career to accommodate more domestic work and childcare, I feared that the version of myself I loved the most had been crushed and lost under the weight of unpaid, and often underappreciated, invisible labor at home. And I worried that the resentment I was holding toward my husband might cause me to lose my marriage, too.

Thankfully, my marriage didn't end. And I wasn't forever lost. Instead, I decided to start a new chapter in my life by borrowing a page from fellow author Ada Calhoun, who encourages us to "tell the story of our mistakes, our lives, in a new way, in which we are the heroine worth rooting for." I told my story not only for myself but for millions of women struggling in their partnerships, afraid to use their voices, rattled by guilt and fear. Eventually, my breaking point was "redeemed" by the good that followed it—creating a widespread Fair Play community for policy and domestic change that I feel, as McAdams said, compelled and mandated to grow.

And it has grown. Into a movement that sparked a new

dream: to inspire others to rediscover and live in their Unicorn Space. To give themselves permission to be unavailable. To burn guilt and shame. To become once again curious. To live by deeply held values and actively go after BIG, AUTHENTIC dreams that can be shared with the world. This is my redemption story and it's not over. It continues with you, with every Uni who bravely steps forward and makes the pursuit of an authentic life story his/her/their living legacy.

As a parallel redemption story, I have finally learned how to turn! Yes, turn on the dance floor and move like my heroes, Shige-boh and the Senior Monsters. The secret was a lot of small steps, rigorous practice, and a pair of extra-wide gold-glitter sneakers that accommodate my aging feet. It's too late for *In Living Color* but look for me and my cousin Jessica on TikTok.

I've learned that these redemptive moments work like an antidote to the laborious plot points of daily life. And when the story dramatically changes direction with the introduction of a new villain—like, say, a worldwide pandemic—I know now that if I continue plodding along toward the next marker of completion, and dancing every step of the way, I will get there. At which point, I can take a moment to celebrate with a piece of cake before resuming my journey to realize and share my next dream. Whatever that may be.

Make the pursuit of an authentic life story your living legacy.

As I was writing these final pages, in addition to identifying my redemptive arc, I challenged myself to go deeper, as I've encouraged you to do. What is *my* living legacy? I recalled a practice that Professor Dan McAdams uses: "Can you summarize your life in six words? For me," he said, "it's 'Raise daughters. Write books. Love Becky.' (Becky's my wife.) It's really trite, but it's also central to legacy."

Hmmmm, I thought, *what are the words that summarize my life today?* The answer came in a flash from my twelve-year-old Zach, the resident Gen Z voice in the house, who I hadn't realized was quietly sitting next to me as I pondered aloud.

"The Three C's." He rolled his eyes. "Your three favorite words. You say them on nearly every Zoom call: *curiosity, connection,* and *completion.*"

I laughed. "Well, look who's paying attention. And you're absolutely right. Those are my three favorite words." (And notably three shy of McAdams's exercise.) Nevertheless, I considered having them tattooed on my rib cage as Robin Arzón had done with two of her favorite words: *resilient stock.*

But Zach was on to something, and I contemplated: Is this the legacy I want to live and leave behind? Be curious. Make meaningful connections. Stay in active pursuit of my goals and dreams. And when I complete one, redream another. Yes, this *is* the legacy I want to live and leave behind, and if the Three C's make it into my obit, I'll forever rest in peace.

*Eve Rodsky, a woman who was endlessly **curious** and eager to make **connections**. A strong believer that although you are not obligated to **complete** the work, neither are you free to abandon it.*

It needs some tweaking, I admit. But I'm only forty-four, and I hope no one is writing my obit for many, many years to come. In the meantime, with my steady Three C's legs, I'm ready for whatever comes next—which brings me back to my conversation with oceanic explorer Bob Ballard. As our interview was wrapping up, he shared this funny anecdote: "I had just found the *Titanic* and I was on the *Today* show, the *Tonight Show*, and the 'Day after Tomorrow' show," he joked. "And my mom calls and she says, 'You know, your father and I have been watching you on TV. All our neighbors are talking about you. But you know what? It's too bad you found that ship.'

"'Why do you say that?' I asked her.

"And Mom says, 'You're a great scientist . . . you've made so many important discoveries, and now they're only going to remember you for that rusty old boat.'"

Ballard laughed at the memory and leaned forward and said with conviction, "Not true. You see, life is a series of strategic tacking maneuvers. You get up in the morning, you know where you want your boat to go, but the winds aren't blowing in the right direction. So you change your tack, which in sailing terms is the best way to get from one point to another. And then the winds change again. And you tack again and again until finally, you cross over the finish line *sideways*. Amelia Earhart's plane is still out there. I've tried once, and I'll try again. I'm going to find it . . . and then, I'll be remembered for that."

CROSS THE FINISH LINE SIDEWAYS

As I often do after an exciting interview, I share the highlights with my kids. When Ben walked into my office the next day to ask me about a math problem, I forgot to chide him for interrupting me and instead greeted him with enthusiasm. "Ben, you wouldn't believe who I got to talk to—the man who discovered the *Titanic* and who's now searching for Amelia Earhart's plane. He's done all these amazing things in his life, but he says the most rewarding thing he does is to go into classrooms like yours and inspire kids to go after *their* dreams. Cool, right?"

"Sure." He shrugged. "Hey, I just added a few more dreams to my list: NFL tight end, children's book author, and also a lawyer working for social justice. You know," he said casually, "like a warrior for peace."

I smiled widely. *That's my boy.*

"Hey, Mom," he continued, "when you finish this book, what are you going to do next?"

Drink a bottle of wine and take a long nap, I thought to myself but answered responsibly, "I'm not sure yet what my next dream will be—maybe I'll write another book, maybe I'll do something else—but what I am sure about is that I will continue the journey. I will keep dancing. I will keep dreaming. I may cross the finish line sideways, but I will continue to create for creativity's sake."

"Cool." Ben nodded with approval.

"Now leave me alone." I smiled sweetly. "Mommy has work to do."

Create for creativity's sake.

The journey continues for Unis everywhere—

Jessica is actively dancing and planning her next adventure to Iceland.

Blessing is growing two companies—one into a vibrant support community for mothers, the other to support them through technology.

Aisa is planning to travel to India to visit her uncle and learn from him in person.

Darby is practicing for a small in-person Dahli Mamas rock concert.

Tiffany is still cooking her mother's recipes but decided to pivot off the cookbook and instead write and illustrate a children's book series that retells Christian stories.

Zoe is writing a television show based on female friendships. The protagonist loves travel, especially to regions known for their spices, and her character's love interest is an antiques dealer.

Acknowledgments

Thank you to my husband, Seth, for your belief in me and for holding so many damn cards while I wrote this second book—during a pandemic, no less. Thank you to my mother, Terry Mizrahi—you always prioritized living in your Unicorn Space even as a single mother and taught me the value of sharing myself with the world.

Reese Witherspoon, Sarah Harden, Amanda Farrand, Erin Stover, and the entire Hello Sunshine team for believing in me and working so diligently and thoughtfully to champion the Unicorn Space messages. Thank you for being the place where women are at the center of the story.

Thank you to my writing partner and "work wife," Samantha Rose. Having a mind-meld with someone doesn't happen often and it's happened with you. Your professionalism, writing style, humor, and patience are unparalleled. You are the best. Let's keep working to change the world together!

Thank you to Yfat Reiss Gendell. This sequel is a testament to your belief in me. Your limitless talents for writing, deal making, editing, advising, and beta-testing the system make you a unicorn.

Thank you to my partners on the wonderful Putnam team. I'm eternally grateful to my editor, Michelle Howry. Your gifted organizational mind and thoughtful guidance have made the process of writing this book a true joy. Every line of feedback was extraordinarily meaningful and made the manuscript better and better. I am extremely thankful to the all-star team of publisher Sally Kim, president Ivan Held, alongside director of publicity Alexis Welby, director of marketing Ashley McClay, publicist Ashley Hewlett, and editorial assistant Ashley Di Dio. A special thank-you to head of managing editorial Meredith Dros, associate managing editor Maija Baldauf, head of sales Lauren Monaco, marketing team members Emily Mlynek and Nishtha Patel, copyeditor Erica Ferguson, production editor Claire Sullivan, director of art and design Tiffany Estreicher, art department directors Anthony Ramondo and Monica Cordova, subrights director Tom Dussel, and Sanny Chiu for the awesome cover design.

Thank you to Jennifer Younker. I couldn't have written this book without you. You move mountains to get the trains to run on time, and you also make everything feel easy especially when things are truly hard.

Thank you to Lindsey Mayer-Beug for the inspired interior illustrations.

Thank you to Sarah Rothman, Meredith O'Sullivan Wasson, Anna Bailer, and Matthew Avento at the Lede Company for all your hard work amplifying the messages of this book.

Thank you to Professor Darby Saxbe, Julian Goldhagen, Rachel Wynn, and Julie Burstein for your contributions to the manuscript. Your comments to the manuscript and insights based on your profound knowledge were invaluable.

Thank you to the following experts for taking time from your busy writing, teaching, and professional lives to speak to me for this book: Dr. Stephen Treat; Professor Dan McAdams; Dr. Amber Thornton; Dr. Laurie Santos; Natalie Nixon, PhD; Dr. Pooja Lakshmin; Dr. Stew Friedman; Dr. Sheryl Gonzalez Ziegler; Dr. Jennifer Petriglieri; Professor Kennon Sheldon;

Alexis Jemal, PhD; Dr. Victoria Simms; Professor Femida Handy; Dr. Lisa Damour; Professor Daniel Carlson; Mia Birdsong; Arianna Huffington; Greg McKeown; and Dan Stillman. Your deep professional expertise informed the writing of *Find Your Unicorn Space*.

Thank you to two additional incredibly insightful mental health professionals who inform the practice of Unicorn Space in everyday lives—psychologist Dr. Phyllis Cohen and psychotherapist Marcia Bernstein, LCSW.

Thank you to my wonderful in-laws, Laurie and Terry Rodsky, for always being there to help Seth and me with so much E in our CPE. Your support and encouragement means the world to me—and your unconditional love of Zach, Ben, and Anna is a priceless gift in their lives. Thank you to my brother-in-law, Eli Rodsky, and sister-in-law, Michal Cohen, for always being there for Zach, Ben, and Anna. Thank you to our most wonderful nanny, Cecilia Interiano, who is living Fair Play with us every day.

Thank you to Zoe Schaeffer, who supported my journey by helping with early editing and critical feedback.

Thank you to Hillary Sherer, PhD, for thoroughly and diligently combing through the academic literature to support and verify the statistics and studies quoted in the book and much more.

Bibliography

Alboher, M. (2007). *One Person/Multiple Careers: The Original Guide to the Slash Career*. A HeyMarci.com Production.

A Little Late with Lilly Singh. (2021, March 23.) "Freeze Your Kids with This New Technology." YouTube video. https://www.youtube.com/watch?v=5qMr6IvkjaQ.

Altman, M. (2020, July 14). "Who Helps Out in a Crisis?" *The New York Times*. nytimes.com/2020/07/14/us/women-men-pandemic-disasters-help.html.

Baer, K. (2020). *What Kind of Woman*. Harper.

Beghetto, R. A. (2020). "How Times of Crisis Serve as a Catalyst for Creative Action: An Agentic Perspective." *Frontiers in Psychology* 11: 600685. doi.org/10.3389/fpsyg.2020.600685.

Behson, S. (2020, May 7). "Working Parents, Save Time for Hobbies." *Harvard Business Review*. hbr.org/2020/05/working-parents-save-time-for-hobbies.

Berger, J. (2020). *The Catalyst: How to Change Anyone's Mind*. Simon & Schuster.

Birdsong, M. (2020). *How We Show Up: Reclaiming Family, Friendship, and Community*. Hachette Go.

Bonger, N. (2017). "The Commodification of Wellbeing." In R. Hougham & B. Jones (Eds.), *Dramatherapy: Reflections and Praxis* (253–270). Macmillan Education.

Borritz, M., Bültmann, U., Rugulies, R., Christensen, K. B., et al. (2005). "Psychosocial Work Characteristics as Predictors for Burnout: Findings from 3-Year Follow-Up of the PUMA Study." *Journal of Occupational and Environmental Medicine* 47 (10), 1015–1025.

Brooks, A. C. (2020). "How to Build a Life: A Column about Pointing Yourself Toward Happiness. *The Atlantic*. theatlantic.com/projects/how-build-life.

Brown, B. (2013). *Daring Greatly: How the Courage to be Vulnerable Transforms the Way We Live, Love, Parent, and Lead.* Avery.

Burnett, B. & Evans, D. (2016). *Designing Your Life: How to Build a Well-Lived, Joyful Life.* Knopf.

Carson, S. (2010). *Your Creative Brain: Seven Steps to Maximize Imagination, Productivity, and Innovation in Your Life.* Jossey-Bass.

Codina, N. & Pestana, J. V. (2019). "Time Matters Differently in Leisure Experience for Men and Women: Leisure Dedication and Time Perspective." *International Journal of Environmental Research and Public Health* 16 (14), 2513.

Cohen, S. (2004). "Social Relationships and Health." *American Psychologist* 59 (8), 676.

Collins, J. (2001). *Good to Great: Why Some Companies Make the Leap . . . and Others Don't.* HarperBusiness.

Conner, T. S., DeYoung, C. G., & Silvia, P. J. (2016). "Everyday Creative Activity as a Path to Flourishing." *The Journal of Positive Psychology* 13 (2), 181–189. doi.org/10.1080/17439760.2016.1257049.

Connley, C. (2021, January 11). "A Year Ago, Women Outnumbered Men in the U.S. Workforce, Now They Account for 100% of Jobs Lost in December." CNBC. cnbc.com/2021/01/11/women-account-for-100percent-of-jobs-lost-in-december-new-analysis.html.

Corry, D. A. S. (2014). "Harnessing the Mental Health Benefits of the Creativity–Spirituality Construct: Introducing the Theory of Transformative Coping." *Journal of Spirituality in Mental Health* 16 (2), 89–110. doi.org/10.1080/19349637.2014.896854.

Csikszentmihalyi, M. (1990). *Flow: The Psychology of Optimal Experience.* Harper & Row.

——. (2019). "Foreword: The Rewards of Creativity." In J. C. Kaufman & R. J. Sternberg (Eds.), *The Cambridge Handbook of Creativity* (2nd ed.) (xvii–xviii). Cambridge University Press. doi.org/10.1017/9781316979839.

Doran G., Miller, A., & Cunningham, J. (1981). "There's a S.M.A.R.T. Way to Write Management's Goals and Objectives." *Management Review* 70 (11), 35–36.

Druckerman, P. (2019). *There Are No Grown-ups: A Midlife Coming-of-Age Story.* Penguin Books.

Duckworth, A. (2016). *Grit: The Power of Passion and Perseverance.* Scribner.

Dweck, C. S. (2006). *Mindset: The New Psychology of Success.* Random House.

Edwards, S. M. & Snyder, L. (2020, July 10). "Yes, Balancing Work and

Parenting Is Impossible. Here's the Data." *The Washington Post.* washingtonpost.com/outlook/interruptions-parenting-pandemic -work-home/2020/07/09/599032e6-b4ca-11ea-aca5-ebb63d27e1ff_ story.html.

Empson, L. & Howard-Grenville, J. (2021, March 10). "How Has the Past Year Changed You and Your Organization?" *Harvard Business Review.* bg.hbr.org/2021/03/how-has-the-past-year-changed-you-and-your -organization.

Ewing-Nelson, C. (2021, January). "All of the Jobs Lost in December Were Women's Jobs." National Women's Law Center. nwlc.org/wp -content/uploads/2021/01/December-Jobs-Day.pdf.

Fancourt, D. & Steptoe, A. (2019). "Effects of Creativity on Social and Behavioral Adjustment in 7- to 11-Year-Old Children." *Annals of the New York Academy of Sciences* 1438 (1), 30–39. doi.org/10.1111 /nyas.13944.

Finkelstein, J. (2020, June 5). "I'm a Gay CEO, and This Is Why Parental Leave Will Promote Gender Equality." *Fast Company.* fastcompany .com/90513225/im-a-gay-ceo-and-this-is-why-parental-leave-will -promote-gender-equality.

Forgeard, M. J. C. (2013). "Perceiving Benefits After Adversity: The Relationship Between Self-reported Posttraumatic Growth and Creativity." *Psychology of Aesthetics, Creativity and the Arts* 7 (3), 245–264. doi.org/10.1037/a0031223.

——. (2019). "Creativity and Healing." In J. C. Kaufman & R. J. Sternberg (Eds.), *The Cambridge Handbook of Creativity* (2nd ed.) (319–322). Cambridge University Press. doi.org/10.1017/9781316979839.

Fray, M. (2016, January 25). "She Divorced Me Because I Left Dishes by the Sink." *Huffington Post.* huffpost.com/entry/she-divorced-me-i -left-dishes-by-the-sink_b_9055288.B.

Fredrickson, B. L. (2004). "The Broaden-and-Build Theory of Positive Emotions." *Philosophical Transactions of the Royal Society London B* 359, 1367–1377. doi.org/10.1098/rstb.2004.1512.

Friedman, S. D. & Westring, A. F. (2020). *Parents Who Lead: The Leadership Approach You Need to Parent with Purpose, Fuel Your Career, and Create a Richer Life.* Harvard Business Review Press.

Gadoua, S. P. (2020, August 12). "'I Work with Couples About to Divorce, Here Are Their Top 5 Problems.'" *Newsweek.* newsweek.com/work -couples-about-divorce-top-5-problems-1524044.

Gilbert, D. (2014, March). *The Psychology of Your Future Self* [Video]. TED. ted.com/talks/dan_gilbert_the_psychology_of_your_future_ self?language=en.

Gilbert, E. (2015). *Big Magic: Creative Living Beyond Fear.* Riverhead Books.

Goddard, C. (2018). "The Significance of Transitional Objects in an Early Childhood Classroom for Children and Teachers." *Dimensions of Early Childhood* 46 (1), 6–9.

Hardy, B. (2019, January 17). "Accountability Partners Are Great. But 'Success' Partners Will Change Your Life." *Medium.* medium.com /@benjaminhardy/accountability-partners-are-great-but-success -partners-will-change-your-life-8850ac0efa04.

———. (2020). *Personality Isn't Permanent: Break Free from Self-Limiting Beliefs and Rewrite Your Story.* Portfolio.

Holt-Lunstad, J., Robles, T., & Sbarra, D. A. (2017). "Advancing Social Connection as a Public Health Priority in the United States." *American Psychologist* 72 (6), 517–530. doi.org/10.1037/amp0000103.

Hooks, B. (2004). *The Will to Change: Men, Masculinity, and Love.* Atria Books.

Horowitz, J. M., Graf, N., & Livingston, G. (2019, November 6). "Marriage and Cohabitation in the U.S." Pew Research Center. pewresearch.org /social-trends/2019/11/06/marriage-and-cohabitation-in-the-u-s.

Huffington, A. (2020, October 30). "Why This Is the Perfect Time to Redefine Success." LinkedIn. linkedin.com/pulse/why-perfect-time -redefine-success-arianna-huffington.

Jeffers, S. (1987). *Feel the Fear . . . and Do It Anyway.* Fawcett Columbine.

Juhn, C. & McCue, K. (2017). "Specialization Then and Now: Marriage, Children, and the Gender Earnings Gap Across Cohorts." *Journal of Economic Perspectives* 31 (1), 183–204.

Kapos, S. (2021, January 15). "The Government's Vaccine Whisperer." Politico. politico.com/newsletters/women-rule/2021/01/15/the -governments-vaccine-whisperer-491431.

Kaufman, J. C. & Sternberg, R. J. (Eds.). (2019). *The Cambridge Handbook of Creativity* (2nd ed.) Cambridge University Press. doi .org/10.1017/9781316979839.

Konrath, S. & Handy, F. (2020). "The Good-looking Giver Effect: The Relationship Between Doing Good and Looking Good." *Nonprofit and Voluntary Sector Quarterly* 50 (2), 283–311.

Krogerus, M. & Tschäppeler, R. (2012). *The Decision Book: Fifty Models for Strategic Thinking.* W. W. Norton & Company.

Libby, K. (n.d.). "My Brain Was Damaged. Making Art Helped." *The Riveter.* theriveter.co/voice/how-art-helps-heal-trauma-covid-19.

Lisitsa, E. (2013, April 23). "The Four Horsemen: Criticism, Contempt, Defensiveness, and Stonewalling." The Gottman Institute. gottman

.com/blog/the-four-horsemen-recognizing-criticism-contempt
-defensiveness-and-stonewalling.

Lyubomirsky, S. (2008). *The How of Happiness: A New Approach to Getting the Life You Want.* Penguin Press.

McKeown, G. (2014). *Essentialism: The Disciplined Pursuit of Less.* Crown Business.

Merle, A. (2019, June 17). "The Best Type of Exercise Uses Your Body— and Your Brain." *Quartz.* qz.com/quartzy/1646275/the-best-types-of -exercise-for-brain-health.

Millwood, M. (2019). *To Have and to Hold: Motherhood, Marriage, and the Modern Dilemma.* HarperCollins.

Mineo, L. (2017, April 11). "Harvard Study, Almost 80 Years Old, Has Proved That Embracing Community Helps Us Live Longer, and Be Happier." *The Harvard Gazette.* news.harvard.edu/gazette /story/2017/04/over-nearly-80-years-harvard-study-has-been -showing-how-to-live-a-healthy-and-happy-life.

Mitchell, J. F. (2004). "Aging Well: Surprising Guideposts to a Happier Life from the Landmark Harvard Study of Adult Development." *American Journal of Psychiatry* 161 (1), 178–179.

Nagoski, E. & Nagoski, A. (2019). *Burnout: The Secret to Unlocking the Stress Cycle.* Ballantine Books.

Nichols, M. H. (2020). *All Along You Were Blooming: Thoughts for Boundless Living.* Zondervan.

Nixon, N. (2020). *The Creativity Leap: Unleash Curiosity, Improvisation, and Intuition at Work.* Berrett-Koehler Publishers.

Oakley, B. (2017). "Learning How to Learn: You, Too, Can Rewire Your Brain." *The New York Times.* https://www.nytimes.com/2017/08/04/ education/edlife/learning-how-to-learn-barbara-oakley.html.

Owens, Z. (Host). (2020, October). "Cheryl Strayed, This Telling." Podcast episode. In *Moms Don't Have Time to Read Books.* zibbyowens.com/ transcript/cherylstrayed?rq=cheryl.

Payne, K. K. & Gibbs, L. (2013). "Economic Well-being and the Great Recession: Dual Earner Married Couples in the U.S. 2006 and 2011." PowerPoint Slides (FP-13-05). National Center for Family & Marriage Research. bgsu.edu/content/dam/BGSU/college-of-arts-and -sciences/NCFMR/documents/FP/FP-13-05.pdf.

Ranji, U., Frederiksen, B., Salganicoff, A., & Long, M. (2021, March 22). "Women, Work, and Family During COVID-19: Findings from the KFF Women's Health Survey." Kaiser Family Foundation. kff.org/womens -health-policy/issue-brief/women-work-and-family-during-covid-19 -findings-from-the-kff-womens-health-survey.

Rao, T. (2019, January 28). "A Day of Rice Cakes for the Lunar New Year." *The New York Times.* nytimes.com/2019/01/28/dining/lunar-new -year-vietnamese.html.

Rominger, C., Fink, A., Weber, B., Papousek, I., & Schwerdtfeger, A. R. (2020). "Everyday Bodily Movement Is Associated with Creativity Independently from Active Positive Affect: A Bayesian Mediation Analysis Approach." *Scientific Reports* 10 (1), 1–9.

Runco, M. A. (2014). *Creativity: Theories and Themes: Research, Development, and Practice.* Academic Press.

Rusbult, C. E., Finkel, E. J., & Kumashiro, M. (2009). "The Michelangelo Phenomenon." *Current Directions in Psychological Science* 18 (6), 305–309.

Samuels, C. (2020, July 7). "What Is the Sandwich Generation? Unique Stress and Responsibilities for Caregivers Between Generations." *A Place for Mom.* aplaceformom.com/caregiver-resources/articles/ what-is-the-sandwich-generation.

Saxbe, D. E., Repetti, R. L., & Graesch, A. P. (2011). "Time Spent in Housework and Leisure: Links with Parents' Physiological Recovery from Work." *Journal of Family Psychology* 25 (2), 271.

Schulte, B. (2020, June 27). "How Not to Optimize Parenthood." *Slate.* slate.com/technology/2020/06/parenthood-technology -optimization-future-tense-fiction.html.

Schwartz, J. (2017, August 4). "Learning to Learn: You, Too, Can Rewire Your Brain." *The New York Times.* nytimes.com/2017/08/04/ education/edlife/learning-how-to-learn-barbara-oakley.html.

Seeman, T., Miller-Martinez, D. M., Merkin, S. S., Lachman, M. E., et al. (2011). "Histories of Social Engagement and Adult Cognition: Midlife in the U.S. Study." *The Journals of Gerontology, Series B: Psychological Sciences and Social Sciences* 66B (S1), i141–i152. doi.org/10.1093/ geronb/gbq091.

Sehgal, K. (2017, April 25). "Why You Should Have (at Least) Two Careers." *Harvard Business Review.* hbr.org/2017/04/why-you -should-have-at-least-two-careers.

Senior, J. (2014). *All Joy and No Fun: The Paradox of Modern Parenthood.* Ecco.

———. (2020, March 24). "Camp Is Canceled. Three More Months of Family Time. Help." *The New York Times.* nytimes.com/2020/05/24 /opinion/coronavirus-parents-work-from-home.html.

Seppälä, E. (2014, April 11). "Connectedness & Health: The Science of Social Connection Infographic." Emma Seppälä. emmaseppala.com /connect-thrive-infographic.

———. (2020, March 23). "Social Connection Boosts Health, Even When You're Isolated." *Psychology Today*. psychologytoday.com/us/blog /feeling-it/202003/social-connection-boosts-health-even-when -youre-isolated.

Sevilla, A. & Smith, S. (2020). "Baby Steps: The Gender Division of Childcare During the COVID-19 Pandemic." *Oxford Review of Economic Policy*. doi.org/10.1093/oxrep/graa027.

Silvia, P. J., Cotter, K. N., & Christensen, A. P. (2017). "The Creative Self in Context: Experience Sampling and the Ecology of Everyday Creativity." In M. Karwowski & J. C. Kaufman (Eds.), *Creativity and the Self* (275–288). Academic Press.

Sinek, S. (2009). *Start with Why: How Great Leaders Inspire Everyone to Take Action*. Portfolio.

Smith, E. E. (2013). "Meaning Is Healthier Than Happiness." *The Atlantic*. https://www.theatlantic.com/health/archive/2013/08 /meaning-is-healthier-than-happiness/278250/.

Solnit, R. (2010). *A Paradise Built in Hell: The Extraordinary Communities That Arise in Disaster*. Penguin Books.

Spalding, D. (2019, January 3). "Why Equal Parenting Is Still a Myth." *Motherly*. medium.com/motherly/why-equal-co-parenting-is-still-a -myth-d4ad732b106d.

Stone, B., Heen, S., Patton, B. (2010). *Difficult Conversations: How to Discuss What Matters Most*. (2nd ed.) Penguin Books.

Teng, E. (@etengastro). (2021, January 12). "am I working at my regular capacity? no. but am I prioritizing and taking care of the most important tasks? no. but am I at least taking care of myself and my mental health? also no." Twitter. twitter.com/etengastro/ status/1349066485310894082.

UCL News. (2020, May 27). "Parents, Especially Mothers, Paying Heavy Price for Lockdown." *UCL News*. ucl.ac.uk/news/2020/may/parents -especially-mothers-paying-heavy-price-lockdown.

UN Women. (2017). "Women in the Changing World of Work: Facts You Should Know. interactive.unwomen.org/multimedia/infographic/ changingworldofwork/en/index.html.

Ury, W. (2007). *The Power of a Positive No: How to Say No and Still Get to Yes*. Bantam Books.

U.S. Bureau of Labor Statistics. (2020, June 25). "American Time Use Survey Summary." bls.gov/news.release/atus.nr0.htm.

Valenti, J. (2020, October 1). "'Am I the Asshole?' Reveals America's Sexist Underbelly." *Medium*. gen.medium.com/aita-reveals-americas -sexist-underbelly-4609aa56658d.

Vanderkam, L. (2020, August 2). "Working from Home Poses Serious Dangers for Employers and Employees Alike." *Fortune*. fortune .com/2020/08/02/coronavirus-remote-work-home-burnout.

Wagner, T. (2012). *Creating Innovators: The Making of Young People Who Will Change the World*. Scribner.

Zamarro, G. & Prados, M. J. (2021). "Gender Differences in Couples' Division of Childcare, Work and Mental Health During COVID-19." *Review of Economics of the Household* 19, 11–40.

Index

INDEX

INDEX